RISING TIDES

'It is accessible and thoughtful . . . The distillation of his learning from two decades in politics'
Daily Mail

'Read this brilliantly chilling new book – and your world will never be the same again'
Mail on Sunday

Liam Fox trained as a surgeon and worked as an army doctor for ten years and is the former Secretary of State for Defence. He is the Member of Parliament for North Somerset. *Rising Tides* is his first book. He lives in Somerset.

RISING TIDES

Facing the Challenges of a New Era

Liam Fox

New updated edition

HERON
BOOKS

First published in Great Britain in 2013 by Heron Books

This updated paperback edition published in 2014 by Heron Books
an imprint of

Quercus Editions Ltd
55 Baker Street
7th Floor, South Block
London W1U 8EW

A CIP catalogue record for this book is available
from the British Library

PB ISBN 978 1 78206 742 9
EBOOK ISBN 978 1 78206 741 2

10 9 8 7 6 5 4 3 2 1

Printed and bound in Great Britain by Clays Ltd, St Ives plc

Typeset by Ellipsis Digital Limited, Glasgow

To my brother, who has shown us what courage is

and

to all those who give of themselves to keep us safe

There is a tide in the affairs of men.
Which, taken at the flood, leads on to fortune;
Omitted, all the voyage of their life
Is bound in shallows and in miseries.
On such a full sea are we now afloat,
And we must take the current when it serves,
Or lose our ventures.

Julius Caesar Act 4, Scene 3

CONTENTS

INTRODUCTION

I have had dreams and I have had nightmares, but I have conquered my nightmares because of my dreams.

Jonas Salk (1914–95)

I have always found Salk's words particularly apt, even comforting. As a doctor I admired him as the man who conquered the scourge of polio. As a politician, I respected his ability to express the optimism that can help bring us through the toughest trials.

Throughout most of our history we have had the luxury of focusing on our domestic problems and, apart from catastrophic global events such as the two world wars of the twentieth century, our involvement with the outside world has been something of a voluntary choice. That is all changing today. The era of globalization means that our economies, our trade, our security and even our politics have more shared risk than ever before.

How do those who make those decisions affecting our world today and that of future generations come to their conclusions? The interplay of history, ideology, geography and religion constantly shapes and reshapes our world, demanding continual responses to emerging problems. How do our decision makers ensure that they are able to see problems in their proper context and weigh up the consequences of the actions they may take? Equally, how do they learn the appropriate lessons from history so that they do not repeat the mistakes of the past? What are the issues that they find most challenging and think about most?

Is it the great new idea that will empower their citizens or take their country forward, or is it a new plan to cooperate in global economics or protect threatened ecology? Which of the long list of threats are at the top of the list of their concerns? Who do they believe constitute the greatest risks and from where? They know the truth that the people who want to harm us do not lack the intent, merely the capability. The job of the decision makers is to ensure that this remains the case.

As someone who trained and practised as a doctor I was steeped in the rhythm and patterns of the medical approach to information. The first task was to ask the appropriate questions and gather all the data possible about the patient and their complaint. The second task was to assess the information and reach a diagnosis based on the most likely probability. The third task was to determine the course of treatment in the light of best accepted practice and the most up-to-date information available. Crucially, this is not just a process about raw data but also about context. It includes an assessment of the patient's family history, their social circumstances and their past medical history. It is an attempt to avoid seeing patients as a particular pathology with a name tag, but rather to create a more rounded picture so that the most appropriate outcome can be achieved. It is that process of analysis that I have always tried to bring to bear throughout my medical and political careers. I am not going to pretend that it was always successful, but it provided a useful framework for decision making, avoiding jumping to conclusions or reacting to sudden threats with supposition or prejudice.

Just like in medicine, in economic, security and foreign affairs we seldom see anything that is completely new. I am not one of those who believe that history repeats itself in the most literal sense, but I do believe that the types of problems we face are repeated in time and realm. J.R.R. Tolkien, reflecting on death in battle in *The Two Towers*, says, 'He wondered what the man's name was and where he came from; and if he was really evil at heart, or what lies or threats had led him on the long march from his home; and if he would not rather have stayed there in peace.' Is that not exactly the sort of question we ask ourselves when confronted by the perpetrators of transnational terrorism? Human behaviour may change with the passage of many years of evolution, but in the short timescales in which we examine our crises the well-documented patterns of human responses to similar situations are likely to be within a well-defined band of probabilities. An understanding of history is therefore just as important to the decision maker in relation to national security issues as a full understanding of the patient's background and medical history is to the clinician. It is a pity that history is regarded by so many as irrelevant in an age where instant justification and gratification have largely become the social norms. Just as doctors need to see the problems of their patients in the appropriate context, so policymakers need to see the global issues in appropriate historic and cultural contexts if they are to make not only the best possible assessment of the situation but also formulate the most appropriate response.

I must, however, make a confession at the outset. I love history and consequently the chapters of this book may go a bit over the top on historical background. I would urge readers to feel free to skip over any detail that may seem excessive, but I believe that history brings some context to the subjects covered, something I think is often missing in contemporary debate.

Why is context so important? Try this simple test. Imagine a glass of cool clear water sitting on a table. What does it mean to you? If like me you grew up in the west of Scotland or live in the English West Country, it is unlikely to make you think of much more than the prevailing wet weather or the occasional flood. If you are reading this in sub-Saharan Africa, it is likely to remind you of the constant lack of this most basic resource. If you are a Chinese politician, it might make you think about the more than sixty cities of the country in drought conditions and the social unrest that this might provoke and the political upheavals that may ensue. To a desert dweller it might seem incredible, even offensive, that in Britain we each flush gallons of the stuff away every day. In rain-soaked northern Europe it may not occur to us that a shortage of water may be the factor that takes nations into conflict with one another in the future. Understanding why things are as they are and how they have reached this point is vital if we are to make sense of the complex world around us. In an age when globalization not only creates greater interdependence but brings an unavoidable importation of strategic risk, we need to understand as well as know – and they are not the same.

In this book I will explore the generic types of challenges we face and illustrate them with reference to particular cases. It is of necessity a more superficial view than can be found in academic tomes but is deliberately so. This is not a book for the experts. Those with far greater knowledge of the subject matter may well find it oversimple. If this is so, it is to help clarify the narrative. Most economists might as well be talking Swahili as far as most of the general public is concerned, yet what happens to our money in the global markets will affect the prosperity of ourselves and our families. The security community has a habit of talking in its own obscure language – no different perhaps from financiers, lawyers or, yes, doctors – but too often it leaves the public out of the debate. People only buy burglar alarms if they really believe there are burglars 'out there' and, likewise, only demand improved security from their governments if they understand the scale and range of the threats in the world. In looking at the issues of failing states, international terrorism, tensions in the Islamic world and the ever greater competition for scarce natural resources I want to describe and discuss these issues for a wider audience so that the quality of our national and international debates might improve.

All of the information in this book is open-sourced and readily available for anyone with a computer and a search engine. In fact, anyone with an interest in any of these subjects could have written this book; I hope I have saved some people the trouble.

I have been able to call on the experiences of a number of those who have been in the hot seat and taken some of these decisions in real life. In Britain former prime minister Sir John Major, who helped me greatly in the years in opposition, reflected on issues such as Bosnia and the Northern Ireland peace process. Another former prime minister, Tony Blair, gave me not only his view on the current situation in the Middle East but provided a great deal of useful background. Former foreign and defence secretary Malcolm Rifkind shared some of his extensive historical knowledge and personal perspective on such a wide range of issues that together we might have written a separate book.

In the United States former secretary of state Condoleezza Rice, now returned to academia, gave me her frank assessments of the conflicts within Islam and wider global security issues. My great friend Bob Gates, former US secretary of state for defense, with whom I have spent more hours than either of us cares to calculate at international meetings, was his usual frank and wise self on issues of international security and the structures we will require in the future. The redoubtable Donald Rumsfeld, another former secretary of defense, was as forthright as usual in his typically disarming way on a whole range of subjects. Our last meeting gave me the opportunity to ask whether or not he had written the 'known unknown' passage which has become so famous. He told me, 'There were fifteen smart people in the room for three days – I don't know who actually wrote it.' When I asked if he minded it being attributed to him he said, 'Liam, I don't care if you attribute Confucius to me.' The whole project has been enormously entertaining and educational for me and I hope some of that flavour comes through to the reader.

Finally, my friend His Royal Highness, Crown Prince Salman of Bahrain has been his usual generous self in discussing global issues from the perspective of the Gulf. As one of the great advocates of democratic and social reform in the region his voice is enormously welcome in this debate, and his command of English puts most of us to shame.

I hope that, having read this book, and having put up with the meanderings that it sometimes takes, you might have a little more understanding of the difficulties that face those who have leadership positions in the world, as they balance up the range of options and outcomes available to them. They too have dreams and nightmares.

Chapter One

GLOBALIZATION

Rising Tides may seem a strange title for a book on the subject of globalization and the challenges it presents. It is intended not as any analogy with the effects of climate change but is a reference to William Shakespeare's *Julius Caesar*, when Brutus is attempting to convince Cassius that it is a good time to enter into battle with Mark Antony and Octavius. I would love to say that the idea was my own, but it was my wife who suggested that this was the best fit for this project.

Globalization is probably as old as mankind itself.

Its true process arguably began when the first inhabitants of the African continent wandered off to find new lands to feed and shelter themselves as their population increased. The phenomenon that has been increasingly described as globalization since the mid-1990s represents an acceleration of the trend in which the world is increasingly compressed economically, culturally and politically. If Francis Fukuyama had called his book *The End of Geography* rather than *The End of History* he probably would have been closer to the mark.

While the international business community has been quick to embrace the potential that globalization has brought for increased economic activity, most politicians have been either less enthusiastic or simply slower in making the necessary adaptations to the new reality. There are probably two reasons for this. The first is that many politicians see the increasing interconnections that the new environment has brought as a threat to many of their concepts of sovereignty. The second is that, while globalization may bring enormous opportunities in terms of trade, there is also an unavoidable importation of strategic risk. As we become more interdependent we interact with many more players in many more parts of the world than in any time in history. This makes us more vulnerable to external shocks and less able to insulate ourselves from instability in distant parts of the global economy or from transnational security threats which may arise in a far-flung corner of the world. Phenomena ranging from the economic and security implications of the 9/11 attacks, through the vulnerability that the SARS outbreak in Asia in 2003 demonstrated, to the economic reverberations following the Japanese tsunami showed that the era when we believed events happened 'over there' is behind us.

The whole history of globalization tells us that the rate of its progress continues to accelerate. The impact of the Silk Road, with its mixing of cultural ideas and knowledge, was followed by the great age of conquest by the European powers including the exploration of the New World. The expansion of the maritime empires of Portugal, Spain, the Netherlands and especially Britain saw the rapid development of global trade. Constant improvements in modes of transportation have made the exchange of goods, peoples and ideas ever easier. Technological advances have been shared (often reluctantly) with others, and the interchange of knowledge has produced ever faster material and scientific progress.

The real acceleration, however, came after the Second World War.

The Bretton Woods Conference set out a new framework for international monetary policy, commerce and finance and introduced international institutions designed specifically to facilitate greater levels of trade. The General Agreement on Tariffs and Trade (GATT) gave way to the World Trade Organization (WTO). Other institutions grew up around the need for greater economic cooperation and the security guarantees that were needed to ensure stability: the United Nations, NATO, the European Union, the World Bank and the IMF. Yet they developed for a different world from the one we have today. The devastation of the Second World War gave way to the military stand-off of the Cold War and the ideological clash between the capitalist West and the communist bloc. Communism may now be seen as largely an intellectual hiccup of the twentieth century, doomed to failure in a world full of differing individuals instead of rigidly conforming ideologues devoid of concepts of difference or choice, but its demise did not always appear inevitable. Following the collapse of communism and the end of the period of bipolarity, there was what some have described as 'America's unipolar moment'. Condoleezza Rice contests this thesis: 'The so-called bipolarity [of the Cold War] was overestimated – it tended to ignore the rising China and the Sino-Soviet split. It was an important strategic concept but it never really felt like that. So, it never felt as unipolar as it seemed.' Real or not, this has given way to a new world in which multipolarity, even if it is only in its infancy, seems the inexorable direction of travel. There are those who believe that the next century will look more like the nineteenth than the twentieth century. Malcolm Rifkind is cautious: 'The nineteenth was multipolar, but only among the European [colonial] powers. Now, for the first time in the history of mankind, there is a multipolarity of power, mass industrialization and mass consumption of resources.'

There are as many different definitions of globalization as there are writers on the subject. Manfred Steger, professor of global studies at

RMIT University, has described five dimensions: economic, political, cultural, ecological and ideological. In 2000 the International Monetary Fund identified four basic aspects of globalization: trade and transactions; capital and investment movements; migration and movement of people; and the dissemination of knowledge. To these we should probably add global environmental challenges such as climate change, pollution, ecological threats, the competition for finite commodities and the rise of transnational terrorism. None of us can isolate ourselves from these changes or their interactions. Even those who choose the ostrich head-in-the-sand option of isolationism will be unavoidably affected by the actions of those who continue to increase the rate of global interaction. Though some would hate to admit it, the isolationist option is now consigned to history.

Economic globalization means the increasing interdependence of national economies, the advent of global production, wider and more complex markets, expanded competition, the generation and stimulation of new technologies and the rise of worldwide corporations and industries. Developed economies interact with less developed ones by means of foreign direct investment, the reduction of trade barriers and, increasingly, migration. New players have challenged the long-standing dominance of the Western nations. Chinese economic reform, begun under Deng Xiaoping in the 1980s, saw Shanghai become the world's busiest port by the middle of the first decade of the new millennium. India's economic liberalization did not begin until the 1990s and yet already more than 300 million people have lifted themselves out of extreme poverty, probably the greatest emancipation from want that has ever occurred in the history of mankind. Those countries which embraced the concept of globalization early have tended to benefit most. The Enabling Trade Index, first published in 2008 by the World Economic Forum, measures how well countries facilitate trade in goods across borders and on to their eventual destinations. It comprises four sub-indexes: market access, border administration, transport and communications infrastructure, and business environment. Top of the list, as in the majority of rankings of the most globalized countries, sits Singapore, followed by Switzerland and Hong Kong. The Nordic states are close behind with the United Kingdom and the United States in the lower parts of the top twenty.

Globalization has seen the rise of MNEs (multinational enterprises), companies with worldwide approaches to markets and production such as McDonald's, Toyota and BP. This is already producing, unavoidably, competition in global taxation rates, with companies moving to where smaller proportions of their profits are expropriated by national governments. In turn, this is creating further demand for (and a supply of) tax havens – defined by the US Government Accountability Office as having nil or nominal taxes; lack of effective exchange of tax information with foreign tax authorities; lack of transparency in the operation of legislative, legal or administrative provisions; no requirement for a substantive local presence; and self-promotion as an offshore financial centre. This rather pejorative description is unlikely to change the global reality that money tends to go where it can be made and can be moved.

Cultural globalization is manifested in a number of ways. The fact that you can have a (broadly similar) Coca-Cola or Big Mac almost anywhere in the world now barely merits a mention. That is unless you are the dictator of North Korea or the supreme leader in Iran. It is said, only half jokingly, that Iran's leader is so afraid of the cultural impact that opening up to the rest of the world would bring that he fears McDonald's more than Mossad. Closed countries can only hold back globalization for so long before the inevitable march of history catches up with them. Not only has the cultural aspect of globalization produced a whole host of cross-fertilizations in the arts and resulted in new international social trends and fashions; it has also created new markets for those who previously had a limited audience, a trend massively exacerbated by the Internet and satellite television. This cultural cross-pollination has also been accompanied by growth in global tourism. The World Health Organization estimates that 500,000 people or more are in the air at any one time, travelling from one part of the globe to another. In 2013 there were over 1 billion international tourist arrivals worldwide, a growth of more than 5 per cent on the previous year. The value of international tourism was placed at a staggering $1000 billion. All of this is facilitated by the ever more dominant English language. Around 3.5 billion people worldwide have knowledge of English, and as well as being the dominant language of the Internet (itself the most powerful tool of all for globalization), English accounts for around 35 per cent of the world's mail, telexes and cables and 40 per cent of the world's radio programmes. Sorry, Paris!

All this increased activity and interdependence has occurred at a time of phenomenal global population growth and the inevitable competition for limited resources. At the end of the Black Death in the mid-1300s the global population stood at around 370 million. With the huge rise in the birth rate, peaking in the late 1980s at around 138 million per year, and higher life expectancy as poverty is gradually eliminated, nutrition improves and medical care becomes more widely available, current projections indicate a global population of up to 10.5 billion by 2050. From 1950 to 1984 more efficient agricultural practices around the world increased production increase by over 250 per cent. However, further progress is limited by the availability of land and increasing problems, in places like China, with water supply and land pollution.

Of course there is a dark side to the globalization process. Increased ease of transportation and communication not only helps tourists and entrepreneurs; it also brings new opportunities for disease, crime and subversive ideas and activities. The great religions of the world were among the earliest groups to see the potential for a virtually unlimited global market, and the propagation of religion through missionaries, evangelists and forced conversions has changed the shape of our world and influenced cultures far from the origin in time and place of the religions themselves. Extreme elements, such as hard-line violent Islamic fundamentalists, have been able to utilize the tools of mass communication to take their messages of hate further, often to poor and perhaps resentful communities. The events of 9/11 in Manhattan, the Madrid train bombings and the London Underground attacks have highlighted the danger of transnational terrorism with non-state actors replacing nation states as the biggest threat to our security. SARS showed how health threats can be spread around the globe, perhaps before we are even aware of the risk. The years taken for the Black Death to produce its grisly toll would be much compressed today. Human trafficking for sex slavery, cheap or forced labour, or even for organ extraction, is an industry estimated to be worth around $32 billion per year in international trade. In 2008 the United Nations estimated that nearly 2.5 million people from 127 different countries were trafficked into 137 other countries around the world. Even more profitable is the global drugs trade, which is estimated to generate more than $320 billion a year in revenues with around fifteen million regular users of heroin, cocaine and synthetic drugs worldwide. Increased global trade has also had a catastrophic impact on some of the world's rarest animals and plants, with poachers willing to take ever greater risks for ever higher rewards. The use of body parts from endangered species, for example in Chinese medicine, has put even more pressure on animals such as the tiger (already competing for its traditional habitat with the growing human population) and the rhinoceros, 90 per cent of whose global population has disappeared in the past forty years.

In this book I will look at five aspects of globalization in greater detail: global money including migration, trade and debt; the threat that transnational terrorism is having across borders; the risk that failing states will endanger the security and economy of an ever more interdependent and sensitive world; the risks and opportunities of the global struggle within Islam, which has replaced the clash of capitalism and communism as the most unstable ideological problem; and how competition for basic commodities, especially water, shows how interdependence could turn to conflict if we do not manage our global resources properly.

How, in each of these cases, do we ensure that policy is made in an informed and consistent way? As a doctor I was trained to look at as much information as was available before coming to a diagnosis, or more accurately a list of possible diagnoses ranked by their probability. That process enables a treatment plan to be set out so that the patient has as much knowledge as possible about likely outcomes. I use this analogy as most people would agree that policy should be based upon empirical data as far as possible rather than supposition, prejudice or guesswork. Even then policymaking is likely to be about the best possible, rather than the perfect, solution and is seldom likely to be risk-free. Decisions about actions (possibly with unintended consequences) are weighed against the risks of inaction and being a passenger as events unfold. Good decision making requires proper understanding of the context of the problem – a knowledge of the history involved; the cultural, financial and social considerations; any security implications – and a willingness to become submerged in a great deal of detailed information. Commenting on the Iraq War, Malcolm Rifkind told me that he believed Margaret Thatcher would have handled it differently: 'Thatcher was ideological but rooted in detail. She would have wanted daily briefings on everything that was happening on the ground. There is a real need to combine vision with grasp of detail if you are to be a statesman and not just a politician'.

Perhaps a good general example to consider lies in the debate at the heart of much of Western political life – how do we achieve an appropriate balance between liberty and security, freedom and authority? This is also at the core of the dispute between those advocating greater state economic control and those who tend towards a more laissez-faire approach. It is an essential political debate that will determine how the global era is ultimately shaped.

We in the West (especially in the US and the UK) should begin by assessing our own history and how we have come to be who we are, how our values and experience have shaped those around us and how we should take our values forward in the globalized environment. For example, as I have already stated, the European powers were responsible through trade and colonization for much of the impetus that eventually blossomed into today's globalization, while those who shaped the United States constitution had an impact that would lead to the defeat of the Soviet empire in the twentieth century as much by political debate as by the economic and military might which were themselves made possible by the success of a free capitalist system.

The freedom and liberty we now all too often take for granted in liberal pluralistic democracies have survived assaults across the ages by autocracy, absolute monarchy, communism, dictatorship, fascism and theocracy. What is it that makes these concepts so resilient and how do we mould them, if at all, in light of the challenges we face in this new globalized era? How, among the rising tides of global change, do we ensure that we continue to swim not sink?

In order to achieve a political environment in which it is possible to have a rational debate about the balance of liberty and authority several things need to be in place. We need to be frank about the nature and extent of the threats we face without exaggerating or excusing them, whether these threats are economic, religious or ecological. We need to accept the mistakes of history (no country ever gets everything right) and learn from them. Yet we must not confuse our own tolerance and liberal values with weakness in the face of threats, allowing ourselves an excuse not to act when we know deep down that we must.

It is important for us to remember that we are not simply passengers on a globalization conveyor belt but are able to influence its direction and destination. Some will say that the forces we are dealing with are too great – an easy way to abdicate our responsibilities at home and abroad. In the West, again especially in the UK and the US, we are defined by our belief in liberty and the rule of law; it is what enabled us to rescue Europe from both fascism and communism in the twentieth century. It was our moral resolve as much as our military hardware that enabled us to win against Nazi Germany and the USSR. So the challenge is to ensure that our value systems survive, and the biggest challenge we now face is how we maintain our values in the debate about the balance between liberty and security in a world where new threats are constantly emerging.

The intellectual debate surrounding liberty and freedom has been the dynamic which has propelled much of our social and political progress and, through our relationship with the rest of the world, shaped much of the direction of global thinking. Debate has also moved beyond the rights of man into other areas including social and economic matters. Late-seventeenth- and eighteenth-century Enlightenment philosophers such as John Locke, Benjamin Franklin and David Hume shaped the political and philosophical discourse of the day, and are shaping it still. Adam Smith's 'invisible hand' still provides the foundation and assumptions on which our economic system is based and operates, and which, since the fall of communism and the success of what has come to be known as the Washington Consensus, has become the dominant, if not universally accepted, model. That is not to say that all the currently emerging economic powers share every one, or in some cases any, of our liberal, pluralistic and democratic values, but events are seemingly pushing them in that direction however much they might want to resist. As one expert on China put it to me, 'China portrays ideas of democracy and the rule of law as being Western or foreign. They do not see that they are universal values.' The beauty of this process is its vibrancy and resilience. It never ceases even though certain events, and consequently some governments – both historically and in modern times – have tried to restrict the freedoms enjoyed by individuals.

So how did we end up where we are? Forgive a short diversion into history, but it is important to understand how the architecture of liberty, both political and economic, came about. Democracy in the United Kingdom, Europe and the West traces its roots back to the Magna Carta. None of those barons in 1215 could have imagined that their actions would be the cornerstone upon which would ultimately be built the construct that we today see embodied not only in a free and democratic Britain but in those many countries, not least the United States, which derive their political systems from a common heritage. Yet even before the Magna Carta there was a little-heard-of document called the Charter of Liberties from which the Magna Carta derived many of its concepts. This document dates back to 1100, when Henry I of England ascended the throne. Under the Charter of Liberties Henry formally bound himself to subject the powers of the throne to the law. More than a hundred years later the Magna Carta took the process one step further. By its terms certain rights of the King's subjects including the writ of habeas corpus – perhaps the most enduring aspect of the document today – were explicitly protected

The English Civil War of 1642–51 was a peculiar episode in that, with typical British eccentricity, the prize – the crown – was given back to the loser a few years later in the Restoration of 1660. Yet the trauma of the period was perhaps given proper expression later in the English Bill of Rights of 1689. This document, in conjunction with the Magna Carta, the Act of Settlement (1701), and the Parliament Acts (1911 and 1949) forms the basis of English constitutional law. Some of the most notable parts of the Bill of Rights included: freedom from royal interference with the law – forbidding the sovereign from establishing his own courts or serving as a judge; freedom from taxation by royal prerogative without agreement by Parliament; freedom to petition the monarch; and freedom from cruel and unusual punishments and excessive bail. Many of these issues are directly applicable to emerging democracies today, which need be helped and encouraged into the democratic family of nations.

There is little doubt that the Bill of Rights inspired similar documents across Europe and North America. For example, the Declaration of the Rights of Man and Citizen in France transformed France from an absolute monarchy after 1789, while the US Bill of Rights in 1791 guaranteed Americans freedom of speech, press, and religion, the right to keep and bear arms and the freedom to petition; and prohibited unreasonable search and seizure and cruel and unusual punishment. This is one of the most influential documents on rights and liberty in history and was eventually followed by other advances such as the abolition of the slave trade and universal suffrage, if not without the expenditure of a great deal of time, argument, sweat, blood and tears. In Britain the Slave Trade Act 1807 abolished the trade but not slavery itself. This did not occur until the Slavery Abolition Act of 1833, but even this excluded 'the Territories in the possession of the East India Company', the 'Island of Ceylon' and 'the Island of Saint Helena'. The huge scale of human trafficking today in many parts of the world is testament to the fact that these arguments still need to be made and won, generation after generation and in every part of the globe. Universal adult suffrage in the United Kingdom was also slow. From the Reform Act of 1832, which extended voting rights to adult males who rented land at a certain value, to the Representation of the People Act of 1928, which made women's voting rights equal with those of men, the struggle was a gruelling one.

When put into this historical context then, we can see that the path has not been short nor the journey fast, and the progress to what we define as freedom and liberty in the West has been incremental. An understanding of our own history, and a healthy dollop of humility, should prevent us from delivering some of the nauseatingly condescending lectures that Western politicians seem prone to, as well as preventing us from optimistic expectations which border on the frankly naive. More than 900 years have passed since the Charter of Liberties and eighty since universal suffrage arrived in the United Kingdom. It is unrealistic to expect the same freedoms and rights we enjoy in the West to be achieved overnight in places like Iraq. I often say that the United Kingdom was liberal long before it was democratic – something we tend to forget during our nation-building exercises. There has been a tendency to raise expectations to unachievable heights. We cannot expect to bring Jeffersonian democracy to a country like Afghanistan in just a few years. However, if freedom and the rule of law have been the defining values of our own political system over time, and define us today, I believe that we must see them as our greatest gifts to the globalization process.

Nations facing serious national security threats sometimes make provisions aiming to ensure the safety of the state and its citizens to the detriment of civil liberties. Abraham Lincoln, for example, was not slow to suspend habeas corpus during the American Civil War when he felt that it threatened the greater goal. Yet we must take care.

The current threat from Islamist fundamentalism could easily be used to enact measures that would ultimately have the effect of making us less like ourselves and more like the people we oppose. There are those who argue that civil liberties must be protected even at the risk of diminished security; there are those who argue that security must be paramount even if it means the sacrifice of liberty. But deciding between them is a false choice. There are those who believe that any diminution in civil liberties is inevitably the beginning of the slippery slope towards authoritarian rule. I do not believe that history suggests that our society is on a one-way trip to authoritarianism. In those periods of recent history when there has been a severe restriction on freedom, such as internment in the Second World War in the United States or during the troubles in Northern Ireland, the pendulum has usually swung back decisively.

Internment in Northern Ireland did not last as it was recognized to be a recruiting tool for extremists and ineffective in reducing violence. This is not to say that we can ever be complacent. Unchecked, the state can achieve a critical mass of authority which can produce the appalling effects which the citizens of North Korea or Zimbabwe could attest to today. And civil liberties can be eroded subtly. Incremental changes in the 1930s took Germany from democracy to dictatorship while many, both inside and out, were in a state of denial. On the other hand, excessive zeal by the state can result in the creation of martyrs, the emboldening of radicals and the emergence or strengthening of a fifth column – exactly the opposite of the intended effect. The essence of McCarthyism, that security always trumps civil liberties, can result in stains on the history of even the most tolerant nations.

It was the late Supreme Court justice Arthur Goldberg who said of America, 'While the constitution protects against invasions of individual rights, it is not a suicide pact.' So a balancing act is required, a balancing act that requires us to avoid oversimplifications and to accept some uncomfortable realities. For example, we need to appreciate that in dealing with any threat, internal or external, force alone will never be enough. We need proper information-gathering to produce intelligence which can be properly assessed in a contemporary cultural and political context. We need proper law enforcement. We need to understand cultural differences and avoid unnecessary provocation while never failing to robustly defend our value system. Intelligence in all its aspects is key to our success: intelligence in understanding the historical roots of conflict, intelligence in our diplomacy, and intelligence in gathering information about potential threats and subversive individuals.

Ultimately, all conflicts, whether physical or intellectual, are wars of ideas. The failure to recognize the ideological threat of the Nazis and the failure to act produced the horrors of the Second World War. By contrast, the ideological strength exhibited by the West in the Cold War not only prevented a potential nuclear calamity but ultimately resulted in the liberation of the peoples of eastern Europe. Now we face a different threat. Since the London Underground bombings and more recent terrorist events including the horrendous murder of Drummer Lee Rigby many people in Britain find themselves asking whether we now have, hidden in our society, those who wish to undermine or replace our system of government and to actively challenge our value system. The answer to this question is almost certainly yes. It is clear from both intelligence and experience that Islamist fundamentalists have the will to inflict carnage in the name of their ideology. Yet the infiltration they seek to achieve is in many ways no different from the tactics used in United States during the Cold War. Communist spies walking the streets of America occasionally succeeding in penetrating institutions and labour unions. The answer to that attack lay not in McCarthy's witch-hunt but in the creation and maintenance of a patriotic mindset and political culture strong and robust enough to deny the viral entryism of the Soviet ideology.

How do we assess the conflict between liberty and authority in our own society given the anxieties and threats we face? What are the ground rules that should influence the legislative framework which governs our lives? The essence is surely the maintenance of equilibrium. Just because the state takes powers it will not necessarily use (or abuse) them, but there need to be strong and independent safeguards to counterbalance any increase in the authority of government and its agencies. If the state is given more power then we must preserve equilibrium by giving citizens increased oversight.

What are the rules we should set for government if it wishes to increase its authority in the name of security, and how do we frame our debate in a way that gives a clear message to those who may look to us for a lead as they play their own part in global security? First, governments should only increase their powers over their citizens if there is no alternative. Privacy and freedom should never be curtailed if there is another way to proceed. Second, there should be clear time limits and safeguards – legal, institutional and technical – to protect citizens from the potential abuse of the state. Third, any changes should be shown not only to be necessary but also effective, with both the sensitivity and specificity required for the task. However, we should never accept the argument that reductions in civil liberties are acceptable just because they are effective. Freedom thrives in open societies with robust debate. There is nothing worse for liberty than a compliant press, a cosy political consensus or a risk-averse judiciary. I know this is true precisely because almost all politicians long for at least one of these less troublesome alternatives to an intrusive press, party tribalism or awkward judges.

The endless balancing of freedom and security, of liberty and authority, will occupy the attention of politicians and public in the years ahead just as we sought balance in the past and seek it now.

It should encourage us, however, that whatever obstacles have been placed in its way, the process which began in 1100 is as robust today as it has ever been. If we understand the detail of the influences that have led the free West to its dominant position in this crucial debate about how the world should develop then we are better placed to understand the context of the issues that will inevitably confront us as a wider global community.

In a totally different way we need to understand that there are certain rules of economics that cannot be indefinitely defied however much they inconvenience contemporary policymakers. Take the issue of debt, for example. I will look in detail at this issue and the position that many Western countries currently find themselves in because economic strength is the wellspring of political and international influence. Economic failure leads to the collapse of prosperity and political fortunes. The point is that all these issues are inextricably linked: economic well-being, global political influence, the quality of life offered to our citizens, the ability of liberty to flourish within safe and secure societies, the need to recognize our mutual interdependence in a world where natural resources are unavoidably finite and where, in the words of a Kenyan proverb, we do not own the world but borrow it from future generations.

I hope that by examining some of the issues that we face as a global community we might achieve a better understanding of why we are where we are, avoid repeating the mistakes of the past and give the best stewardship we can to this exciting but challenging globalized era. The following chapters separate the issues for the sake of simplicity but they are hugely intertwined. Indeed, one of the most basic problems of government is that subjects are compartmentalized into pigeon holes which work to the advantage of incumbent bureaucracies but are sub-optimal at best for producing the holistic approach to problems necessary for better outcomes.

The ability to shape the future is in our hands.

There truly are tides in the affairs of mankind which, if taken at the most propitious time, can lead us to a better future. If we fail to take advantage of the opportunities we may create a nightmare scenario for which history will not forgive us.

Chapter Two

TROUBLES WITH NEIGHBOURS

If you are selling a house, one of the questions you expect to be asked by any potential purchaser is 'What are the neighbours like?' We all know that having good and considerate neighbours can make our lives so much better while neighbours from hell can be a living misery. Unfortunately the ability to choose our neighbours is not a gift that we are given when it comes to the countries we live in and the part of the globe we inhabit. The impact of globalization lies not only in the pure economic or military spheres but in the risk of contagion that may come if some of our global neighbours, either through failure or intent, cause massive instability to themselves or those around them.

Troublesome states, those international neighbours who seem to cause everyone else persistent difficulties, come in a range of forms and produce various problems. They may create economic complications, they may cause political instability or they may pose a military threat – sometimes even all three. They fall into a number of categories. Those we may describe as rogue states tend to threaten world peace itself and are usually associated with the acquisition of weapons of mass destruction. Such countries are usually ruled by dictatorships or other authoritarian regimes, often sponsor terrorism beyond their borders and show scant regard for human rights. Sometimes states like this may even act in a way that is likely to be detrimental to their own interests – even their own ultimate survival. At the moment North Korea is seemingly intent on becoming the poster child for this group. This almost pantomime regime, wickedly parodied in the film *Team America: World Police*, would be a lot easier to disregard if it were not for its constant sabre-rattling and its possession of nuclear weapons. Another kind of undesirable is what we might call the pariah state; Robert Mugabe's continuing vandalism of the state of Zimbabwe has produced a good example. The pariah has many of the attributes of the more dangerous rogue state in terms of the treatment of its domestic population but has insufficient power or influence to export its instability to neighbouring countries.

To this list of the undesirables next door I would add a third category – the failing state. Unlike the previous suspects, the trouble caused by such countries may not be intentional; it is often a consequence of the failure of their political, security and/or economic architecture. Nature abhors a vacuum, and when economic and governmental systems fail, anarchy or terrorism can all too easily be sucked in. We are already battling with these forces in places like Somalia and Yemen, but I believe there is one country that stands out in terms of the risks it poses as a failing state, and that is Pakistan.

When I originally had the idea to write this book, I thought of calling it *The 4 a.m. Moment – What Keeps World Leaders Awake*. I wanted to explore the fears of those who took real global decisions, in and out of government, but quickly ran into a major problem. The answer of most of those I contacted was the same – Pakistan. When I asked which country was liable to keep them awake at night the answers were typically 'Pakistan as a failed nuclear state', 'Pakistan's political implosion', or 'Pakistan is a source of global terrorism'.

Having dealt with Pakistan as a member of two different British governments, separated by over a decade, I see Pakistan equally as a strategic ally and a strategic liability – an unusual if unenviable position to be in. Let me say at the outset that I don't have any personal animosity towards Pakistan or its people and indeed have enjoyed both my visits there and the people that I have been fortunate enough to meet. Having said that, on balance I think I agree that it is probably the most dangerous country in the world. This is not as a result of any malign intent but as a consequence of its inherent political instability, the unpredictable and sometimes malevolent behaviour of its intelligence services, its willingness to share nuclear technology with rogue states and non-state actors alike and its potential to export terrorism. That does not mean we should be over-pessimistic or fatalistic about the future for Pakistan but instead realistic about the risks that it poses to itself, its neighbours and the wider world. If we are to find ways to defuse some of its problems then we need to understand the roots of Pakistan's difficulties: its inherent complexity, its historical origins and the influences that affect it. This will give Pakistan the best chance of succeeding as a state – something that is in all our interests.

I have always wondered why it is that India and Pakistan, coming from an immediate past with so much in common, not least 200 years of British rule, should have followed such different trajectories. Why is it that India has managed to progress economically and politically to become the world's largest democracy with a rapidly growing economy, while Pakistan languishes under periodic military dictatorships with an economy massively dependent on international aid? I hope that by considering some of the longer historical influences as well as the more recent political past we might be able to see the context in which this divergence has occurred. For those of us in Britain there is the added complication of having over one million UK citizens and inhabitants of Pakistani origin. The 7/7 bombings, perpetrated by third-generation descendants of Pakistani immigrants seemingly well integrated into British society, have inevitably nurtured both fear and anger among the British people and complicated the already tricky business of integration.

However, I have no time for those who see Pakistan as a lost cause we should abandon to its fate. As I have said in other chapters, there is no quick route to international security and stability. We need to win the war of ideas as well as the other wars. We need to ensure that we can detect, deter and deal with threats adequately, but we must also encourage and support those whose desire for freedom will ultimately produce greater stability and prosperity, particularly those who promote democratic reform and an economic model that will give a more equitable share of the country's wealth to its rapidly growing population (this applies as much in Pakistan as anywhere else).

Before coming to any judgement, it is necessary to understand the historical and cultural influences that have given rise to today's Pakistan. It is a fascinating and complex story, and although it may initially seem like a historical tangent, Pakistan's subtle weave of military, ethnic and religious strands make the country what it is today, for better or worse. Seeing Pakistan in its full three-dimensional context is worth a bit of effort.

Pakistan: the Troublesome Neighbour

The Arabs Come to India

When people talk about Islamic influence in the Indian subcontinent, it tends to be as though history began in the seventh century, ignoring the fact that in pre-Islamic times the Arabian peninsula was well known to the Hindus and that Arab traders used to visit the Malabar region of India. Between them they created a trading network connecting the cities of the Mediterranean, east Africa, Egypt and south Asia. I was surprised to learn that before Islam even existed today's city of Mecca was originally Makheswara, a sacred place in the cult of Shiva–Dionysus. I wonder why religions often choose the same places as sacred!

According to the French historian Alain Danielou, the Arabs gradually subjected or assimilated the other elements of the population of Arabia well before the appearance of Islam and, like the Hebrews, had probably invented a philosophy with monotheistic trends. It was into this cultural mix that the Prophet Muhammad was born in AD 570. By the time of his death in 632 the first mosque in India had already been built in modern-day Kerala. In the centuries that followed Muslim influence in India would ebb and flow, depending on a range of different political, cultural, religious and military factors.

The first of these was the power balance between the incoming Muslims and the indigenous Hindus. For some considerable time the Arabs had coveted the trading ports and rich interior of India with all the merchant riches that their natural abundances promised. The initial advance of the Islamic world, which reached from the north of Spain to central Asia, was rapid and violent, but dynamics change, and by the late ninth century, when the power of the Baghdad caliphs began to decline, the Muslims had once again to learn to negotiate with powerful Hindu princes. Within Islam throughout this period there was an alternation between regimes which welcomed tolerance and saw the value of the science, philosophy and art of other peoples, and destructive religious fundamentalism. This struggle continues today with some Muslim states seeing the value of tolerance and pragmatism (usually reflected in their economic and social progress), while others reap the bitter harvest of unyielding medieval orthodoxy, persecution and bigotry.

The second factor was the moderating influence of external powers, especially the Mongols, who introduced a new, and at times deadly, dynamic to the subcontinent. The third was the behaviour of local rulers trying to maximize their own power (or the creation of a dynasty), whose behaviour oscillated between sensible and downright twisted.

Danielou reflects the view of many, although by no means all, commentators on this period in his book *A Brief History of India* when he says, 'throughout the history of India the Muslims were insatiable invaders. The vast scope of their expeditions, over time, pillaged the fabulous riches of India and demoralized those who guarded them.' The annexation of the Punjab in the tenth century drained India's military and economic strength. It opened wide the gates to the north-west and shook the whole social and economic structure. In 1175 Muhammad of Ghour began his conquest of the kingdoms of India. He occupied Peshawar in 1181. One of Muhammad's most talented generals, Qutb ud-Din Aibak, a former slave, went on to take Delhi in 1192, Gujarat in 1197 and the fortress of Kalinjar, in central India, in 1202.

Muhammad of Ghour died without any male heirs (such is the role of sex in history), and Qutb ud-Din died in 1210 after falling from his horse during a polo match (such is the role of sport). Their eventual successor, Shams ud-Din Iltutmish, took Lahore and annexed Sindh before subduing Bengal in 1231. He reigned for twenty-six years and probably did more than anyone else to establish Muslim domination over India. A skilled military strategist and politician, he is also remembered as a patron of both the Islamic arts and of Persian letters.

The centuries that followed saw regimes rise and fall, the insane savagery of Tamerlane's Mongol invasion and the destruction of the country, and the rise of the Muslim Mogul emperors, descended from the second son of Genghis Khan. It was not until the eighteenth century that the Hindus would gain the upper hand but then witness the increasing power of those who were to control India's destiny for the next 200 years, the British.

A simple historical narrative such as this, however, does not enable sufficient understanding of the Muslim legacy in India or reveal the complexity of the relationships within the Islamic community itself.

Culture, Not Just Religion

The early expansion of the Muslims into India was followed by the arrival of the Sufis, who were to exercise enormous influence and to some extent provided a cultural bridge between Islam and the more esoteric beliefs of Hinduism.

Sufism is not a religion in itself, nor indeed a sect, but a more mystical dimension of Islam. It emerged in the eighth and ninth centuries largely as a reaction to the excesses of court life. Sufis believe that Islamic knowledge cannot be gained solely from books but should also be learned from teachers passing down a tradition descended from the Prophet himself. They believe that the Koran and the Hadith (sayings or specific approvals or disapprovals directly attributed to the Prophet) have deep and secret meaning and symbolisms which need to be interpreted. This is in contrast to the literal reading which has always been at the heart of mainstream Islam.

Sufis were powerful missionaries whose adherence to non-violence and tolerance had strong parallels in Indian philosophical literature. (Ghandi, it might be argued, was something of a product of this cultural tradition.) They exerted considerable influence, particularly in poetry, on Arabic, Persian, Urdu, Sindhi and Punjabi writing. Believing that the external observance of sharia (Islamic canonical) law alone could not satisfy spiritual hunger, they used poverty and asceticism as ways of drawing closer to the spiritual essence of God. They may also have been influenced by the example of Christian hermits and monks, who sought an escape from worldly possessions as a means of distancing themselves from the central authority of the Christian Church and of developing a closer relationship with God. The twelfth and thirteenth centuries saw the high point of Sufi influence. During the Mongol invasions the Sufis helped convert the conquerors and provided emotional comfort to the local populations, attracting followers from the untouchable communities and from artisans. Many of the conversions they achieved seem to have had as much a political as a religious flavour, with a distinct liberationist attraction for the downtrodden. By the nineteenth and twentieth centuries their fortunes had changed and they suffered considerable persecution from their co-religionists. The Salafists and the Wahhabis attacked them for their lack of adherence to orthodox Islam, while others saw them as hindering the development of Islamic society with their superstitious beliefs. In Turkey Kamal Atatürk went as far as confiscating their lands and property and abolishing the Sufi orders in 1925.

Attacked by both the traditionalist and modernizing wings of Islam, Sufism has lost its potential to bring Muslims and Hindus together. Would it have made much difference? Possibly not, but we will never know. Is such cross-fertilization more likely in a globalized world? Global communication, the development of the Internet and the increasing propensity for world travel will surely result in new cross-influences. That may be problematic for isolationists but it brings a ray of hope to the rest of us.

It was not only the intellectual environment that was influenced by the interaction of these great forces.

The physical world too bears witness to cultural contact. The architecture that we recognize today as Islamic has strong resonances of Byzantine style. The Dome of the Rock in Jerusalem is a prime example, and architecturally, if not religiously, shows a deeply shared heritage. When the Ottoman Turks captured the city of Constantinople and the magnificent Hagia Sophia, the largest Christian cathedral before the building of the new St Peter's in Rome (1506–1666), they incorporated elements of Byzantine architecture into their own works including the Suleiman Mosque, and converted Hagia Sofia itself into a mosque. It is today a majestic museum, testament to its unique role in history and the emphasis placed by Atatürk on secularism and tolerance. It is impossible to walk through its stunning spaces, as I have on many occasions, without marvelling at the skill of its builders and decorators and without a hint of gratitude to its Muslim conquerors that they left at least some of the exquisite Byzantine mosaics behind so that we can more easily imagine its former glory. It is for me one of the must-see places in the world.

The Mogul empire, which lasted in India from 1526 to 1764, used a mix of Islamic, Turkish, Persian and native Indian architecture characterized by the beautiful symmetry of its buildings and courtyards. Undoubtedly the best-known example is the 170-metre-high white tomb instantly recognizable as the Taj Mahal. Built for the beloved wife of Shah Jahan, Mumtaz, who died in 1631, it was the culmination of previous experiments with symmetry, gardens and water, and is one of the most admired and loved monuments in the world, haunting in both its history and execution. (Most of us will have to do with a simple headstone!) More than a piece of architecture, it is a reminder of the cumulative power of religions and cultures over the centuries. I remember seeing it for the first time and being stunned by how much more beautiful and impressive it is in real life than in any picture (placing it in my mind alongside the Grand Canyon and the paintings of Van Gogh). Those religions and cultures would meet a new and alien power in the shape of the British empire, And the clash would ricochet throughout history.

The British in India

In the year 1600 Queen Elizabeth I of England granted the newly formed East India Company a fifteen-year charter, giving it a trading monopoly with the east. Little did the Elizabethans understand the enormous consequences that this act would have for Britain and its interests. The charter began a period of increasing British involvement in India that would grow to full colonial control, an interchange of cultural and political influences which would leave both countries permanently altered, and ended with India being split into two nations and the creation of Pakistan. The story of British involvement in India is not merely an interesting narrative but one whose repercussions echo to this day and figure in current geopolitical considerations.

After the English Civil War and the execution of Charles I in 1649, a new charter was granted to the company by Oliver Cromwell. Over time the company changed its nature, moving from a purely commercial entity into one which emphasized territorial acquisition. Management of the East India Company centred on Bombay, which rapidly became the hub for British trade in the region. Following the effective demise of the Mogul empire in 1739 it became increasingly apparent that only the British had the military and political ability to control the Indian subcontinent. Bit by bit, feuding states and territories were incorporated into the area of direct British administration, with other regions remaining within the control of local rulers under company patronage.

Unsurprisingly, the pace of British domination and the spread of new cultural and political values led to a violent backlash with frequent revolts. There was also a growing culture of corruption among officials with an increasing, and increasingly obvious, gap between the opulent lifestyle of the East India Company elite and that of the local inhabitants. This process was to culminate in the great mutiny of company sepoys in 1857.

What was the trigger to this great upheaval? At least in part, the answer is fat! The new 1853-pattern Enfield rifle being issued to the East India Company's British and local troops came with cartridges greased with either beef or pork fat, which had to be bitten in order to be loaded, horrifying both Hindu and Muslim soldiers alike. If this innovation had been intended to offend it did the trick perfectly. Far more likely it was simply indicative of a disregard for cultural sensitivities and the inevitable consequences ensued. The uprising began in May, spread rapidly across several parts of the country and resulted in the massacre of many Europeans including women and children. It was eventually put down (with considerable loss of life), but the whole episode brought about a rethink of British policies towards India and an end to the control of the East India Company, whose behaviour and corruption had done so much to provoke the rebellion.

Thus began the era from 1858 to 1947 commonly known as the British Raj, a period romanticized in British popular culture, in literature and film, across a spectrum from E.M. Forster's *A Passage to India* to television's *It Ain't Half Hot Mum*. Probably more than any other period of British history it has been subject to airbrushing, which often prevents us from fully understanding the significance it has for the world in which we find ourselves today.

The British Raj

The first major consequence of the events of 1857 was that the East India Company was deemed too discredited to continue the governance of India and it was decided that the Crown, under Queen Victoria, should take over a vast area which covered what is now India, Pakistan and Bangladesh and for a time even included Burma and Singapore. The British Raj in India actually consisted of two separate entities. British India was the name given to the territories governed by the Queen through the governor general, while the wider term India referred to British India plus the territories of the local princes or chiefs under the suzerainty of Her Majesty. These princely states, also known as native states, were very numerous – there were 565 when India and Pakistan became independent from Britain in 1947 – but many were very small. What they had in common was that, in reality, they possessed little real power with all major responsibilities being exercised by the British.

That is not to say that there were not great successes during the period. Education flourished in the universities created in Calcutta, Bombay and Madras. By 1890 there were around 60,000 Indian graduates with about one third of these entering the law and another third joining the public administration, resulting in around 45 per cent of mid-level civil service appointments being held by Hindus, 29 per cent by Europeans and 7 per cent by Muslims. The most senior appointments were, as would be expected, almost uniquely held by the British, but the universities created a new group that was educated and ambitious for both themselves and their country.

Unsurprisingly, improved levels of education and social status had an impact upon politics in India. The emergence of a new middle class of Indians, bolstered by their improved financial prospects, especially in the prestigious civil service, fostered a growing demand for greater freedom and independence from Britain. At the end of December 1885 seventy of these educated men (it was, of course, an exclusively male preserve) assembled in Bombay and founded the Indian National Congress. At first discussions were confined to British policy towards

India, but deep divisions soon emerged. Essentially, there were two distinct groups: those who shied away from public agitation and were primarily focused on social reform, and those who put nationalism squarely at the front of their objectives and gave debate on social reform a very low priority. It is worth emphasizing the point that this pattern, relegating social policy to an also-ran, would be a consistent part of the nationalist political dynamic right up to Partition in 1947 and, some would argue, beyond. Additional political complications resulted from attempts by the nationalists to appeal to an explicitly Hindu political identity, in order to unite them against the British, an approach which naturally provoked fear in minority groups such as the Muslims and would later be used by figures such as Muhammad Ali Jinnah to justify the creation of a separate Muslim state.

It was in this increasingly febrile climate that in 1905 the British viceroy Lord Curzon split the biggest administrative subdivision in British India – the Bengal Presidency – into the Hindu-majority province of West Bengal and the Muslim-majority province of East Bengal and Assam. This was, in so many ways, the shape of things to come. In protest, the Bengali Hindu middle class used its new-found economic power to boycott British goods, with the campaign cutting British textile exports to India by 25 per cent. The boycott turned into a more aggressive expression of dissent and gradually violence spread beyond Calcutta into the villages and countryside. The actions of the Bengali Hindus caused fear and alarm in the Muslim community, and its political response was the formation of the All-India Muslim League in 1906. Not only did the Muslims support the partition of Bengal but, increasingly, their focus turned to the influence of the nationalists in Congress and their ever more frequent references to the cult of Kali, which raised fears of ethnic and religious persecution.

And so, as tension between the two communities simmered away in India, back in Britain debate continued about how this part of the empire should be governed. A milestone was reached with a plan for self-government in the provinces, seen by the British as a huge move forward and in line with enlightened views of the day. India would remain entirely within the British empire, with constitutional politics used to bring on board a generation of educated, moderate Indians. How would India have developed if this plan for gradual democratization and the devolution of power had been put in place? We will never know, for whatever chances there were of this venture succeeding were destroyed with the outbreak of the First World War, which forced the focus of the British government back onto the European continent.

The war brought with it new military and economic requirements as the British empire creaked and strained amidst the cost of the carnage on the European continent. Indian revenues were needed to help fund the fighting in Europe, and to maintain order in India in what was now a national emergency for Britain new security powers were introduced, which brought the process of political reform to a shuddering halt. While this might have been comprehensible to the British, it made little sense to those who did not understand why their rights should be curtailed because of a war on the other side of the world in places most of them had never heard of. To make matters worse, after the end of the war there was an unemployment crisis as a result of returning veterans who found themselves with few rights and little, if any, income.

With the war in Europe over and the Treaty of Versailles having dismantled the defeated empires, the British were once again able to turn their attention to the Indian question. The reforms resumed and eventually resulted in the Government of India Act of 1919, by which functions such as education, public health and local self-government were transferred to the provinces. In an attempt to reassure minority opinion, the new regional legislatures reserved numbers of seats for defined groups such as Sikhs, Muslims and Indian Christians, but this further irritated the Hindu majority. This is a conundrum that is encountered time and time again in trying to deal with ethnic disputes: any attempt to protect minority rights can be seen by the majority population as an unacceptable restriction on its ability to do anything and everything it wants.

Despite this, and other setbacks, the general thrust of British policy continued on these lines for the next two decades with increased autonomy being exercised by the Indians, culminating in the Government of India Act of 1935. This had two radical elements: the first was a provision for the establishment of a Federation of India, to be made up of British India and some or all of the princely states; and the second, and more significant, the introduction of direct elections, increasing the franchise from seven million to thirty-five million people. This was not, however, a dramatic lurch towards self-rule as the level of autonomy at provincial level was limited, with the governors keeping important reserve powers and the British authorities having the power to suspend.

In line with previous British policy, special protection was to be given to Muslim minorities with the electorate divided into nineteen social and religious categories. Congress was ready for the new arrangements, building up its membership from under 500,000 in 1935 to what would be over 4.5 million by 1939. It achieved considerable success in the provincial elections of 1937, much to the surprise and no doubt dismay of British officials. In response, the Muslim League grew too. By 1944 it had close to a million members with over 500,000 in Bengal alone. In contrast to the leadership of Congress, which in 1939 was outraged at war being declared on India's behalf without it being consulted, the Muslim League supported Britain, and so Jinnah found himself well positioned (some would say he positioned himself well) both to deal with the British from a place of strength and to sideline other Muslim leaders who might have had a different view on the issue of Partition. While the Muslim League supported the British position, either out of principle or self-interest, Congress continued to move in the opposite direction. In July 1942 they threatened nationwide civil disobedience if the British did not immediately withdraw from India – the Quit India campaign. With Britain in the middle of a brutal fight for survival against Nazi Germany and imperial Japan, this brought a predictable response. This was no time to appease the troublemakers on the Indian subcontinent, and on 8 August all national, provincial and local Congress leaders were arrested, with many thousands held until 1945.

Congress was technically a secular movement and was strongly against any division of India on religious grounds. Gandhi in particular was appalled by this notion and tried hard to keep Muslims within the party, a cause he eventually paid for with his life, assassinated soon after partition by a Hindu nationalist who believed that Gandhi was much too accommodating to Muslim interests. Thus the supporters of a united, tolerant and multicultural India lost a powerful advocate. Gandhi once said, 'My whole soul rebels against the idea that Hinduism and Islam represent two antagonistic cultures and doctrines. To assent to such a doctrine is for me a denial of God.' His untimely killing would pave the way for the solution favoured by Jinnah and Jawaharlal Nehru.

Jinnah, like Gandhi, had initially sought greater unity between Muslims and Hindus. In the early days he had been a member of Congress, but by the early 1930s had become convinced that it had become uninterested in or even hostile to Muslim interests. His repeated warnings about the potential treatment of Muslims within an independent India dominated ethnically by Hindus and politically by Congress culminated in the Lahore Resolution, a political statement adopted by the Muslim League in March 1940. This set out a two-nation future for India. He put it this way:

Islam and Hinduism . . . are, in fact, different and distinct social orders and it is a dream that the Hindus and Muslims can ever evolve a common nationality . . . The Hindus and Muslims belong to different religious philosophies . . . They neither intermarry nor even dine together and, indeed, they belong to two different civilizations which are based mainly on conflicting ideas and conceptions . . . To yoke together two such nations under a single state, one as a numerical minority and the other as a majority, must lead to growing discontent and the final destruction of any fabric that may be so built for the government of such a state.

Other prominent voices such as the challenging and idealistic politician Vinayak Damodar Savarkar argued that, although there were two nations in India, they must exist within a single constitution. His view was that a new state would guarantee Muslims freedom of religion and culture but that they must exist within a single system of political representation where all votes had equal weight and no minorities were to be over-represented in relation to their proportion in the population. But the advocates of a multi-ethnic state were either outgunned or outmanoeuvred by the separatists and as the 1940s progressed the case for the partition of India into two separate states became increasingly accepted in the political mainstream and the outcome took on an irresistible momentum.

The Partition of India: Pakistan's Bloody Birth

The end of the Second World War and the shock defeat of Winston Churchill and the Conservatives brought the election of a Labour government under Clement Attlee and fresh impetus to the Indian independence movement. In August 1946 Jinnah called a 'direct action day' which ignited Hindu–Muslim riots across the country.

In Calcutta, where the action began, there were over 4,000 dead on the first day. Neither the British nor Indian governments nor the British army were prepared for the levels of unrest and violence which occurred over the following months. In response to the events and with undue haste Attlee announced in early 1947 that Britain would leave India in June 1948. This had two main consequences. Firstly, the whole process was incredibly rushed and created the perfect conditions for blackmail during the negotiations by the participants who understood well the need to conclude on time. Secondly, the negotiations were carried out with Jinnah (on behalf of the Muslim League) and the nationalists led by Nehru (on behalf of Congress), effectively excluding the more moderate elements within both the Hindu and Muslim communities, many of whom were completely opposed to the division of India into two separate states. With the appointment of Mountbatten as viceroy (with an impatient socialist British government behind him), the stage was set for a monumental and historic division of the subcontinent decided by a British representative who had little understanding of the complexities of the issues together with those who had manoeuvred themselves into acting as the sole representatives of their entire communities.

On 3 June 1947, less than three months after his arrival, Mountbatten announced his plan for the division of India into two new dominions. He also announced the date for independence, bringing it forward from June 1948 to 15 August 1947. The princely states, which had been so valuable to British rule (not least in helping quell and deal with the consequences of the 1857 rebellion) were bounced unceremoniously by Mountbatten into joining one or other of the new dominions, much to their great resentment. One consequence of this timing and process, whose complications we live with today, is the situation in Kashmir, the cause of so much bitterness, division and violence.

Jammu and Kashmir was the largest of the princely states with a predominantly Muslim population but a Hindu ruler, Maharaja Hari Singh. In October 1947 Muslim revolutionaries entered western Kashmir, and the maharaja, being unable to halt the invasion unaided, did the only thing open to him and signed the Instrument of Accession with India. This act of miscalculation, with all its ill-advised interference, not only denied Pakistan territory it had expected at Partition but set an unfortunate precedent for the Muslim state, whose incursions into Kashmir have generally seen it come out on the losing side.

Why did Mountbatten act with such haste? Some believe that he simply did not understand the complexity of the problems and did not appreciate the dangers of such a rapid timetable; others take a completely different view, that he understood clearly how difficult the situation was likely to be – and his inability to control the forces already unleashed – and that he wanted to take the necessary decisions, however unpalatable, as quickly as possible.

At a practical level, the actual drawing of the border between India and Pakistan was carried out by a boundary commission under Sir Cyril Radcliffe – the border would come to be known as the Radcliffe Line. Not only whole provinces but the much smaller districts with a Muslim majority could choose to join the new Pakistan, a process which was to lead to the splitting of both Punjab and Bengal. Pakistan was to consist of two non-contiguous elements – East Pakistan and West Pakistan – separated by India and some 2,000 miles. The commission in both Bengal and Punjab consisted of two Muslim and two non-Muslim judges with Sir Cyril acting as chairman. There was, as might be expected, little agreement between the protagonists, and Radcliffe himself was ultimately forced to make most of the important decisions, something that, according to recently released documents, he seems to have hugely resented. The British province of Punjab was split into the Indian state of East Punjab, consisting of mostly Hindus and Sikhs, and the Punjab province of Pakistan, the mostly Muslim western part. There was controversy over Amritsar and Lahore, with Amritsar going to India while Lahore became part of Pakistan. Bengal was split into West Bengal, which became Indian, and East Bengal, which originally went to Pakistan but following the war of 1971 became today's independent state of Bangladesh.

After such a long gestation, the midwives to history, at the birth of the two new states, were involved in a painful and bloody delivery. There was hardly any part of India which did not have both Hindu and Muslim communities. While over half the Muslims remained in secular, multi-religious India, the Hindus in Pakistan found themselves in a theocratic state which effectively recognized Koranic law. Inevitably there were massive population movements across the new border. Murder, rape, robbery and revenge were widespread. Whole communities and families were (sometimes almost literally) torn apart. Nearly 7.5 million Muslims moved to Pakistan from India while around the same number of Sikhs and Hindus moved in the opposite direction. Unsurprisingly, neither of the new governments was ready or equipped to deal with such colossal movements of population, and the result was massive bloody violence on both sides of the border with as many as a million people dying in massacres, riots or from other causes. The scale of human misery is hard for us to fully understand today. After so many years of living side by side under British rule, albeit often resentfully, the first experience of many citizens of the new independent states was mutual slaughter among those who had for so long been neighbours.

How much blame should be attached to the Attlee government for the division of India and the bloody birth of Pakistan? Why was a socialist government which preached equality and rights at home and which talked about freedom under the law willing to see millions of citizens of what had been a British colony come under the control of a theocratic government? Certainly Britain's economic position after the Second World War made the end of its control in India virtually inevitable, while the British armed forces were not prepared for, nor capable of, controlling the increased levels of unrest and violence in India. Yet I still find it deeply perplexing that Attlee's government was prepared to see so many people move from the richly developed fabric of British law, with its concepts of rights and protections, to the starkness of a law which effectively recognized no rights for those who were not Muslims.

I think it is too easy to be judgemental about Mountbatten. He was drafted in at short notice to deal with a complex problem, of which he had no detailed understanding, by a prime minister whose government was seemingly determined to cut and run. The practical options available to him were very limited, and, given the apparent willingness of his political masters to see India divided into two and to accept the creation of a theocratic state, the pressure to resolve the situation quickly and avoid the descent into civil war must have been considerable, if not irresistible.

The New Arrival

And so Pakistan came into being – or at least what became known as Pakistan, as originally no one really knew what to call it.

Not only was Pakistan not a natural country, rather a state created around a religious and cultural identity, but its name was also an artifice. In 1933 a group of students at Cambridge University published a pamphlet entitled 'Now or Never' in support of the creation of a separate Muslim state. Failing to find any suitable historical name for the new country, they came up with Pakistan, 'composed of letters taken from the names of our homelands: that is, Punjab, Afghania

[North West Frontier Province], Kashmir, Iran, Sindh, Turkestan, Afghanistan and Baluchistan'. Thus, Pakistan was not only an artificial geographical construct but its very name was, and is, an acronym.

The early life of the new state was not auspicious. As a result of the incursions into Kashmir, the new neighbours immediately found themselves embroiled in the (first) Indo-Pakistan War. The refugee problem was immense in scale and the consequent rioting frequent and violent. Liaquat Ali Khan, Pakistan's first prime minister, attempted to create a more stable political framework with the beginnings of a constitution. Abroad, tensions quickly developed with Washington and Moscow, and there was friction with Afghanistan. The next year, 1948, was no better. Jinnah, father of the nation, died of tuberculosis, and unrest continued to plague the new country with Islamic militants attacking religious minorities especially in West Pakistan. In order to reduce tension between India and Pakistan, the two prime ministers met in 1950 to conclude and sign the Liaquat–Nehru Pact, designed to reassure and protect religious minorities on both sides of the border. There were also growing problems in East Pakistan with an increasingly vocal Bengali language movement protesting at Jinnah's insistence on Urdu being the only state language.

To say that it was not a good start is a massive understatement, but it is hardly surprising that it should have been so given that all the political energy of Pakistan's leaders had been devoted to the creation of the state itself with far too little consideration given to what would happen next. In their defence, it was not the first time that this had ever happened, nor would it be the last.

In January 1951 the prime minister approved the selection of General Ayub Khan as army commander-in-chief, the first Pakistani to occupy the post. It was an appointment that was to have extremely important consequences for the prime minister and began the shadow-boxing between politicians and the military which is still a part of Pakistani life today. In the same month as the general's installation, military intelligence foiled an attempted coup d'état by leftist sympathizers led by Major General Akbar Khan and Faiz Ahmad Faiz, a prominent intellectual associated with the Communist Party of Pakistan. The new commander-in-chief and the defence minister, Iskandar Mirza, remained loyal to the prime minister and the attempt collapsed. The pattern had been set, however, for the coups which would become the hallmark of Pakistan's faltering progress in and out of democracy in the decades that followed and which would so hamper its relations with its next-door neighbour.

On 16 October 1951 Liaquat Ali Khan was shot twice in the chest during a Muslim City League meeting in Rawalpindi by an Afghan professional assassin. The motive for the killing was never made known not least because of the – possibly deliberate – incompetence of the ensuing investigation. The main protagonists were given lengthy jail sentences but, in true Pakistani fashion, reprieved when their defence lawyer Huseyn Shaheed Suhrawardy became prime minister in 1957. It was the first of all too many episodes that eroded the people's confidence in the relationship between the military, politicians and the law. In a twist of fate, the city park in which the prime minister was assassinated was renamed Liaquat Bagh and was to be the site of another infamous political assassination, that of former prime minister Benazir Bhutto in 2007.

There are those who argue that democracy in Pakistan was seriously handicapped from the start. Dr Bettina Robotka, a historian at Humboldt University, Berlin, maintains that India simply carried on as the successor government to the British, using all the facilities, structures and institutions left behind, while Pakistan had to start with no institutional set-up prepared. She maintains that those who constituted the population of Pakistan were much less educated and politicized than those of the Indian heartland. Furthermore, British institutions, both educational and political, tended to be centred around cities that went to India with only Lahore falling within the Pakistani border. In her paper entitled 'The Dilema of Democracy in Pakistan', she also blames the Muslim League and its leaders for expending so much energy on creating Pakistan without spelling out what it should be like.

> After the coming into existence of Pakistan the Muslim League was in dire need of a new programme and direction, which it found difficult to develop . . . It was torn between the ongoing power struggles between different Punjabi feudal families after the demise of Jinnah in 1948 and Ali Khan's assassination in 1951. Regional parties with nationalist ideologies were perceived as enemies rather than a new feature in a growing independent party system of Pakistan.

It is a sad fact that today's politics in Pakistan still largely reflects regional, rather than national, interests and priorities with few unifying themes and aims.

The Ahmadiyya, Intolerance and the Military

It is quite difficult now for any outsider to understand that Pakistan was essentially created because Muslim leaders wanted religious freedom and were afraid of Hindu dominance. That this early aspiration has been betrayed by systematic and institutionalized intolerance is one of the greatest failures of Pakistan to date. The tensions and contradictions which existed within the Muslim community at the time of Partition were not only political but also religious. Intolerance, which lay barely beneath the surface, would erupt when Pakistanis turned on each other. The story of the Ahmadiyya stands as both a terrible indictment of Pakistan and its betrayal of religious freedom and as a warning to others about the perils of religious bitterness.

Towards the end of the nineteenth century, Mirza Ghulam Ahmad began an Islamist reformist movement which bears his name. The Ahmadis, as his followers are known, believe that Ahmad, who died in 1908, was the Mahdi, a sort of messiah awaited by some Muslims. They maintain that Ahmad was sent by God to end religious wars and revive basic morality and justice, restoring Islam to its original format and true essence. They believe that the 'pristine and untainted essence of Islam' as expressed by the Prophet Muhammad has been lost over the centuries and see themselves as being responsible for a revival of true Islam and its peaceful propagation.

In February 1953, in the city of Lahore, a series of violent riots began, aimed at the Ahmadiyya community. These followed incitement by Abdul Ala Maududi, a hard-line Sunni theologian, and his Jamaat-e-Islami political party, who had threatened to take action if their demand to declare Ahmadis non-Muslims was not met. Shops and houses belonging to Ahmadis were looted and destroyed and there were widespread incidents of torture, arson and murder. Unable to contain the disorder, the governor general handed control of Lahore over to the army under Lieutenant General Azam Khan, whose seventy-day deployment marked the beginning of military involvement in Pakistan's political life. In the crackdown Muadudi and other leading agitators were arrested and eventually sentenced to death. With his sentence ultimately commuted, however, Muadudi would continue with his unbending and destructive views, encouraging General Zia to overthrow the government of Zulfikar Ali Bhutto in 1977 and establish an Islamist military government. By General Zia's infamous Ordinance XX, passed in 1984, Ahmadis were forbidden to call themselves Muslim, banned from worshipping in non-Ahmadi mosques and performing the Muslim rite of prayer, prevented from publicly quoting from the Koran, and prohibited from preaching in public, seeking converts or distributing religious materials.

The attack on the Ahmadis was ironic for two main reasons. The first was that Jinnah had sought a separate Muslim state specifically to prevent religious persecution against the minority Muslims in India. The second was that one of the founding fathers of Pakistan and the country's first foreign minister, Muhammad Zafrulla Khan, who went on to make Pakistan's case on Kashmir at the United Nations, was himself a leading Ahmadi. For Maududi and his followers religious zealotry trumped any concept of national unity, a view that still threatens the stability of the Islamic world today.

In 1974, as religious intolerance in Pakistan grew, its parliament passed a law declaring Ahmadis non-Muslims, and the constitution was amended to define a Muslim as 'a person who believes in the finality of the Prophet Muhammad'. Even now Pakistani citizens are required to sign an oath when applying for a passport or national ID card declaring Mirza Ghulam Ahmad a false prophet and all Ahmadis non-Muslims. This codified intolerance has resulted in the persecution and social exclusion of Ahmadis, the worst example of which was the suicide attacks in May 2010 on those attending Friday services in which ninety-five Ahmadi worshippers were killed and over a hundred injured.

This is the fate to which millions of people who had lived under British rule and British law have ultimately been consigned as a result of the decisions taken at Partition and the inability of Pakistan's political class to confront – in some cases actually condoning – Islamist intolerance and persecution. Many have chosen to leave Pakistan and large numbers of Ahmadis settling in countries like the United Kingdom, where they make up a large proportion of today's Pakistan-derived Muslim population. Today they can be found in over 170 countries.

The persecution of religious minorities including continuing violence against the Shia Muslim population of Pakistan tells us that bigotry has not lessened. Those Western countries who shower Pakistan with aid need to ask themselves whether their taxpayers, from whom this money comes, condone such attitudes and actions. While Pakistan continues in ever decreasing circles of intolerance it is difficult to see how it can ever progress in the way that many of its politicians claim to want.

Alain Danielou gives an even more pessimistic view of the consequences of Pakistan's illiberality in the following description:

an artificial country without traditions or unity, Pakistan's only cohesive element is religion. It can only perpetuate itself as a theocratic and military state, based on an inquisition and the severity of Koranic law. The West appears not to understand that this return to a mediaeval concept is by nature incompatible with modern notions of freedom, democracy, and the rights of man. Pakistan can only keep going as an armed camp and could never become a peaceful state.

What I find particularly disturbing about the attitudes of Maududi and his followers, views still being propagated today, is that they recall the prejudice, mutual suspicion and political manipulation that characterized Europe in the 1600s, when religious intolerance spilled over into politics, accusations of witchcraft were widespread, and the Thirty Years' War between Catholics and Protestants claimed millions of lives. That was 400 years ago; it would be unforgivable if in the twenty-first century contradictions and tensions within Islam were to see a repeat of that dark chapter of history.

Division and Strife

In the aftermath of the anti-Ahmadi riots of 1953, Pakistan's faltering democracy stumbled on, but separated by 2,000 miles of Indian territory, the eastern and western parts of the country became increasingly polarized. In 1955 Pakistan's western territories and East Bengal officially became respectively West Pakistan and East Pakistan. Legislative elections then showed how profound the political differences had really become. In East Pakistan communist influence was strong, with the Awami League (allied with both the Communist Party and the Workers-Peasants Party) sweeping the board, while the Republican Party gained the majority of seats in the West. The Awami League's Huseyn Suhrawardy became prime minister, but from the outset he was beset by a number of problems. Ethnic tensions continued to simmer with Bengali gaining equal status with Urdu as a state language in the 1956 constitution. Leading capitalists, especially in West Pakistan, sought to block extensive nationalization, while the communists in the East recoiled at attempts at a closer relationship with United States. Suhrawardy lost both momentum and support and resigned in 1957, the first of four prime ministers to leave office before President Mirza imposed martial law in 1958, suspending the constitution. When General Muhammad Ayub Khan became chief martial law administrator it was the end for the democrats and Mirza remained in office for only two further months. The generals had arrived.

In 1962 Ayub Khan became president and promulgated a new constitution for a new 'presidential republic', with an electoral college of 80,000 to determine who should occupy the top role. If democracy was on its knees then even this cloud had its silver lining. Over the next seven years and not for the last time under military rule, Pakistan's economic performance and infrastructure development improved markedly. Diplomatically too, the country saw much-improved relations with the US and regional allies. This period also saw an acceleration of Pakistan's nuclear ambitions, and ultimately its capabilities. The drive to acquire nuclear weapons both as an international status symbol and to match the challenge of India continued irrespective of whether the leadership was left or right, civilian or military – a fact which we should bear in mind when dealing with Iran today.

The 1965 war with India, which resulted in military stalemate, began the decline in popularity which ultimately led to Ayub Khan's resignation in 1969 – another victim of Pakistan's inability to appreciate the military might and reach of its next-door neighbour. The war also magnified the growing tensions between the two constituent parts of the country, with West Pakistan effectively accusing East Pakistan of failing to take a sufficiently active role in the conflict. But even as Ayub Khan handed over power to another general, Yahya Khan, real political power in the West was swinging towards the Pakistan People's Party (PPP), a socialist grouping founded by the popular and charismatic Zulfikar Ali Bhutto.

The results of the election showed with even more brutal clarity than before the increasing differences between the two parts of the country. In East Pakistan, with over 31 million of the country's 57 million voters, the Awami League under Sheikh Mujibur Rahman won 167 of the 169 seats available with no seats at all won by the PPP. Conversely, in West Pakistan, with 25.7 million voters, the PPP won 85 seats with none at all going to the Awami League. Faced with seemingly insurmountable divisions, the president refused to hand over power to Rahman, triggering a mass uprising in East Pakistan which developed into, sequentially, the Bengali Liberation War, the Indo-Pakistan War of 1971 and ultimately what we know today as the state of Bangladesh.

India had of course taken full advantage of the instability in Pakistan and in March 1971 announced its open support for the Bengalis' struggle. Both overt and covert hostilities continued and accelerated, and open warfare broke out between India and Pakistan on 3 December 1971. Once again, the conflict was to prove short-lived; the overwhelmed Pakistani forces in the East surrendered to the Indians only thirteen days later with almost 90,000 troops becoming prisoners of war. As the new state of Bangladesh emerged in the new Pakistan, Yahya Khan resigned and Ali Bhutto and the PPP began a period of left-wing socialist-democratic government that was to last until 1977. Under the new constitution of 1973 Pakistan was declared a parliamentary democracy for the first time with widespread reform of the military designed to bring it under political control. It was to prove a vain hope.

Ali Bhutto's government was characterized domestically by land and education reform, and internationally by deteriorating relations with the United States and improving links with the Soviet bloc and the Arab world. It is most likely to be remembered, however, for the real genesis and development of Pakistan's nuclear weapons programme. Despite his reforms, however, Bhutto showed himself weak in the face of religious extremism, and in 1974 he bowed to increasing pressure from fundamentalist religious parties and declared Ahmadis non-Muslims, thus feeding the beast that was eventually to devour him. Indecisive and controversial elections in 1977 resulted in violent civil disorder and a bloodless coup which saw the return of the military to power in the shape of General Muhammad Zia ul-Haq supported by, and indebted to, Maududi and his Jamaat-e-Islami hard liners.

Bhutto was subjected to a two-year-long and highly controversial trial by the Pakistan Supreme Court before being hanged at 2 a.m. on 4 April 1979. The execution was carried out in secret, and the only people outside the regime who were aware of it were Bhutto's wife and his daughter Benazir, who were granted a visit the previous day and told that it would be their last. The execution was not only yet another stain on Pakistan's tarnished reputation as a democracy but something that the young Benazir would never forgive. It would also have a profound influence on the political life of Pakistan for decades to come.

Zia ruled Pakistan for eleven years characterized by reversal of the socialist policies of Ali Bhutto with widespread privatisation and deregulation of the economy, and with the government intentionally devoid of politicians of any party. On the international stage, Zia was able to use the Russian invasion of Afghanistan as a convenient tool to cosy up to the United States, finding an ally keen to use Pakistan as a conduit for the financing and supply of the anti-Soviet insurgency. The consequences for Pakistan were twofold – a huge inflow of American money and a huge inflow of Afghan refugees. The latter provided a ready source of pupils for the madrasas – religious colleges used by the Muslim far right to indoctrinate their students with fundamentalist, and in some cases jihadist, ideology. Martial law was lifted in 1985 and non-partisan elections held with Zia choosing Muhammad Khan Junejo as prime minister. The relationship followed the well-established pattern in Pakistan of distrust and intrigue between the political and military elites, and the government was dismissed in May 1988. However, before the elections scheduled to replace the sacked government could take place, General Zia died when the military aircraft on which he was travelling crashed on 17 August 1988.

Killed along with Zia were the US ambassador, Arnold Raphel, and the chief of the Pakistani Joint Chiefs of Staff, General Akhtar Rehman. The CIA, the KGB, Mossad and Benazir Bhutto's brother were all suspected, and the *Sunday Times* reported that the pilot had told a confidant, 'The day Zia flies with me, that will be his last flight.' Investigations led to no clear conclusion about the cause of the crash, and speculation continues both in Pakistan and on the numerous websites which conspiracy theorists now frequent.

The In-Out Roundabout of Benazir and Nawaz

The next period in Pakistan's politics saw an oscillating battle between the centre-left Benazir Bhutto and the centre-right Nawaz Sharif, with each being elected twice only to be removed from office on both occasions on charges relating to corruption or national security. The intense competition between these two strong personalities resulted in a score draw and a wasted decade for the country.

Following the death of General Zia, Benazir Bhutto became not only Pakistan's first woman prime minister in 1988, but also the first woman to become head of government in a Muslim-majority state. Her first period in office coincided with the end of the Russians' occupation of Afghanistan and the withdrawal of Soviet troops. Relations with the United States were initially good but American interest waned as the Russians left. To make matters worse, revelations about Pakistan's nuclear project resulted in the imposition of US sanctions and the atmosphere between the two countries cooled rapidly. With the economic situation also deteriorating, President Ghulam Khan dismissed the Bhutto government in 1990 and new elections were held. These saw the election of Nawaz Sharif and his Islamic Democratic Alliance, ostensibly a more conservative and free-market alternative to the centre-left policies of Bhutto. Within a short time, however, Sharif was also in dispute with the president, who again attempted to dismiss the government. This time the intervention of the Supreme Court enabled Sharif to see off Ghulam Khan and, in alliance with Benazir Bhutto, Sharif forced the resignation of the president. It was something of a pyrrhic victory, however, for within a matter of weeks Sharif himself was forced to relinquish office.

In the elections of 1993 the roundabout turned again, and Benazir Bhutto found herself once more prime minister. In her second term she aggressively promoted reform of the military and the economy albeit with mixed results. In a period of increasing tension with India, she pushed forward with Pakistan's nuclear programme and sought to improve relations with the United States and other Western countries. The government was ultimately undone this time not by economic or international problems but by whispers and allegations about the involvement of Benazir's husband, Ali Zardari, in the death of her younger brother, Murtaza, a character who might generously be called colourful and controversial.

Following the fall of Bhutto for a second time, the 1997 elections saw a massive win for Nawaz Sharif and a real opportunity to overhaul Pakistan's creaking economic and political systems. It was around this time that I first met him. Flushed with his electoral triumph, he talked to me in Islamabad in an atmosphere of great optimism. As parliamentary under secretary of state at the Foreign and Commonwealth Office in John Major's government, I told him what high hopes we had for his government and that he had a once-in-a-lifetime chance to shape his country's future and bring both stability and prosperity. He seemed to fully understand the position in which he found himself and initially moved at a rapid pace. Determined to increase the power of the prime minister and to diminish the risk of being dismissed from office once again, Sharif began reforms to the constitution which saw him clash with the president, the chairman of the joint chiefs of staff and the chief justice. This time, Sharif had the upper hand and all were forced to resign.

It was regional, not domestic events, however, that would shape his second term. In 1998 India carried out its first nuclear test since

1974 and declared itself the world's sixth atomic power. In response, on 30 May 1998 Sharif announced that Pakistan had carried out six successful nuclear tests and had become the seventh. And so the rivalry that had become increasingly bitter in the years since Partition became a nuclear competition, engendering apprehension well beyond the borders of the two states. In the short term Sharif's popularity rocketed with the news about the nation's nuclear capability, but the international economic sanctions that followed his announcement combined with the Asian financial crisis of the late 1990s saw Pakistan's economic performance decline once more and with it Sharif's political support.

The events that ultimately sealed Sharif's fate took place in that cauldron of Indo- Pakistani tension, Kashmir, in what came to be known as the Kargil Incident. When Pakistani-backed Kashmiri militants infiltrated positions on the Indian side of what had become known as the Line of Control (LOC) – the effective border between the two states – the threat of conflict between what were now two nuclear powers became very real indeed. Indian troops moved quickly to retake the positions and international condemnation led Sharif to attempt to distance himself from any involvement in the affair. On 12 October 1999 he moved to dismiss the man he had appointed as chairman of the joint chiefs, General Pervez Musharraf, and replace him with the head of Inter-Services Intelligence (ISI). Musharraf, who was out of the country at the time, immediately boarded a flight for Karachi. In a last desperate attempt to retain power, Sharif ordered the closure of the Jinnah Terminal at Karachi airport to stop Musharraf landing. This was the last straw for the military, who took control of the airport and ousted the Sharif government. So ended another turbulent and unsuccessful period of democratic rule with the return of the military.

This period is, I think, more tragic than most, if only because of the golden opportunities that political fortune had given Sharif. If a strong government with a large parliamentary majority and popular support could not make a decent fist of democratic government in Pakistan, who could? Now that he is once again back in charge of Pakistan's government, maybe it will be third time lucky.

The Generals Are Back (Again)

With Sharif having overplayed his hand and finding himself facing serious charges in court, Musharraf set about economic reform with a more free-market agenda designed to rescue Pakistan from the doldrums in which it seemed intractably becalmed. Most commentators would accept that he achieved a modest amount of success on this front. In 2004 a new political arrangement in Pakistan was ushered in with a division of responsibilities between two roles. Musharraf as president focused on foreign affairs and internal security. In particular he focused on the American 'war on terror' with which his presidency would be so identified. His prime minister, Shaukat Aziz, took charge of domestic policies such as the economy, education and energy.

US secretary of defense Donald Rumsfeld, with whom Musharraf worked, certainly takes a more generous and optimistic view of Pakistan than some of his colleagues or successors. In May 2011 he told the Fox News *On the Record* programme,

They have been enormously helpful in some respects and not helpful in others. We ought to keep working that relationship and try to improve it. The question isn't, are they good or bad? It is mixed. The question is, what is the trajectory? Which way are they going? Are we improving our relationship in a way that it is more beneficial to the United States? We have political, economic and security interests and we need to balance them and recognize we have to deal with countries that are different than we are. They are not 100 per cent helping us. But nonetheless, on balance, it is a useful relationship.

I know from many discussions I have had with him that this is a view he continues to hold and the inherent contradictions between the roles of useful ally and strategic liability provide ongoing anxiety to policymakers on both sides of the Atlantic.

But Musharraf's alliance with the US and his support of the international mission in Afghanistan were not met with universal approval at home. The religious parties who had such influence under the Zia presidency resented the post-9/11 stance his government adopted, and several assassination attempts were made on Musharraf's life, some clearly utilizing inside knowledge. Internationally this period was characterized by growing concern about the role of Pakistan in global nuclear proliferation, with the scientist A.Q. Khan a particular focus of attention. Kashmir also continued to be a source of tension with India, and another military confrontation was narrowly averted when Kashmiri militants, very plausibly with ISI support, carried out an attack on India's parliament.

As 2007 drew to a close, political events in Pakistan took a turn for the worse. On 3 November President Musharraf sacked Chief Justice Choudhry and fourteen fellow judges, declaring a state of emergency. On 25 November Nawaz Sharif made another return from exile and this time succeeded in filing nomination papers for the forthcoming election – as did his old sparring partner Benazir Bhutto, who filed for three seats. On 28 November Musharraf retired from the army and was sworn in for a second presidential term.

A month later, on 27 December 2007, Benazir Bhutto was assassinated while leaving a rally in Rawalpindi. This was tragic but not entirely unexpected. I had had lunch with her in Dubai just a few weeks earlier. In her favourite Persian restaurant – where she delighted in ordering 'the best feta cheese in Dubai' and then whispering ' imported from Denmark' – we discussed the risks of her return to Pakistan. 'You know they will try to kill me, don't you?' she said in a completely calm and controlled tone. 'Who?' I asked. 'Who exactly are "they"?' She was quite clear. 'The ISI. They want me dead.' I asked, if the risk was so great, why she was going back at all. 'The country needs me,' she told me, and then with almost a smile, 'Being killed is part of the risk you take in Pakistan. It's how we operate. It happened to my father and my brother. I will take my risk.' I remember the horror and revulsion I felt on hearing the news of her murder and wondering whether there was any hope for a country so totally enmeshed in violence, instability and corruption. Her words haunt me still.

In February 2008 Pakistan held another general election and the PPP, formerly led by Bhutto, and the Pakistan Muslim League (Nawaz) were able to form a coalition government united by its anti-Musharraf sentiments. They moved towards impeaching Musharraf, and on 18 August the weakened president resigned as so many of his predecessors had been forced to do. Another cycle in the military–democracy saga had been completed and the tables turned again. This time it was Bhutto's husband, Ali Zardari, whose suspected role in her brother's death had brought about one of her downfalls, who was the beneficiary, and he was elected president. Yousaf Raza Gillani became prime minister at the head of a multi-faceted coalition government and the eighteenth constitutional amendment stripped the presidency of its greatest powers, especially the ability to dissolve parliament by decree. And so Pakistan became a parliamentary democracy in a new iteration and with a new constitutional settlement. Will it be any more durable than any of its previous incarnations? Only time will tell.

When I asked Tony Blair about Pakistan's problems he told me,

The weakness of the country's institutions is the first failure. We don't understand how much we take for granted with the functioning systems of government that we have. There is a dynamic of instability when institutions get removed. The problem in Pakistan, and countries like that, is that when you reduce the centralizing power the tendency is towards instability with tribal traditions and the forces of religion and ethnicity liberated and running in different directions.

Bob Gates was much more focused on how Pakistan's weaknesses might affect India:

For India, Pakistan's instability must frighten them even more than it frightens us. The danger of another terrorist attack [on India] is less a risk of conflict with Pakistan, than a conflict inside India between Muslims and Hindus. We tried to get more confidence building measures between them and to promote a nuclear dialogue. It's not clear if they are still in use'

The Islamic Bomb?

Whatever concerns anyone has had about Pakistan and its relationship with its much larger neighbour have been magnified enormously by the development of nuclear weapons on both sides of the border and the claims by some in Pakistan that what they possess is not only a national nuclear weapon but 'the Islamic bomb'.

The story of how Pakistan came to be a nuclear power cannot be fully understood without first understanding the tale of Dr Abdul Qadeer Khan – better known as A.Q. Khan – Pakistani scientist, patriot, national hero and eventual political embarrassment. He was born in 1936 in Bhopal, which was then part of the British Indian empire. After the trauma of Partition, despite initially trying to remain in Bhopal, the family moved to West Pakistan to avoid the harassment of their Hindu neighbours. After school education in Lahore and Karachi, Khan took his degree in Europe and joined a research laboratory in Amsterdam subcontracted to the URENCO group. This had been set up by the governments of the United Kingdom, Netherlands and Germany under the Treaty of Almelo to provide uranium enrichment for civil nuclear purposes. Khan was involved in work to improve the efficiency of the centrifuges used for uranium enrichment, had access to most of the restricted areas in the facility and was given the technical drawings of the centrifuges to carry out his work.

The war with India in 1971 which gave rise to the state of Bangladesh was traumatic for Pakistanis both at home and abroad. It resulted not only in national humiliation but also in increased anxiety about Indian domination and gave credence to the notion that nuclear deterrence was the only way to hold India in check. Reflecting on this in May 2011, Khan told *Newsweek*, 'Pakistan's motivation for nuclear weapons arose from a need to prevent nuclear blackmail by India. Had Iraq and Libya been nuclear powers, they wouldn't have been destroyed in the way that we have seen recently. If Pakistan had atomic capability before 1971, we would not have lost half of our country after a disgraceful defeat.' Clearly, for him, the sense of humiliation had not abated with time.

Pakistan's path to nuclear power really began in January 1972 when Zulfikar Ali Bhutto created the Pakistan Atomic Energy Commission (PAEC) under its chairman Munir Ahmad Khan, its task to create a nuclear bomb for the country. When on 18 May 1974 India carried out its first nuclear test – code-named Smiling Buddha – less than three years after Pakistan lost half its territory, Bhutto demanded that the timetable for nuclear capability be reduced from the original five years to three.

A.Q. Khan wrote to Bhutto, setting out his own experience and suggesting uranium rather than plutonium for Pakistan's nuclear bomb. Bhutto seems to have been impressed by the young man, despite the ISI regarding him as an 'incompetent', and he wrote back, encouraging his interest. In 1974 Khan said goodbye to URENCO and returned to Pakistan to run a parallel and rival nuclear programme to that of Munir Ahmad Khan. Bhutto was determined to get to a viable weapon by the quickest route possible. The rivalry between the two leading protagonists would continue for many bitter years. In December 1974, at a meeting with Prime Minister Bhutto, Munir Khan and the government's chief scientific adviser, A.Q. Khan once again advocated the use of uranium. This was a minority view at the time as the Pakistani government was expecting the French to provide them with a plutonium reprocessing plant. However, under American pressure the French then killed the deal, also losing multi-billion-dollar contracts in other industrial areas, and A.Q. Khan was presented with an unexpected tactical advantage over PAEC.

With Bhutto's support, Khan took over the existing enrichment programme, renamed it the Engineering Research Laboratories (ERL) and situated it in the city of Kahuta, which had the attraction of being remote enough to be able to be sealed off completely by the security forces. Then, with the help of theorist Ghulam Dastigar Alam and more than a little assistance from his former colleagues in Europe, Khan worked to deal with the practical issues relating to centrifuges with some success.

Even when Ali Bhutto was overthrown in 1977, Khan's appointment as director of ERL was personally endorsed by the president and the project was renamed the Khan Research Laboratories (KRL). Relations between the PAEC and the KRL continued to fester. Spokesmen for the former described A.Q. Khan variously as an 'egomaniacal lightweight' and a 'showman'. A.Q. referred to Munir and his colleagues as cheats and liars, and reportedly told Bhutto, 'they have no love for the country. They are not even faithful to you. They have told you a pack of lies – no work is being carried out and Munir Ahmad Khan is cheating you.'

Things came to a head in 1998 when India, after a twenty-four-year gap, carried out further nuclear tests. This reignited feeling in Pakistan that it faced a potentially existential threat, and Prime Minister Nawaz Sharif faced demands from A.Q. Khan, the military and public opinion to authorize their own nuclear testing programme. At the same time he came under huge pressure from the West not to succumb to such coercion.

Given the difficult domestic political position, Sharif's decision was a foregone conclusion. On 28 May 1998 Pakistan successfully detonated its first nuclear devices followed by a smaller detonation two days later. Although the details remain secret, it has been widely speculated that it was the KRL's highly enriched uranium that led to the successful detonation of the first devices. Whatever the truth, the night before the first successful Pakistani test, rumours began to circulate that Israeli jets had taken off with the objective of destroying the facility at Kahuta as well as the test site at Chagai. Although this intelligence was completely false, Pakistan rolled out its missiles and scrambled its jets. This brought the nightmare scenario of a nuclear clash between India and Pakistan into the realms of reality, one of the reasons why so many of those I interviewed for this project regard this as such a credible global danger. There are claims that the prospect of a nuclear exchange was genuine, at least for a few hours, with many fearing that this was just the kind of situation which could provoke a knee-jerk nuclear response.

Despite his high personal profile, his self-importance and the top-level patronage he enjoyed, A.Q. Khan did not control the test nor was he given public credit for it. It was the boss of the test site Samar Mubarakmand who received the red-carpet treatment on his return to Islamabad, met by the prime minister and cheering throngs of supporters. A.Q. slipped quietly back to his house having been met by a small group of friends, the awful thought dawning on him for the first time that he may have been both used and outlived his usefulness.

When Benazir Bhutto was prime minister, Pakistan had signed a treaty with North Korea which seems to have paved the way for centrifuge technology to be exported to Pyongyang in return for the missile technology that Pakistan badly needed as part of its weaponization programme, at least according to Khan's version of events. In 1987, after Iran's request for help with its nuclear programme was rebuffed by General Zia, A.Q. Khan secretly handed over information to help Tehran on its quest towards centrifuge technology. Subsequent inspections by the IAEA indicated that Iranian centrifuge technology had come from the same foreign source as that which had produced the Pakistani capability. Also, when Libya's nuclear programme was voluntarily dismantled in 2003, A.Q. Khan's name was one of those listed as a supplier. The man who had once been an indispensable adviser and was still a national figure was becoming an embarrassment to the government of Pakistan. At the end of January 2004 he was dismissed from his post and supposedly placed under investigation by the Zia government, which was desperate to distance itself from him. In early February 2004 he appeared on Pakistani state television and confessed to running a proliferation ring and transferring technology to Iran, North Korea and Libya. The government of Pakistan was of course seeking to make it clear that even if A.Q. had run an atomic military programme for them, in many cases by stealing foreign technology, they had no knowledge of his involvement in technology proliferation to other states.

Despite repeated calls from the IAEA and international allies, all requests to interrogate A.Q. Khan about his involvement in nuclear proliferation and knowledge of such activities by a series of Pakistani governments were denied. Investigations were finally suspended in 2007 and Khan was never charged with any crime. But if the Pakistani government at best turned a blind eye and at worst colluded with the activities of A.Q. Khan, how much do the Western countries from which the technology originated need to take their share of the blame, and how much did the United States really know about Pakistan's nuclear programme? While it's clear that a number of European governments were casually complicit in Khan's nuclear activities there are numerous indications that the United States government was well aware of the existence of the Pakistan project from the time of Bhutto onwards. It is difficult to imagine that the US security forces did not know anything when Pakistan was effectively a client state. How much did Washington just not want to know because of its need to keep Pakistan onside following the Soviet invasion of Afghanistan, because of its Cold War importance and later as an ally in the post-9/11 war on terror? No doubt we will learn in time.

The Risks of a Nuclear Pakistan

According to a research paper prepared for the US Congress in February 2013, Pakistan is estimated to have an arsenal of around 90–110 warheads. The report states,

> Islamabad is also expanding its production capacity by building additional nuclear facilities, including the construction of two new heavy water reactors . . . The completion of these would effectively double the amount of plutonium Pakistan produces for weapons, enabling it to build approximately 19–26 weapons per year . . . Pakistan is currently estimated to possess approximately 2.75 tons of highly enriched uranium and between 90 and 180 kilograms of weapons plutonium. Available delivery vehicles

include ground launched ballistic missiles, cruise missiles and dual use fighter aircraft . . . Pakistan declared its intention to acquire nuclear powered submarines from China in April 2012.

How do we assess the risks of a Pakistani state with nuclear weapons and how worried, if at all, should we be? Broadly, the risks (which apply to any state which develops nuclear weapon technology) fall into three groups: the possibility of deliberate use, most likely against another nation state; the possible loss of control of existing weapons; and the export of nuclear expertise or technology to hostile states or non-state actors.

In recent years Pakistan and India have attempted to build mutual confidence by abstaining from nuclear testing, establishing a hotline and agreeing to exchange advance notifications of any ballistic missile flight tests. Despite these moves, Dr Bruno Tertrais, a senior research fellow at the Foundation for Strategic Research in Paris, in a paper of July 2012 commented,

In summary, the risk is that a combination of nationalist passion (on both sides), self-confidence, misunderstanding (compounded by the fact that both leaderships believe they understand each other) and miscommunication (despite the existence of dedicated channels, which are not used in crisis time) would turn a small scale crisis into nuclear war.

The level of threat is largely determined by the nuclear threshold that each country includes in its military doctrine. The Tertrais paper sets out how in 2001 Lieutenant General Khalid Kidwai described the circumstances in which Pakistan might believe its existence as a state was threatened. It makes chilling reading, even if the Pakistani government refuses to confirm its veracity. He described four thresholds: spatial, military, economic and political. On the spatial threshold he said that, 'the penetration of Indian forces on a large scale would elicit a nuclear response. The threshold could be low (30–60 miles) in Kashmir and in Punjab.' Militarily, he declared, 'the destruction of a large part of Pakistani land or air forces could lead to a nuclear response if Pakistan believed that it was losing the cohesiveness of its defence and feared imminent defeat.' On the economic threshold, 'economic strangulation could lead to a nuclear response. This refers primarily to a blockade of Karachi, but could also concern the stopping of the Indus River's water flow, or the capture of vital arteries such as the Indus River and the Karakoram Highway.' Finally, on the political threshold for nuclear conflict the general said, 'Destabilisation of the country fomented by India could also be a nuclear threshold if Pakistan believed that the integrity of the country was at stake.' For many people coming to the subject for the first time these thresholds might seem alarmingly low. Should they be worried at how easily a nuclear conflict might be triggered? Indeed they should.

The second type of risk, the possibility of the loss of control of nuclear weapons, is probably the least acute of the three, although it is likely to remain a favourite with thriller writers. There are a number of reasons for relative confidence. The first is that most of the weapons are believed to be stored in the northern and central parts of Pakistan, the areas most strongly controlled by the government and the military and so least likely to come under the control of a rogue military unit or terrorist group. It is likely that fissile materials are stored near installations such as Kahuta or Khushab in the Punjab. The second reason is that Pakistan's weapons are probably stored in a disassembled form, so any group wishing to acquire one would need to attack simultaneously a number of different sites to obtain both the fissile core and the warhead itself. The third reason is coding, which is now carried out during the manufacturing process, and the key to which is given to the launch officer only a few moments before use or to pilots during flight. Just how effective this is was questioned in the Tertrais paper, which raises a number of technical issues. Are the arming mechanisms buried deep in the warhead design, or is it possible that the coding could be bypassed? Do the codes include disabling features? Is there a specific code for each warhead or set of warheads, or just a general nuclear release enabling mechanism? Finally Tertrais asked whether physically arming a warhead would depend on a code transmitted down the chain of command at the last minute, or would those codes already present at the base be sufficient?

The third type of risk, the export of nuclear expertise or technology to hostile states or non-state actors, has already been touched upon. Since the Pakistani government was rocked by the A.Q. Khan scandal in 2004 there has been no known, deliberate, state-approved transfer of WMD technology. However, stories have continued to appear around the world suggesting that all might not be as it appears. In 2009 *The Australian* newspaper suggested that Pakistani nuclear scientists had twice met Osama bin Laden. Professor Gregory of Bradford University, was quoted as stating that two senior Pakistan Atomic Energy Commission scientists, Sultan Bashirrudin Mahmood and Chaudhry Abdul Majeed, had travelled to Afghanistan in 2000 and again shortly before 9/11 for meetings with Osama bin Laden himself, the content of which has never been disclosed. In 2011 the *Guardian* reported that Pakistani generals had sold nuclear secrets to North Korea. It reported that a senior North Korean official claimed that in 1998 $3 million was given to Pakistan's former army chief, General Jehangir Karamat, and another $500,000 to Lieutenant General Zulfikar Khan, who was involved in Pakistan's nuclear tests. According to the newspaper, the generals had sold uranium enrichment technology to North Korea in return for millions of dollars in cash and jewels.

As Pakistan's relentless expansion of its nuclear programme

continues, it is inevitable that more and more people will possess both technical and operational details. It has been suggested that as many as 70,000 people have access to, or knowledge of, some element of the Pakistani nuclear weapons production, storage, maintenance and deployment cycle. This encompasses everyone involved in the manufacturing of fissile materials, weapons design, assembly and maintenance, and those who guard and transport the weapons.

So, to return to my question, how worried should we really be?

The Nuclear Threat Initiative is a non-profit, non-partisan organization with a mission to strengthen global security by reducing the risk of use and preventing the spread of nuclear, biological and chemical weapons. It was founded in 2001 by entrepreneur Ted Turner and former US senator Sam Nunn, whose contribution to nuclear weapons security worldwide cannot be overstated. The NTI Index assesses the contribution of thirty-two states with one kilogram or more of weapons-usable nuclear materials 'toward improved global nuclear materials security conditions'. The assessment uses five categories: (a) quantities and sites, (b) security and control measures, (c) global norms, (d) domestic commitments and capacity, and (e) societal factors. Pakistan is rated thirty-first for reasons including political instability and corruption, the risk of terrorists being able to seize materials, the non-ratification of several international agreements and doubts about the Pakistani government's willingness or ability to address the nuclear materials security conditions in bulk-processing facilities, in transit or in storage.

The Security Conundrum

Those who deal with Pakistan in international affairs often wonder where real power in the country lies. Does it reside with the democratically elected politicians, with the unelected military or with the unaccountable intelligence service, the ISI? This is a genuine difficulty because politicians in Western democracies normally have clear equivalent counterparts in other governments with whom to do business. Likewise, the military are used to dealing with their military counterparts and the intelligence services their own opposite numbers. In Pakistan distinctions are blurred and foreign politicians need to learn to talk not only to their political counterparts but also to be those elements of the military or ISI who have real influence over events.

At our last lunch, when considering the risks of her own return to Pakistan, Benazir Bhutto was emphatic: 'What the army knows, the ISI knows. They are effectively one and the same.' This is probably an oversimplification, though given her history and experience it was an understandable thing for her to say. The ISI is widely believed to have been responsible for the rigging of the 1990 election to ensure the defeat of the PPP. While there is no proof of this, the fact that there is such hostility from one of the main democratic parties in Pakistan towards its own intelligence service is a fault line in the political system. There is no doubt, however, that the ISI has wielded considerable, if variable, influence over the course of Pakistan's history. Its role has gradually expanded, especially under military rule. Under President Ayub Khan it began monitoring opposition politicians and gathering political intelligence, and this increased under General Zia especially in relation to Benazir Bhutto's PPP and the Pakistan Communist Party.

The ISI, which is headquartered in Islamabad, is headed by a director general nominated by the army chief of staff but appointed by the prime minister. Its three wings – internal, external, and analysis and foreign relations – are split into departments including the Joint Counter Intelligence Bureau, whose responsibilities include the surveillance of Pakistan's diplomats and diplomatic agents abroad, and the SS Directorate, comparable to the CIA Special Activities

Division, whose role is to monitor terrorist groups operating inside Pakistan who pose a threat to the state.

When the Soviet Union invaded Afghanistan on Christmas Eve 1979, the hitherto strained relations between the United States and Pakistan became a secondary consideration for Washington, and cooperation between the CIA and the ISI rapidly increased with the latter being used to train fighters and to channel money and arms to the mujahideen. It is estimated that between 1983 and 1997 the ISI trained between 80,000 and 90,000 Afghans and dispatched them to Afghanistan to fight with the Taliban. It is unclear exactly how much support the Taliban received in the years running up to 9/11 but it is likely that Pakistan was giving aid right up to when the events in Manhattan triggered the US war on terror and political reality required President Musharraf to support the United States. There are many who believe that elements of the Pakistani state continue to support the Taliban. In 2011 the chairman of the joint chiefs of staff of the United States, Mike Mullen, stated,

The fact remains that the Quetta Shura and the Haqqani Network operate from Pakistan with impunity. Extremist organizations serving as proxies of the government of Pakistan are attacking Afghan troops and civilians as well as US soldiers . . . For example, we believe the Haqqani Network – which has long enjoyed the support and protection of the Pakistani government . . . is, in many ways, a strategic arm of Pakistan's Inter-Services Intelligence agency.

The fact that Admiral Mullen's comments were not disowned by the White House is indicative of the ambivalent role the ISI is seen to play.

This is not, however, to overlook the examples of cooperation and success against terrorism and insurgency to which the ISI has contributed. It works alongside the Pakistan armed forces in the north-west of the country against the TTP (Pakistan Taliban) and has lost up to a hundred personnel. Secretary of State Hillary Clinton acknowledged this when she said, 'I think it is important to note that as they have made these adjustments in their own assessment of the national interests, they're paying a big price for it.' The ISI has also been instrumental in neutralizing some of the most wanted al-Qaeda and Taliban militants. On 7 February 1995 they captured Razmi Yousef, the 1993 World Trade Center bomber, when they raided the Su-Casa guesthouse in Islamabad, while symbolically, on 11 September 2002, they captured Ramzi bin al-Shibh, responsible for the 2000 USS *Cole* bombing and one of the planners of the 9/11 atrocities, during a raid in Karachi. On 1 March 2003, in a joint raid with CIA operatives in Rawalpindi, the ISI succeeded in capturing Khalid Sheikh Muhammad, the principal architect of 9/11, uncle of Razmi Yousef, mastermind of the Bojinka plot and involved in the Bali nightclub bombings as well as the murder of Daniel Pearl.

Despite these successes, there is continued suspicion that the ISI continues to play both sides. In their article for *Global Security Studies* entitled 'A Pakistani Fifth Column?' David H. Gray and Grant Holt state, 'The agency specializes in utilizing terrorist organizations as proxies for a Pakistani foreign policy, covert action abroad, and controlling domestic politics.' More controversially, a report by Matt Waldman of the Crisis States Research Centre at the LSE claimed that Taliban commanders inside Afghanistan are closely managed by the Pakistani intelligence service. Waldman, who interviewed a number of Taliban commanders in Afghanistan, says that the ISI orchestrates, sustains and strongly influences the movement. He claims it gives sanctuary to both Taliban and Haqqani members, and provides huge amounts of training, funding, munitions and supplies.

According to Waldman, 'The ISI even arrested and then released two Taliban leaders, Qayyum Zakir, the movement's new military commander, and Mullah Abdul Raouf Khadem, reportedly now head of the Quetta Shura, who are among the three or four highest ranking in the movement below Mullah Omar.' The reaction to the report from Pakistan was ferocious, particularly in relation to claims that President Zardari had met, reassured and even authorized the release from prison of senior Taliban leaders.

Drifting Apart? What Next for the US–Pakistan Relationship?

Two events in the first half of 2011 were to strain US–Pakistan relations almost to breaking point. The first occurred on 27 January, when two young men on a motorbike pulled alongside a Honda Civic stopped at traffic lights in the Mozang Chungi district of Lahore. Moments later, the two men, Faizan Haider, aged twenty-two, and twenty-six-year-old Faheem Shamshad, were shot dead by the man in the Honda, Raymond Allen Davis. A few minutes after that a motorcyclist not in any way connected to the initial incident was killed when a Toyota Land Cruiser with fake registration plates hit him as it drove into oncoming traffic. From these established facts, the detailed versions of the events that were to spark such a storm differ widely.

According to Davis, one of the men brandished a pistol, and, fearing for his life, the American shot and killed both of them with his Glock automatic. The version of the investigating police was very different. Although they confirmed that both men were carrying sidearms, no eyewitnesses supported the allegation that either brandished a pistol, and no shots had been fired from the weapons. Furthermore, the police maintain that the men were sitting on their bike in front of the car, with their backs towards Davis, when they were shot. After Davis radioed for back-up, a Toyota Land Cruiser attempted to reach the scene. When prevented from doing so by a traffic jam, it crossed the central reservation and drove into oncoming traffic, where it hit a young man, Ebadur Rehman, who later died in a Lahore hospital.

Whatever the truth – whether the two men shot worked for the ISI and whether Davis and his associates were CIA operatives, the repercussions were swift and enormous. The killings were described as 'a clear-cut murder' by the Lahore police chief, Aslam Tareen, and public reaction was predictably voluble and hostile, especially when Davis claimed diplomatic immunity.

The American government was insistent that Davis was covered by the Vienna Convention on diplomatic relations and should neither have been arrested nor prosecuted. Intense political and diplomatic pressure flowed from Washington to Islamabad. The Pakistani foreign minister, Shah Mehmood Qureshi, refused to confirm Davis as a member of staff at the US embassy in Islamabad: 'I could not certify him as a diplomat. The kind of blanket immunity Washington is pressing for Davis is not endorsed by the official record of the Foreign Ministry.' Qureshi was relieved of his post shortly afterwards.

The initial crisis was resolved and charges were dropped against Davis when payment of around $2.5 million was made to the families of the dead men, although Hillary Clinton denied that the US government had paid the money. However, on 6 February 2011, ten days after the shooting incident, the widow of twenty-six-year-old Shamshad, one of the motorcyclists shot by Davis, took her own life in Lahore with an overdose of pills – another tragic human price paid for the incident. Relations between the United States and Pakistan quickly grew frosty. On 12 February the US postponed the planned trilateral talks between Afghanistan, Pakistan and the United States scheduled for 23–24 February. The reason given was 'political changes in Pakistan'. It was against this backdrop of poor and still deteriorating relations between the two countries that on 2 May 2011 a CIA-led operation attacked Osama bin Laden's compound in Abbottabad, killed him and buried his body at sea within twenty-four hours.

Over several months the CIA agents had staked out the compound using a rented house in Abbottabad as their base. With information derived largely from the US National Geospatial-Intelligence Agency they were able to create a three-dimensional plan of the house, devise mission simulators for pilots and assess the number, gender and height of the residents of the compound including a six-foot four-inch tall male – the known height of bin Laden. Despite all the detailed information available, however, no part of the US intelligence network was ever able to get a photograph of bin Laden at the compound before the raid.

Deciding against a heavy bombing raid partly because of the risk to adjacent civilians, President Obama asked for plans to be drawn up for a helicopter operation. While the mission was officially described as a 'kill or capture' one, CIA Director Leon Panetta told the media, 'Obviously under the rules of engagement, if he in fact had thrown up his hands, surrendered and didn't appear to be representing any kind of threat, then they were to capture him. But they had full authority to kill him.' It was agreed that the Pakistanis could not be trusted sufficiently to be informed of the raid in advance.

After the raid, the government of Pakistan came under close scrutiny and was widely suspected of having known about bin Laden's whereabouts. The Pakistanis, once again, chose to ask themselves the wrong questions. Their leaders, rather than asking how the world's most wanted man had been able to live in a large compound less than a mile from the Pakistani Military Academy, many chose to ask how the United States was able to carry out such a mission without being intercepted by Pakistani forces. The impression was of a government, military and society with completely different aims from the rest of the international community. India, as might be expected, used events to its propaganda advantage, implying that the fact that bin Laden had been able to live so long inside Pakistan was proof that others, including those responsible for the Mumbai terror attacks, continued to be sheltered in the country. Bob Gates was a little more understanding about why the Pakistani military was so upset about American military action within its territory: 'The Abbottabad raid induced panic about US intent on seizing the nuclear weapons. The military were very hurt by the attack and I wonder if the US really understands the humiliation of Abbottabad.' Personally, I find it inconceivable that the ISI and elements of the military in Pakistan would not have known of bin Laden's location. However, given the distance and distrust that exists between the Pakistani military-intelligence community and elected politicians, it is conceivable that no member of the government was aware of his whereabouts. Information subsequently published on the WikiLeaks website suggested that up to twelve officials of the ISI knew about bin Laden's compound in Abbottabad.

David Ignatius, writing in the *Washington Post* in February 2012, asked a very pertinent set of questions that still require answers:

How did bin Laden come to Abbottabad in 2005 and what did Pakistani officials know about his whereabouts? . . . Who owned the compound in 2005, and how was it readied for the new guest? . . . One intelligence source tells me that the architect who worked on the compound was regularly employed by the ISI; the architect reportedly was told only that a 'highly placed VIP' was coming . . . What about the recent claim by former general Ziauddin Butt, former chief of the ISI, that the Abbottabad safe house was used by the intelligence bureau, another Pakistani spy agency? . . . Who did bin Laden contact while he was at Abbottabad?

These questions have never been answered to anyone's satisfaction. Furthermore, it is alleged that while in Abbottabad, bin Laden communicated with Muhammad Omar, leader of the Taliban, and with the Kashmiri militant group Lashkar-e-Taiba. If the ISI monitors both these groups as closely as they contend – and as closely as we would expect – how would such communications have been possible without their knowledge? That these questions have not been answered by the Pakistani intelligence community suggests either a lack of knowledge bordering on staggering incompetence or more than a little double-dealing.

What Next?

So what does the international community do with a country like Pakistan – with its inherent political instability and potential to become the world's first failed nuclear state – in our ever more complex and interdependent globalized world? What are we to do with an ally whose intelligence service appears to be involved in double-dealing yet whose cooperation we require in order to deal with transnational terrorist threats? How do we encourage economic reform in a country which still requires enormous amounts of international aid but whose governmental structure remains almost wholly incompetent? How, in an age of such personal mobility, do we interact with a state which has become a byword for the radicalization of the young through its madrasas and whose exported terrorism straddles the world from India to the United Kingdom?

I asked Bob Gates what the United States can do to reduce Pakistan's paranoia about its own security.

I'm not sure that the US is best placed to do this. China and Saudi might have a better chance of helping. China is concerned about their own domestic fundamentalism so their considerable leverage could be very important. The King [of Saudi Arabia] is not as fundamentalist as some of his citizens. The Turks might be helpful, given the military role in maintaining the integrity of the state. None of these are a threat to Pakistan.

He was concerned about the lack of understanding that the United States has of individuals in the Pakistani military.

One of my worries [as secretary of defense] was that we knew people like Kayani, but the twelve-year gap after Pressler [US sanctions in response to the nuclear programme] meant that we did not know the lower ranks of the Pakistan military. We don't know how radicalized they are in relation to their senior officers. I'm not confident that it's an army that will hold together under all pressures. If the focus is India, OK, but what if the pressures are internal?

I'm sure that, as ever, Bob is absolutely right.

If we are to have a successful outcome in our dealings with Pakistan then we will have to deal with the fundamental causes of Pakistan's insecurity. The first is its relationship with India and the deep suspicions that come from the history we have already looked at, the result of which is an ingrained fear that India would like the end of the Pakistani state altogether. The second is its relationship with the United States, which has oscillated between close cooperation and estrangement as global and regional events have shifted in recent decades. As long as Pakistanis believe that the United States does not have a long-term strategy for their relationship and that Pakistan may at some point be dumped politically and economically, as it has been in the past, then there is little basis for the trust required to steer

Pakistan in the right direction. The third is the instability of its internal institutions, which has created long-running competition between politicians and the military for control of the country, complete lack of transparency in the ISI and the economic weakness which flows from the lack of good governance.

Ostracizing, isolating and punishing those states who cross the 'red lines' of international behaviour may work with rogue states with whom we have little or no common interests but are likely to be counter-productive when used against a state like Pakistan, from which we require collaboration on regional cooperation and stability, cooperation with our security goals and ultimately an end to a dependency relationship which sees it requiring larger and larger amounts of international aid in order to provide its own citizens with the basic necessities of life. Dealing with a country which is simultaneously a strategic partner and a strategic liability is a skill that we need to develop in an era which is likely to produce multiple power centres across the globe with competing interests combined with increased interdependence.

The reason that I have lingered on Pakistan is that I believe it will be one of the most important puzzles for the international community to solve if we are to maintain peace and stability not only in the country itself and its immediate region but also to stop the export of transnational terrorism both physically and ideologically. It is, I believe, not an insoluble problem though it may be a difficult one which will take a great deal of time and effort to get right.

To return to the earlier analogy about neighbours, we must remember that the Pakistanis can be helpful as well as difficult. The problems they pose for us are not for the most part because they want to cause trouble but because they are not in full control of their own household. If we want to find a really good example of a real neighbour from hell – the ones you really don't want to live next door to – then a much better example lies 3,000 miles north-east of Islamabad in North Korea. That's where to go if you want to see what a true, basket case rogue state looks like.

Neighbour from Hell: North Korea

After the Second World War, competing claims of sovereignty in the Korean peninsula led to the North Korean military invading the South on 25 June 1950, leading to a full-scale conflict. Eventually, with the endorsement of the United Nations, countries allied with the United States intervened on behalf of South Korea. The armistice that ended the fighting on 27 July 1953 restored approximately the original boundaries between North and South Korea. More than one million civilians and soldiers were killed in the war. A heavily guarded demilitarized zone on the 38th Parallel still divides the peninsula. Technically, the two countries are still at war because no peace treaty was ever signed.

At a breakfast meeting with Donald Rumsfeld he produced for me a satellite picture taken at night of the Korean peninsula. 'You don't need a map to know which is the North and which is the South,' he said, pointing at the photograph, where an invisible line separated the bright lights of the developed South, with its towns and cities, from the pitch blackness of the tragedy that is North Korea. 'With the same people, from the same history, you now have one side in a command economy and one side with a free-market economy. Look where the light is and who is in darkness.'

The roots of its problems run deep. North Korea, the country where hunger is widespread, is now the world's most militarized state, with a total of 9,495,000 active, reserve and paramilitary personnel. Behind China, the US and India, its active-duty army of 1.21 million is the fourth largest in the world. It is a nuclear-weapon state and has an active space programme – the epitome of bad spending priorities in a nation of widespread poverty. It is almost impossible to understand why these programmes can be a priority in a country where a combination of a series of floods and poor economic decisions led to a famine which lasted from 1994 to 1998 and killed an estimated 240,000 to 1,000,000 people.

This was not an inevitable disaster. In fact, in North Korea recovery from the war was quick: by 1957 industrial production had reached 1949 levels. Until the 1960s economic growth was higher than in South Korea, and North Korean GDP per capita was equal to that of its southern neighbour as late as 1976. So what went wrong? The answer lies in its deeply repressive political environment, which has suppressed individualism, enterprise and innovation and substituted a personality cult which might be comical were it not so malign and dangerous. The hereditary dictatorship that is North Korea revolves around its founder (and eternal president) Kim Il-Sung and his late son Kim Jong-Il. It remains to be seen whether the current leader Kim Jong-Un is able to continue the worship-fest.

All forms of political expression are tightly controlled in North Korea. Government supporters who deviate from the official line are subject to 're-education' in one of the labour camps specifically set aside for the purpose. Those who are 'rehabilitated' are able to resume their previous positions on release on the assumption that they are unlikely to make the same mistakes again. More difficult dissidents and 'class enemies' regarded by the state as irredeemable are incarcerated, along with members of their close family, in camps in 'total control zones', where they endure lives, often not long ones, of hard labour. Those children who are unfortunate enough to be born in the camps suffer the same fate.

North Korea is regularly accused of having one of the worst human rights records on the planet. Amnesty International has reported severe restrictions on freedom of association, expression and movement, arbitrary detention, torture and other ill-treatment resulting in death, and executions. They estimate 200,000 political prisoners and their families exist in the camps in 'the most inhuman conditions imaginable'. Human Rights Watch has referred to the North Koreans as 'some of the world's most brutalized people'. According to defectors, the conditions in the camps where political undesirables are imprisoned are appalling, with inmates subjected to torture, starvation, rape, forced labour, forced abortions and even medical experimentation. Estimates suggest that forced labour, executions and the camps were responsible for over one million deaths in North Korea from 1948 to 1987.

While this hell has been unleashed on the people of North Korea, the leadership has indulged itself in an ever more extravagant and bizarre personality cult. Kim Il-Sung is still officially revered as the nation's 'eternal president', and touching songs such as 'No Motherland Without You', composed in praise of his son Kim Jong-Il, remain popular favourites – unsurprising when any remark to the contrary is likely to result in re-education or worse. When Kim Il-Sung died, the hysterical nation was shown in inconsolable distress and weeping at massive staged public events. The scenes were repeated in December 2011, when Kim Jong-Il died from a heart attack, and the spectacles have continued with mass public adoration of the rotund Kim Jong-Un. The general disposition of the leadership was shown when North Korean defectors claimed that Kim Jong-Un had given out copies of Adolf Hitler's *Mein Kampf* to officials on his birthday. The government response was that it was determined to 'physically remove the despicable human scum who are committing treason'.

Tensions between North Korea and its southern neighbour have frequently been exacerbated by provocative actions by Pyongyang. North Korea was widely suspected of a 1983 bombing that killed members of the South Korean government and the destruction of a South Korean airliner. North Korea finally admitted that it was responsible for the kidnapping of thirteen Japanese citizens in the 1970s and 80s when five of them were returned to Japan in 2002. In March 2010 forty-six South Korean seamen died in the sinking of the warship *Cheonan*, thought to have been caused by a North Korean torpedo. The government in Seoul responded by cutting trade, and the situation worsened further when on 23 November 2010 North Korea bombarded Yeonpyeong Island and the surrounding waters near the Yellow Sea border, killing two marines and two civilians with around eighteen others wounded.

While events such as these have from time to time disturbed the international community, it has been North Korea's nuclear programme that has caused the greatest worry. In June 2009 Pyongyang declared that it would proceed with its uranium enrichment programme, the first time the project had been publicly acknowledged. As a result, the process known as the Six Party Talks was begun in order to find a peaceful solution to the growing tensions between the two Korean governments, the People's Republic of China, Japan, the Russian Federation and the United States. The Institute for Science and International Security now (2013) estimates that North Korea possesses between twelve and twenty-seven nuclear weapon equivalents, including uranium stockpiles. In addition it has uranium mines containing an estimated four million tons of high-grade uranium ore.

As well as nuclear technology, North Korea has invested in chemical weaponry and is believed to be able to produce nerve, blood, blister and choking chemical agents in bulk. This might explain why, in a starving nation, large sums have been spent on training the civilian population in the use of gas masks, suits, detectors and decontamination systems. North Korea also maintains at least eight industrial facilities capable of producing biochemical weapons with current estimates of around

5,000 tons of biological and chemical agents. Another of the world's more unsavoury regimes, Iran, was one of the first buyers of North Korean missiles, and sales to Iran are estimated at around $2 billion annually.

Tensions were particularly high in the spring of 2013. On 7 March North Korea announced its intention of launching a pre-emptive nuclear strike against the United States in a statement which called the Americans the 'sworn enemy of the Korean people'. The following day it announced that it was withdrawing from all non-aggression pacts with South Korea, closing the border crossing and cutting off the hotline to the South. On 13 March North Korea confirmed it had ended the 1953 armistice and declared it was 'not restrained by the North–South declaration on non-aggression'. International analysts generally took the view that this dangerous game was part of a strategy by the new leader to assert his control over North Korea and indicative of an internal power struggle. Nonetheless, four missiles were launched in May, which fell in the waters off the Korean peninsula. Although none of North Korea's neighbours was seen as seriously at risk, such actions are inevitably viewed in the context of the aggressive rhetoric of the leadership and the considerable military capability that the country possesses.

In December 2013, Kim Jong-un had his uncle and political mentor Jang Song-thaek executed as a traitor and his body reportedly fed to a pack of hungry dogs, something that was eventually officially denied. In April 2014 he was 're-elected' as the country's leader in an election where no one else was allowed to stand, and having disposed of eleven high-ranking government officials over the previous weekend. It is reported that his latest insanity has been to insist that North Korean men replicate his haircut, colloquially referred to as the 'Chinese smuggler haircut', though, as with most events in North Korea, it is virtually impossible to corroborate.

North Korea has the highest percentage of military personnel per capita of any nation in the world, with approximately one enlisted soldier for every twenty-five citizens. The Korean People's Army possesses a very large arsenal, including over 4,000 tanks, some 18,000 artillery pieces and around 10,000 defence and anti-tank guided missiles. There are over 900 vessels in its navy and 1,748 aircraft in the air force, of which 480 are fighters and 180 bombers. The country also has a wide range of equipment designed for asymmetric warfare.

How is such a regime to be controlled? What is the role of China in particular? Donald Rumsfeld is sanguine: 'It is not in China's interests to see a conflict on the Korean peninsula, but it might be in China's interests to have a state of tension that has the US tied up and maybe wrongfooted.' What does he think about the potential use of a nuclear weapon?

> The global community clearly is not in a position to prevent nations acquiring the knowledge to construct nuclear devices – which is widely available – but greater efforts must be taken to prevent weapons assembly, including by securing vulnerable nuclear material. While, of course, the lawful and peaceful pursuit of nuclear power should continue, there is an imperative to enforce and demand greater transparency in nuclear programmes to clearly demonstrate peaceful use.

While such a course might be possible in states currently trying to achieve nuclear status, North Korea is already there. 'It is likely but not inevitable that there will be multiple nuclear states,' says Rumsfeld. 'It says something about our respect for the capability of these weapons that they have never been used since World War II.' Nonetheless, no one believes there is any room for complacency when dealing with a regime as deeply unpleasant, and possibly as deluded, as North

Korea. Of course we must employ all the diplomatic and economic tools available to us, including utilizing the influence of China, but the increased military precautions being undertaken by the US, China and South Korea are completely justified. We may not be able to help the poor suffering souls of North Korea in the short term but we can certainly bring pressure to bear in order to seek better behaviour from their leaders, and we must take the military steps necessary to send an unequivocal message that any aggression on their part will be met with an overwhelming military response.

Above all, we must keep in mind that whether the problem is a potentially failing state like Pakistan or an unstable and crazy regime like that in North Korea, we would all be affected by a disastrous outcome, so it is in all our interests to do everything we can together to prevent that scenario from occurring. The implication of globalization is that, whether we like it or not, it is everyone's business.

Chapter Three

THE GULF, ISLAM AND
THE GLOBAL CROSSROADS

At the end of the last glacial period, around 20,000 years ago, the ice sheets reached their maximum extent, hugely affecting the world's climate and resulting in drought, desertification and a massive drop in sea levels. Between 12,000 and 9,000 years ago much of what is today the floor of the Gulf would have been exposed. The marine life that is so abundant today has developed only over the past 8,000 years or so. Today, this inland body of water of some 156,000 square miles averages around 115 feet in depth with the seabed between Abu Dhabi and Qatar much shallower at around 50 feet. The Gulf and its littoral are now the world's largest single source of crude oil with large gas finds also having been made. At the beginning of the millennium the Gulf nations of Iraq, Iran, the United Arab Emirates (UAE), Qatar, Bahrain and Saudi Arabia produced around 25 per cent of the world's oil and held nearly two thirds of known global oil reserves and 35 per cent of natural gas reserves.

Novices who visit the region, take part in meetings or attend conferences there will quickly discover that even the name of the body of water variously known as the Gulf, the Persian Gulf or the Arabian Gulf is controversial and sensitive. What I will refer to as the Gulf is a fault line where religion, power, money and politics collide. It is the primary venue for the tensions between Sunni and Shia Islam. There is also a political divide between pro-Western states such as Saudi Arabia, the UAE and Bahrain on one side and the growing strength of Iran on the other. Add to all this the geography of the Strait of Hormuz, one of the world's great maritime and economic pinch points, and it is easy to see why this region is regarded as a potential tinderbox.

For 850 years between 625 BC and AD 225 the northern side of the Gulf was occupied by a series of empires including the Parthian and Achaemenid. Under the most famous of the Achaemenids, Darius the Great, a strong maritime tradition was established which saw Persian dominance of the Gulf alongside patrols of the major waterways from the Shatt al-Arab to the Sindh waterways of India. The Persian fleet was instrumental in the opening up of trade with India, long before the birth of Islam and the cultural clash between the two civilizations. Persian dominance would last until the mid-nineteenth century, when the British arrived in the guise of the East India Company and the Royal Navy. From 1763 the British maintained political control, to some extent, over what would become the UAE, Bahrain, Kuwait, Oman and Qatar. British interest in the area increased particularly during the eighteenth and nineteenth centuries as British India took on a greater importance within the empire. Until 1892 Britain had a policy of non-interference in the affairs of what were known as the Trucial States (primarily Bahrain and Oman), but from that point assumed responsibility for their foreign policy and thus their protection. The price of this protection in terms of the local states' ability to develop their natural resources was high. In 1922 they agreed not to allow oil exploration and exploitation in their territories unless permitted by the British government, and in 1937 they were compelled to do business exclusively with a subsidiary of the Anglo-Iranian Oil Company (AIOC).

Britain remained the controlling power in the region until Bahrain, Kuwait, Qatar and Oman became independent in 1971. Only two years later many of the Gulf states found themselves on the other side of the fence from Britain as the 1973 oil crisis got into full swing. On 6 October 1973, on the holiest day of the Jewish calendar – Yom Kippur – Egypt and Syria, supported by a number of other Arab countries, launched a surprise attack on the state of Israel, and a massive Egyptian crossing of the Suez Canal soon saw their forces advance almost unopposed into the Sinai peninsula. Israel quickly mobilized, and three days later the Egyptian advance had turned into a stalemate. The Syrians launched a simultaneous attack on the Golan Heights, but again, after three days, they were pushed back to pre-war ceasefire lines.

It was the aftermath of the war, however, that was to have profound implications for the oil-producing Gulf states and the international community. In many ways the Yom Kippur War simply accelerated a process that had begun some time before with increasing resentment among the oil suppliers that the West was insisting on ever increasing oil imports without any willingness to pay more. In 1973 the Shah of Iran told the *New York Times*, 'You increased the price of wheat you sell us by 300 per cent . . . You buy our crude oil and sell it back to us, refined as petrochemicals, at a hundred times the price you've paid to us . . . It's only fair that, from now on, you should pay more for oil. Let's say ten times more.' With the Western nations hugely dependent on Gulf oil, a strategic weakness was ruthlessly exposed, and when the United States chose to resupply Israel with arms during the war, the Organization of Arab Petroleum Exporting Countries (OAPEC) decided to punish it with an oil embargo that lasted from October 1973 to March 1974.

Some European nations and Japan tried to distance themselves from American policy in the Middle East in a generally crass and undignified attempt to avoid the worst of the oil embargo. It was the price rises rather than the embargo, however, that did the greatest economic damage to European nations, particularly Britain, where it combined with strikes by miners and railway workers to produce a full-scale energy crisis, with Prime Minister Edward Heath being ejected from office in February 1974. Across Europe governments tried a range of measures from restrictions on weekend activities to rationing of electricity to deal with the crisis. The point was made, however, that the boot was firmly, if temporarily, on the other foot – and the foot was an OPEC one.

The Organization of Petroleum Exporting Countries, which then consisted of Iran, Saudi Arabia, Iraq, Kuwait, Qatar and the UAE, along with Venezuela, Indonesia, Nigeria and Ecuador, had, from its start in 1960, succeeded in gradually securing for its members an increasing share of the Western oil companies' profits and more control over levels of production. Their closer cooperation was to prove both timely and globally significant. In August 1971 President Richard Nixon took the United States out of the Bretton Woods Accord and, by doing so, broke the link between the value of the dollar and the price of gold. In response Britain floated the pound sterling. It was followed by a number of other industrialized nations also loosening their monetary policies, the net result being a substantial depreciation in the value of the US dollar. This meant that the oil exporters received less real income as oil was and is priced in dollars. They countered by announcing that henceforth oil would be priced against gold itself.

In response to both the end of Bretton Woods and the Yom Kippur War, on 16 October 1973 OPEC announced its decision to raise the price of oil by 70 per cent – to a then shocking $5.11 a barrel! The next day they agreed to cut production by 5 per cent from the previous month's levels and vowed continued cuts of 5 per cent until their political and economic objectives were met. The response of the markets, anticipating (correctly) the slow pace at which demand would fall in line with higher prices, saw prices rocket to $12 a barrel, and the stage was set for the high inflation and recessions that would plague the global economy for the next decade. Another result of the economic upheaval was the end of capital controls in Western oil-dependent economies to enable the petrodollars of OPEC to finance their current-account deficits, a foretaste of the financial imbalances that were to come in the ensuing decades.

The oil embargo predictably spurred Western nations towards more oil exploration within their own territories as well as energy conservation measures, and subsequent changes in economic policy – including the early cutting of interest rates to prevent recession – resulted in inflation, eventually followed by tighter money supply to bear down on self-created inflationary pressures. None of these developments were to be in the longer-term interests of those who took the embargo decision back in 1973. The Americans quickly recognized the need to improve their energy security and many US companies began to seek ways to develop oil reserves that had previously been deemed too expensive. This process, which involved territories from the wilds of Alaska to the deep seas of the Gulf of Mexico, has continued with today's fracking, which has driven and continues to drive down global gas prices. Across the world countries discovered renewable energy sources including solar and wind power. Not only was Israel unaffected by the embargo due to its own oil industry in the Sinai, but the crisis provided the impetus for the development of the solar water heaters now used in over 90 per cent of Israeli homes.

The effects went beyond the energy industry. The Japanese, whose enormous dependence on Gulf oil had been so painfully exposed, shifted from oil-intensive industries into the new field of electronics, quickly establishing themselves as global leaders in this emerging market. At the same time they took advantage of the move in America away from large gas-guzzling cars by producing smaller more fuel-efficient alternatives. I can remember the first time I visited the United States – as a medical student in 1982 – when the roads were still relatively full of the huge automobiles so familiar from American television and films, and then, a mere three or four years later, being amazed at the number of mid-sized cars, largely Japanese, cruising the American highways. It was an American cultural revolution made in the Gulf.

Did the oil embargo produce the desired effects for its prime movers? The answer is almost certainly not. Western policy did not change in the way the Arab leaders had hoped. Israel continued to receive support from the United States, Britain and their allies. Indeed, 1973 saw the high-water mark of OPEC, whose influence declined steadily so that by 1981 its production was surpassed by non-OPEC nations. Internal divisions also surfaced, with Saudi Arabia putting downward pressure on prices as it sought to regain its market share. The price of oil, which peaked at around $80 per barrel in 1979, fell back to around $38 per barrel within a few years, at one point in real terms reaching pre-1973 levels. The fall was catastrophic for those countries whose economic lifeline was oil but who were otherwise overpopulated and poor. For countries such as Mexico, Libya, Algeria and Nigeria the situation became grim.

As the decade wore on, economic costs were compounded by political irony. In the years of the Cold War the United States and the Soviet Union had vied for influence in the region. The American camp could count on Saudi Arabia, Israel, Turkey and Iran, while the Soviets had Syria, Egypt and Iraq. When President Sadat threw out his Soviet advisers in 1970 it may have annoyed the Russians, but the oil shock of 1973–4 and the subsequent price increases provided the impetus for the development and export of Soviet oil. By 1980 the Soviet Union was the world's largest oil producer, and competition with OPEC was intense. On top of regional fears following the Soviet invasion of Afghanistan in 1979, this resulted in the Gulf nations turning to the United States for precisely the same sort of security guarantees that they had tried to prise away from Israel less than ten years earlier. It was a bitter if not fatal blow for the remnants of Arab nationalism and it would have its own ramifications.

The Ebb and Flow of Arab Nationalism

The Mashreq is the collective name given to the countries north of the Arabian peninsula and east of Egypt, in other words, Syria, Lebanon, Kuwait, Iraq Jordan and Palestine. The Arabic word from which the term is derived means literally 'place of sunrise'. It can be seen as the partner term to the Maghreb, the Arabic-speaking countries west of Egypt in North Africa. Egypt lies in the centre and has ties to both areas – linguistic, ethnic and cultural – and its distinctiveness was to make it a much valued prize in the rush to create a pan-Arab movement.

In the second half of the nineteenth century the countries of the Mashreq were under Ottoman control. Around this time literature began to be produced which condemned the Ottomans for betraying the true nature of Islam by deviating from its true beliefs and practices and thus causing its gradual decline. In the view of some writers the Arab world had seen its greatest military triumphs and cultural achievements with the advent of Islam. Therefore, their argument went, the revival of true Islam would produce the sort of effective constitutional government that, while Islamic in origin, was manifested in the West at the time. This thinking was an amalgam of what, in the twentieth century, would give rise and encouragement to both pan-Arab nationalism and Islamic fundamentalism.

Nationalist ideology celebrated the glories of Arab civilization, the language and literature of the Arabs, and called for rejuvenation and political union in the Arab world. Its central premise was that the Arab peoples, from the Atlantic Ocean to the Arabian Sea, constituted one nation bound together by common linguistic, cultural, religious and historical heritages. Two of the primary goals of Arab nationalism were the end of Western influence over the Arabs and the removal of those governments considered to be dependent for their existence on Western power.

During the First World War the British incited and, through T.E. Lawrence, assisted the Arab revolt in the Hejaz (western Arabia) which saw the defeat of the Ottomans there and the rebel forces under Faysal ibn al-Husayn eventually reach Damascus. The campaign is superbly captured in David Lean's Oscar-winning *Lawrence of Arabia*, which remains one of my most watched favourites. Damascus became the centre of Arab nationalism with Faysal the closest thing to an Arab monarch anyone alive had known, following 400 years of Turkish dominance. Yet the human tensions that would later undermine the movement were present even at the outset, with splits between those who wanted to see the establishment of a pan-Arab state of some sort and those who wanted to work more within present realities, based on tribal tradition and identity.

During the war the British actively encouraged Arab nationalism, not out of any attachment to the cause, but as a means of undermining and defeating the Ottomans, and, as so often in history, the generous promises that were given, largely by Lawrence, did not survive the glow of victory. After the war a secret agreement between France and Britain saw the territories of the region divided between the two imperial powers. This provided the Arab nationalist movement with a new and potent ideology – anti-imperialism – which was to help power it for the next half-century. Effective as it was at the outset, however, it became less powerful as a number of local revolts saw the steady diminution of imperial influence in the region.

In 1931, during a conference in Jerusalem, a pan-Arabist covenant was proclaimed. It affirmed that Arab countries formed an integral and indivisible whole, that those countries whose focus was exclusively on their own local or regional interests should be opposed and that imperialism should be confronted at all times. It was around this time that fears of the growth of Zionism in Palestine began to provide another unifying force for the movement, and in 1932 the Arab Independence Party (AIP) was formed with the aim of resisting the British mandate in Palestine and the increasing number of Jews settling there.

The following years saw rival plans emerge for closer ties among Arab nations, the most successful of which came from the Egyptian government of Nahas Pasha, not least because of the vigour of the Egyptians' much-valued embrace of Arabism, something that the leaders of other regional governments were quick to latch on to. In the autumn of 1944 the leaders of Egypt, Syria, Iraq, Lebanon and Transjordan met to produce what became known as the Alexandria Protocol. This marked the beginning of the central role that Egypt was to play in the peaks and troughs of Arab nationalism in the following two decades, but centre stage was to bring its own stresses and strains.

Of all the figures in history who will be associated with Arab nationalism, the most outstanding is almost certainly Gamal Abdel Nasser Hussein, who as president of Egypt from 1956 to his death in 1970 epitomized the Arabist cause in all its manifestations. As an army colonel, Nasser had planned and led the Egyptian revolution of 1952 which resulted in the overthrow of King Farouk I. Initially governing through the Revolutionary Command Council, he introduced popular land reforms, but following an attempted assassination by the Muslim Brotherhood in 1954 he assumed executive command and his nomination for the presidency was confirmed by a public referendum in June 1956. The Muslim Brotherhood's assassination attempt resulted in a brutal crackdown by Nasser, including the execution of Sayyid Qutb, its leading ideologue, and I would argue the most extreme, which further widened the growing distance between Arab nationalists and Islamic fundamentalists. It is the religious zeal of Qutb and his sympathizers, rather than Arab nationalism, that drives much of the violent concepts of jihad today.

In a bid to free Egypt from what he perceived as imperialist influences, Nasser sought to widen Egypt's aid base by taking money and arms from Soviet bloc countries. This funding differed from what had gone before in that it was independent of treaty ties, base concessions or peace accords, which had been the conditions for Western aid. In August 1956 he played his trump card, nationalizing the Suez Canal, prompting an attack by Britain and France and the invasion of Sinai by Israel. Under much-resented American pressure, the invaders withdrew and America began its own aid programme to Egypt. In Britain the debacle resulted in the resignation of Prime Minister Anthony Eden. Just as the British in the First World War encouraged Arab nationalism in order to undermine and defeat the Ottomans, so now America promoted it as a means of containing communism. In February 1958 the United Arab Republic was formed by the merger of Syria and Egypt, and on 14 July that year the monarchy in Iraq fell to a violent military coup. The nationalist movement had reached its high point. America, not least because of an anti-imperialist policy against Britain and France, finds itself still holding the baby today.

The Palestinian question and opposition to Jewish settlement were the focus of Arab nationalist intent in the years after the Second

World War. With the end of the British mandate over Palestine, a UN partition plan was supposed to come into effect. However, a number of Arab states immediately intervened on the Palestinian side. Belief in their own propaganda, growing internal tensions and unjustifiable overconfidence culminated in the humiliating defeat of the Arabs leading to the 1948 Arab–Israeli War. The result was that the new state of Israel kept almost all the territory apportioned to it by UN General Assembly Resolution 181 and well over half of the area allocated to the proposed Arab state. Transjordan took over what was left of the West Bank and East Jerusalem and the Egyptian military controlled the Gaza Strip. There was no Arab Palestinian state created – only new uncertainties and indignities. Little wonder that the Arabs refer to 1948 as *al-nakba*, the catastrophe.

It was another military defeat, the 1967 Six Day War, that brought the nationalist dream to its knees. What Nasser had called 'the battle of destiny' turned out to be an irreversible setback for the Arab nationalist movement. Not only were the Arabs decisively defeated but many of the political elements that had supported the cause in its earlier days had atrophied. The imperialist threat and presence were greatly diminished and there were unbridgeable differences over attachments to tribal tradition and suspicion between some groups, such as the Iraqi Shia and Sunni communities. The southern Shia population largely saw Arab nationalism as a Sunni project designed to marginalize them in an expanded Sunni domain despite the Shia constituting over half the population of the country. The seeds of escalating tension between the two principal Islamic sects had been sown and would grow as the century drew to its close.

Scholars have pointed to two other elements in the decline of Arabism. The first was the lack of concepts of free political expression, pluralism and the separation of powers within the movement. This left it entirely dependent upon the power and charisma of its leaders with no strength in reserve in the event of a political setback. The second was the continuing and growing Islamic revival, which the secular Arab nationalist movement profoundly rejected. The Islamists, in their turn, rejected the concept of nationalism, believing that the fundamental flaw in the Arabist argument was that it was Islam which had rescued and given glory to the Arab peoples rather than vice versa.

Following the events of June 1967 Nasser was forced to focus on his increasingly fraught domestic difficulties with Israeli soldiers camped only three hours away from Cairo on the eastern bank of the Suez Canal and an economy teetering on the brink. These factors conspired to produce deepening Egyptian dependence on the more conservative Arab states for financial support, and it was the wealthy oil kingdoms who had never supported Nasser's movement who delivered its effective coup de grâce. After Nasser's death, under its new president Anwar Sadat, Egypt changed its name to the Arab Republic of Egypt, turning its back on pan-Arab pretensions and emphasizing Egypt's own long history, cultural heritage and individual identity.

As Arab nationalism faded, radical Islam further emerged. The nationalists had accepted that there was a special place for Islam within the movement but tended to stress only its moral and spiritual elements, rejecting any constitutional or political role. They saw the defining and binding elements of their movement as linguistic and historical ties, not religious links. Radical Muslim groups saw this as blasphemy and nationalists increasingly became their target. In the last three decades of the twentieth century radical Islam became the main threat to Arab regimes with Islamists challenging the governments of Iraq, Syria, Egypt and Algeria.

Iran : The Land of the Aryans

All civilizations have complex histories often compounded by myth and folklore, but a common denominator tends to be the role that symbolic dates play in their development and identity. In the case of Iran the date which probably stands out in the minds of most people is not some long-distant battle but 1 February 1979, the day on which Ayatollah Ruhollah Khomeini returned from exile, marking the end of the Iranian monarchy and with it the birth of the Islamic Republic of Iran. While Khomeini undoubtedly changed the course of Iran and with it the modern world, all too often Iran is incorrectly viewed by the limited myopia of events that immediately preceded and followed the revolution in 1979. This is unfortunate because the long and proud history of Persia, as the country was known for much longer, makes both fascinating reading and also provides valuable insights into events which have shaped the more recent pages of the nation's history. In order to help unravel and understand the enigmatic riddle which is Iran we must begin with its historical roots. While people talk about the Middle East or the Gulf as a complex jigsaw, I have always tended to think of Iran more as a Rubik's cube, probably appropriately for a nation that refined the game of chess from its Indian origins.

Islam's arrival in Persia from Arabia was by the sword in the invasion of AD 637–651. While the military conquest took many years, under the direction of Caliph Umar it eventually prevailed, marking the end of the Sassanid dynasty, which had ruled for some 400 years. The eventual success of the invasion was largely a reflection of the decline of the Sassanid empire rather than as a result of a single event. Years of almost perpetual conflict with the rival Byzantine empire eventually took its toll and left Persia financially weak and lacking the strong leadership which had characterized its rise. To many historians the Sassanid empire was one of the most important of Persian history because of its military and political successes and also its cultural influence, which extended well beyond its expansive borders, themselves reaching as far as modern Russia and China in the east and Turkey and Egypt in the west.

Prior to the Islamic invasion Persia had predominantly been Zoroastrian, with Christianity and Judaism also present. The Zoroastrian religion derives its name from the philosopher Zoroaster, who lived around 1000 BC, but it wasn't until the Achaemenid and subsequent Sassanid empires that it truly flourished. The religion's beliefs centre on the existence of a single universal good against the backdrop of a constant struggle in which the good deeds of humanity are required to hold back the advance of evil forces. Fire and water, which are symbols of purity in Zoroastrianism, play a central role in its rituals. It continues to flourish today with one of its most famous followers being the rock star Freddie Mercury, whose funeral was conducted by Zoroastrian priests.

The arrival of the harsh new religion Islam contrasted sharply with Zoroastrian traditions, so in spite of the forced conversions undertaken by the new rulers, its uptake was probably more evolutionary than revolutionary. Over time the new religion became more established with the fastest growth in numbers occurring in cities and among the nobility (for whom it was a prerequisite for social advancement), but with much lower numbers in rural areas. Historical records suggest that it took some 400 years for Islam to establish itself as the majority religion of the country. Certainly it was not until the fifteenth century, under the Safavid dynasty, that Shia Islam became the official state religion.

As so often happens when a new cultural influence is introduced, the emergence and development of Persia's Islamic identity did not eradicate existing cultural traditions, most of which were deeply rooted in Zoroastrian customs. Instead the two became ever more interwoven over the centuries that followed, and while attacks on Zoroastrian shrines and the destruction of relics did take place, the Persian national identity was never swept away. Not only was there a strong and vibrant religious culture but the concept of nationhood already existed. A recent insight into the importance of ancient customs occurred following the revolution in 1979. Ayatollah Ruhollah Khomeini attempted to ban the traditional celebrations which mark the start of Nowruz, the Iranian New Year, on the grounds that the festival, whose origins are Zoroastrian, was un-Islamic. A suitable analogy is perhaps the banning of Christmas by Oliver Cromwell in Britain after the English Civil War. Unlike Cromwell, however, whose move caused lasting and unwavering resentment, Khomeini realized the futility of his efforts and his plans were soon dropped.

The entrenching of the schism in Islam between Sunni and Shia also played an important part in the development of Persia's identity. That Persians regard themselves as having found a better interpretation of a religion that some would characterize as having been brought to them by barbarians is a theme in their Shia tradition which chimes harmoniously with what many would regard as Iran's pre-Islamic achievements. The ongoing impact and importance of the division within Islam is an important issue to which I will return later. There is of course also a chauvinistic narrative (by no means confined to Iran) of what we might call national exceptionalism, which dictates that Iranians are uniquely capable people, and hence those who have been duped by others are not real Iranians – but we will leave that aside as we have quite sufficient psychological complexity baked into the history.

At the start of the twentieth century Persia, as it then was, was in a state of flux, facing enormous pressures from both outside and inside its borders. Externally the 'Great Game' was afoot between Britain and Russia. These two acquisitive and expanding empires were pitted against each other, with control of Persia's key geopolitical position being among the most valued spoils being played for. Peter Hopkirk's *The Great Game* is one of the most readable historical texts I have ever come across; it gives a remarkable insight into this period and is an absolute must for anyone with an interest in how Britain's involvement in Asia shaped us as well as the other players. (I actually prefer the Russian title for the same events, the 'Tournament of Shadows'. It conjures up, I think, a more complex, mysterious and even romantic image which perfectly suits the subject.) The history of this period saw ruthless foreign interests manipulate Persian domestic affairs to their own advantage and goes a long way in helping to explain why modern-day Iran continues to fear and resent in equal measure the hand of clandestine foreign interference.

Internally, Persia was a politically unstable state, a reflection of both events taking place around it and also the domestic political climate. The lack of stability during this period is well illustrated by the fact that between 1896 and 1909 four different shahs from the Qajar dynasty, which had occupied the Peacock Throne since the late 1700s, ruled the country. Financially too, the country was very weak, with Britain and Russia particularly able to assert pressure as both countries provided substantial loans in exchange for trade concessions – loans that were largely used to fund the extravagances of Mozaffar ad-Din Shah, Persia's ruler from 1896 to 1907. His legendary fondness for travel in opulent style, his appetite for socializing with the royal families of Europe and Russia and his predilection for buying multiple works of art and antiques on his journeys did not come cheap. As a consequence of these excesses resentment among the ruling and middle classes began to grow over both the shah's unchecked authority and the pervasive influence of foreign powers in Persia's domestic affairs. Events came to a head in late 1905 when a dispute over sugar prices spiralled out of control and resulted in what became known as the Constitutional Revolution, a hugely important event in modern Persian history.

It began when two sugar traders caught exceeding the controlled sugar price were punished by having their feet beaten in a practice known as *falaka*. This particularly painful and cruel punishment has been used in many different cultures and is popular with torturers as, while agonizing, it leaves few external bruises. In Act 1, Scene XIX of Mozart's *Magic Flute* Sarastro orders Monostatos to be punished with seventy-seven blows on the soles of his feet and, perhaps more relevantly to this story, a British colonial police officer, Charles Tegart, is reputed to have introduced the practice in an interrogation centre in Jerusalem in 1938 as part of the effort to crush the 1936–9 Arab revolt in Palestine.

Outraged at the treatment of their prestigious colleagues in such a publicly humiliating way for what they felt was a minor infraction, Tehran's *bazaaris*, as the merchants were known, closed down the market, and some 2,000 protestors, comprising merchants, religious students and elders, marched to the Royal Mosque from where the protest's leaders demanded the establishment of an *adalathanah* – house of justice. Initially the shah refused, but after a month of stand-off, during which the bazaar remained closed, he acquiesced. Unsurprisingly, as the months passed, the shah's words were not matched by actions and in the summer of 1906 the protests returned. In the resulting crackdown the authorities shot and killed a cleric who was a *sayyid* – someone believed to be descended from the Prophet Muhammad. The incident provoked uproar which both fanned the flames of protest and fuelled ever greater and more vocal demands for political reform. No longer content with an *adalathanah*, instead the protesters now demanded a majlis, the closest thing to the Western concept of a parliament. Through the coordinated efforts of the *bazaaris* and the religious authorities, Tehran was soon brought to a virtual standstill.

In the face of this resurgent opposition, the shah, in his politically weakened state, had little option but to concede, and in October 1906 the first majlis was convened. Within a year the country's first constitution had been drafted and signed by the shah, whose health was by now rapidly deteriorating. Designating Shiism the state religion and with it formal recognition of sharia law, the constitution's most controversial article by far was the definition of the shah's sovereignty, which was stated explicitly to be derived from, and conferred by, the people. This was a radical departure and similar to the end of the notion of the divine right of kings, which disappeared in England with the beheading of Charles I at the end of the English Civil War. Within days of the new constitution being enacted, Muhammad Ali Shah had ascended the throne following the death of his father. The new shah strongly opposed the constitutional reforms and the constraints they imposed on his authority, but it was external events some months later which would have the greatest impact on Persia.

In August 1907, in spite of long-standing deep mutual suspicions, Britain and Russia agreed a treaty regarding their respective interests in Persia, Tibet and Afghanistan. The timing of the agreement reflected in no small part their mutual desire to counter the perceived and growing threat that Germany represented. The Anglo-Russian Convention divided Persia into three administrative zones: the Russians controlled the north and the major cities; Britain took the south, incorporating the highly prized border area with India, leaving a neutral buffer zone between the two. The inevitable outcome saw the green shoots of Persian democracy put to the sword in the name of the Great Game – the pursuit of their own national interests by outside powers. Britain was regarded as particularly duplicitous by the Persians because it had initially been a strong supporter of the constitutionalist movement only to switch sides when the political tide turned. The legacy of what was seen as unprincipled pragmatism at best was to echo through the remainder of the twentieth century.

The First World War saw a further deterioration in the country's economic and political health, and by the early 1920s Reza Khan, a prominent military figure, had come to recognize that the prevailing environment of paralysis offered opportunities for advancement for a man with ambition and drive. Initially he secured the position of head of the military but was soon appointed prime minister and then declared shah in December 1925. It was the birth of the Pahlavi dynasty.

Reza Shah strongly believed Persia required urgent modernization through social reform and industrialization in order to advance as a credible contemporary nation and he formally renamed the country Iran, which means the land of the Aryans. The term had been in use since the Sassanid era of AD 224 to 651. The introduction of wide-ranging reforms sought to overhaul and modernize central pillars of Iranian society including the country's legal and education systems. Compulsory education was introduced for the first time, coinciding with a nationwide school building programme. Prior to this, education had been the domain of the religious authorities, but for Reza Shah tradition and the backward-looking instincts of the clerics were an unacceptable barrier to modernity and progress. His emphasis on secularism set him on a collision course with the religious establishment that would, decades later, seal his own fate and that of his dreams of Iranian enlightenment.

An often forgotten and central aspect of the reform programme was the redefining of the role of women. Reza Shah took unprecedented steps to liberate and empower women, including opening access to education and in 1936 the abolition of the enforced wearing of the veil, both steps important in themselves, both symbols of a liberating tendency and both opposed by the religious traditionalists. He was also the first and only shah to worship in a synagogue, again a highly symbolic act unthinkable today in the Iran of Khamenei. In terms of industrialization his most ambitious and high-profile project was the Trans-Iranian Railway, which linked the Persian Gulf to the Caspian Sea in the north and which upon completion in 1938 became a hugely important economic artery for the country.

The outbreak of the Second World War further boosted Iran's geopolitical importance, reflecting both its substantial oil resources, whose control both sides saw as a major priority, and its strategic location, which included a vital supply route for the Soviet Union known as the Persian Corridor, for which the Trans-Iranian Railway was vital. Appreciating the risks of miscalculation, Reza Shah officially adopted a position of neutrality. This however masked the admiration he had for Germany and its culture, with whom he believed Iran shared Aryan roots. (It is not at all clear that Hitler felt the same way.) Both nations perceived themselves as having suffered at the hands of Britain and Russia over many years, making them well disposed to developing closer ties. Ultimately it was the shah's unwillingness to formally take sides that was to be his downfall, and in 1941 a combined Anglo-Soviet force invaded to secure an unambiguous, pro-Allied stance from Iran, which had by then become essential to the war effort. The bloodless coup which followed saw the Shah's forced abdication in favour of his twenty-two-year-old son Muhammad Reza Pahlavi.

Reza Shah lived the rest of his life in exile under British supervision, first in Mauritius and then in South Africa, dying only three years later in 1944.

Under the new shah the prominence of the majlis was reinstated, with elections taking place in 1944, reversing Reza Shah's drive to centralize power, which had seen the representative body effectively sidelined. Iran, however, suffered economically in the post-war period and struggled to deal with the combined effects of unemployment and inflation. In spite of his efforts to follow a populist political agenda, it was not long before the shah found himself at odds with public opinion, with clerical figures resisting, as ever, all secularization measures while constitutionalists were calling for further reform. These events culminated in a failed assassination attempt in 1949.

It was in this increasingly turbulent environment that a new political alliance called the National Front emerged. Led by a prominent politician named Muhammad Mossadeq who had served earlier in the majlis, his opposition to Reza Shah's coronation had seen him cast out into the political wilderness in the years which followed. It was the shah's decision to propose the renewal of the 1933 Anglo-Iranian Oil Agreement which propelled Mossadeq and his grouping to prominence. The agreement governed royalty payments by AIOC, 51 per cent of which was owned by the British government. When the agreement was originally signed the royalties had been set at a fixed rate, but over the years that followed the value of the payments to Iran had been steadily eroded by inflation and further reduced by taxes levied by the British, so any suggestion that these conspicuously bad terms should be extended caused a predictable political uproar.

Capitalizing on the nationalist sentiment, in early 1951 Mossadeq proposed in the majlis the nationalisation of the Anglo-Iranian Oil Company. While the motion was rejected, Britain's unwillingness to offer significant changes to the agreement meant that deadlock ensued and resentment brewed. Mossadeq's now enormous popularity made his appointment as prime minister in 1951 an inevitability, or certainly as close as one gets in politics. What was less accurately predicted by contemporary commentators was the determination and speed with which he again moved to nationalize AIOC. The response was swift, and a Royal Navy blockade of Iranian oil exports, with Churchill able to persuade the United States not to interfere, saw oil revenue slow to a trickle. Mossadeq however stood firm. (The whole episode has echoes of today's situation, in which the international community is attempting to restrict Iran's oil exports in response to its nuclear programme.)

Buoyed by unparalleled public support, Mossadeq successfully faced down the shah over the appointment of a minister for war in 1952 and quickly moved to further consolidate his grip on power by slashing the royal budget, exiling the shah's twin sister and purging the military's senior leadership in favour of his own placemen. Inevitably, if not unprecedentedly, Mossadeq was quickly acquiring the same dictatorial style for which he was simultaneously condemning the shah. Events reached a climax in 1953, when the majlis, whose members were increasingly unwilling to support Mossadeq's ambitions, was dissolved and a national referendum called to affirm support for the prime minister.

Given the direction in which events were moving, the shah was persuaded to support US-led plans to remove Mossadeq through a coup. In August a new prime minister was appointed and the shah left the country to wait out the ensuing turmoil. The National Front responded to the shah's actions with calls for the abolition of the monarchy, and with support from the CIA Premier Zahedi rallied the army and took on the pro-Mossadeq protesters. Ultimately the pro-shah forces prevailed, and while the CIA undoubtedly played a pivotal support role, Zahedi would not have been successful without the support of the Iranian people. Mossadeq, once seemingly so powerful, found himself convicted of treason and placed under house arrest, where he remained until his death in 1967.

The shah returned, understandably changed by the experience, and subsequently adopted a far less reformist political posture, acting to centralize power around his imperial court and away from the majlis and the Iranian people.

The Rise of Khomeini

In 1902 Ruhollah Mousavi was born in a small town named Khomein in Markazi province in central Iran and, as is customary, took the name of his town of birth. Khomeini came from a family with an established history of religious scholarship, and in 1921 the young man arrived in Qom, Iran's holiest city, to further his studies in line with his family's expectations and his own sense of duty. By the early 1930s Reza Shah was actively implementing measures designed to dilute Iran's Islamic cultural traditions, which he saw as impeding social and economic progress, in favour of Western secular modernity. In spite of Khomeini's instinctive opposition to these reforms, clerical convention required that he respect the settled will of Qom's leadership to remain passive to events in the country's political sphere.

Some three decades later, in 1963, Muhammad Pahlavi Shah followed in his father's footsteps and introduced an ambitious modernizing programme of his own named the White Revolution. By now Khomeini had risen significantly in the Qom hierarchy, and the appointment of a new grand ayatollah in 1961, following the death of Sayyid Hossein Boroujerdi, had created an environment in which it was easier for him to challenge the convention of non-interference in politics. The proposed rolling fifteen-year reform programme was intended to regenerate the country through a series of economic and social measures. While the initial reforms announced contained measures which were very popular with large segments of the population, the fact remained that the programme would cement further the dominant position of the shah and his regime. A key component of the shah's strategy was the creation of a solid support base for his regime among the peasant class. Proposals included measures to provide affordable government-backed loans enabling agricultural labourers to become landowners for the first time. These were to be complemented by the founding of a Literacy Corps intended to reduce Iran's high illiteracy levels and lay the foundations for a better-educated population. Both of these measures were naturally popular with their intended political audience and reinforced support for the regime.

Conversely, these measures reduced the power and influence of the landowning middle class and the religious establishment, the sections of Iranian society the shah increasingly regarded as a threat to his authority. In order to present these highly politicized reforms as reflecting the people's will, the shah held a referendum to endorse them. The clerics did not take all this lying down. The previous year Khomeini and other hard-line mullahs had petitioned the government over plans to allow women and non-Muslims to vote in local elections. Having initially believed that these plans had been shelved, they found themselves faced with their reintroduction, with a fanfare, in January 1963. Thus a battle of wills ensued, with Khomeini calling for a public boycott of the vote.

The referendum duly delivered 99.9 per cent in support, a level of popular endorsement that North Korea would be proud of today. Rather than accept the result, Khomeini chose to indulge in ever more personal attacks on the shah. This was an important turning point as it marked Khomeini's complete abrogation of the clergy's convention on political non-interference and also indicated his growing personal willingness to take significant political risks. Some senior clerics in Qom were critical of his stance, even going so far as to question the religious justification for his actions. The gamble however was to pay a significant political dividend sooner than many thought possible.

In a speech on 21 March 1963, the eve of the Iranian New Year, Khomeini claimed that the reforms were being introduced to serve the interest of outside powers, a populist claim which resonated well with Iranian paranoia about foreign interference. The speech resulted in the shah's security forces ransacking the Feizeyeh seminary, preferred by Khomeini, leading to injuries and the death of a number of students. Khomeini reacted by stating that these actions showed the shah and his government in their 'true light', pitching his tent on the ground of increasingly overt opposition.

Tension and rhetoric continued to rise in the following months, reaching a peak on 3 June when, in a speech purposely planned to coincide with the highly symbolic Shia religious day of Ashura, Khomeini publicly attacked the shah in unprecedented language, describing him as a 'wretched, miserable man' and claiming that his regime was 'opposed to Islam itself and the existence of a religious class'. In one passage he predicted that if the shah did not change his path then the people would 'offer up thanks for his departure from the country' – a vivid and publicly understood reference to the third Ummayad caliph, Yazid, who has always been seen by Shia Muslims as a tyrant.

On the morning of 5 June Khomeini was arrested at his home in Qom in a dawn raid. As news of his arrest spread to Tehran and other major cities it was met with angry protests. With the situation in danger of spiralling out of control, martial law was declared in some areas with armoured units being deployed in major cities. It took six long days to restore order at the cost of the lives of an estimated 200 protesters in what became known the Uprising of 15 Khordad – the date of Khomeini's arrest in the Iranian calendar.

These events served as a vivid demonstration of both Khomeini's popularity and his power. Accordingly, the question of what to do with him now came to the forefront of the minds of the regime's leadership, with some voices going so far as to call for his execution. In the end Khomeini remained in custody, latterly under house arrest, until the spring of 1964, when he was freed and allowed to return to Qom. Predictably, less than six months later, following his fierce denouncement of the government's decision to grant US military personnel immunity from Iranian laws, the shah finally lost patience with Khomeini, who was forcibly sent into exile.

Khomeini spent less than a year in secular Turkey before the shah allowed him to move to Iraq in the mistaken belief that he longer posed a significant political threat, not least because of the perceived success of the Iranian secret police's campaign to degrade his support base. Khomeini established his new base in Najaf, a city of great importance to Shia Islam, particularly due to the presence there of the Tomb of Imam Ali, the First Imam of Shiism. It provided a very effective platform from which Khomeini continued his attacks within easy reach of both his followers and his potential audience in Iran.

It was during his years in Najaf that Khomeini authored a series of lectures on the principle of *velayat e-faqih* (governance of the jurist), later published as a book, in which he articulated the case for theocratic rule. His argument centres on the premise that until the return of the Twelfth 'hidden' Imam, senior clerics alone are qualified to direct and control all aspects of life in order to protect the sharia, the legacy of the teachings of the Koran. This work would later form the foundation of the constitution of the Islamic Republic of Iran and reflects the Shia view that, as they are able to interpret the hidden meanings of the Koran, they are superior to the Sunnis with their literal application of the holy text.

Events in Iran themselves continued to play to Khomeini's advantage. Following a crackdown on the regime's opponents in the mid-1960s the shah completely turned his back on populism and reform and resolved to stifle all forms of dissent. The four-yearly majlis elections became ever more rigged (and ever less credible in the eyes of the people) and coincided with a vast expansion of the role and scope of the SAVAK, the shah's notorious secret police. By the early 1970s the shah had become a dangerous political contradiction – ever more detached from the needs and aspirations of his people but simultaneously determined to dominate every aspect of their lives.

Following the oil shock, record oil prices in the early 1970s provided the country with an unprecedented level of national wealth, generating for the shah the means to pursue his extravagant grand designs but at the cost of further isolation from the real issues of day-to-day life in Iran. The centrepiece of his new project was Iran's transformation (or perhaps its re-emergence is more apt) as a 'great civilization', which through further reform at home and upgraded foreign relations would assert beyond doubt Iran's rightful place among the world's leading nations. In the eyes of the shah and his supporters this would redress the perceived slights of the old colonial powers and restore Iran's regional dominance, which had been so cruelly suppressed.

A show of unprecedented excess was staged in 1971 to mark the 2,500th anniversary of Iran's monarchy. The five-day celebrations included, among other events, a five-and-half-hour state banquet which was sufficiently lavish to be recorded in the *Guinness Book of Records* and stand as a totem to the shah's increasingly relentless drive for materialistic modernity (and excess). A series of extremely ill-judged and damaging decisions followed. In 1975 a decree was issued dissolving all political parties in favour of the new Resurgence Party, which all citizens were required to join. A body reminiscent of the Soviet politburo was created to oversee the principles of what was oxymoronically named democratic centralism. This Orwellian fantasy met a predictably hostile reaction from a society which had long craved more representative forms of government.

These disasters were followed by a decision to crack down on the *bazaaris* in an effort to deal with the country's rocketing inflation, a classic authoritarian attempt to impose price fixing on a market system. The move coincided with a further attack on Iran's religious establishment which saw the shah anoint himself the country's spiritual leader as well as its political one. Then, in perhaps his most bizarre act, the shah announced the introduction of a new calendar which saw Iran jump from year 1355 on the Islamic calendar to Imperial Year 2535, an innovation intended to reflect the length of time which Iran had been governed by a monarchy combined with the shah's time on the throne. Khomeini and his supporters reacted with predictable fury to what they saw as ever more provocative attacks on Iran's Islamic traditions by an increasingly eccentric despot.

In early 1979, with his health deteriorating, the shah and his family departed on a holiday. Four years earlier he had been diagnosed with leukaemia, and while his illness was a closely guarded secret, its impact on his health had now become evident in a decline which was undoubtedly exacerbated by the events unfolding around him. In a planned move the shah appointed a new, moderate prime minister, Shapour Bakhtiar, in an attempt to defuse the crisis that increasingly gripped the country. On 16 January 1979 a state television crew filmed the shah and his family surrounded by senior military officers at Tehran airport. As the shah turned to board his aircraft a colonel reportedly threw himself at his feet declaring, 'We will not let you go.' The shah replied, 'I'll come back.' Minutes later the shah caught the last glimpse of his country that he would ever see as he and his family departed, never to return to Iran.

With the shah gone and the country descending into near-chaos, the question for Khomeini was no longer if he would return but rather when. His advisers rightly feared that if he were to return by plane the aircraft might be shot down, and in order to guard against this a large delegation of international journalists was invited to travel with Khomeini, who had been living in France since leaving Najaf the previous year. On 31 January Khomeini boarded a chartered Air France Boeing 747 to begin his journey home after over fourteen years in exile. His arrival in Tehran was greeted by a rapturous almost hysterical crowd estimated to be as large as five million. His return signalled, in the most emphatic way, the end of 2,500 years of Iranian monarchy, which the shah had celebrated with such excess less than a decade earlier, and the birth of the Islamic Republic.

The Iran–Iraq War

In September 1980, less than a year after Khomeini was appointed to the newly created post of supreme leader of the Islamic Republic, Iran was invaded by Iraq. The ensuing horror of the Iran–Iraq War would last almost eight years and cost almost one million lives. The conflict was to have a profound and defining effect on how the young republic would come to see both itself and the world around it in the years ahead.

Following his return Khomeini had acted swiftly to decapitate the remaining leadership of the shah's military through a series of bloody purges and executions. The inevitable consequence was that the country went from possessing one of the world's largest, best-trained and equipped militaries to a poorly organized revolutionary fighting force bereft of experienced leadership and barely able to operate its hardware. This was in stark contrast to neighbouring Iraq, which had become increasingly militarized following Saddam Hussein's ascent to power. Saddam was contemptuous of Khomeini, who had called for him to be deposed by a popular revolution of Iraq's Shia majority. These factors, combined with Saddam's desire to establish Iraq as the regional superpower with control of the region's extensive oil resources, were the catalyst for the invasion.

In order to understand the political context in which this conflict began it is helpful to first appreciate the impact that the Iranian hostage crisis had on prevailing attitudes at the time. On 4 November 1979 a group of pro-revolution students from Tehran University (including future president Mahmoud Ahmadinejad) scaled the walls of the US embassy, which, with the help of other protesters, was quickly overrun. Embassy staffing levels had been reduced, reflecting concerns about anti-American sentiment following Khomeini's return, but fifty-two staff remained and were taken hostage.

The original aim of the students' plan had been to use the hostages as leverage in an attempt to pressure the US into forcing the shah to return to face 'justice' in the new Iran. While the students were to fail in this aim, and the shah died of his illness in Egypt in 1980, the situation which developed provided Khomeini with a powerful political tool which enabled him to both publicly humiliate the US while pressing hard in secret talks for the return of frozen Iranian assets. The situation was further complicated when a high-risk US clandestine military operation to rescue the hostages failed spectacularly and in the most public of ways due to a series of operational accidents, resulting in the death of a number of the military personnel involved. For President Jimmy Carter, who had personally authorized the mission, the debacle was the final nail in the coffin of his re-election hopes.

Eventually, after 444 days of captivity and following the return of $7.9 billion in frozen assets, the hostages were released on 20 January 1981. The date coincided with the inauguration of President Ronald Reagan and, in a last act of contempt, Khomeini humiliated Carter by withholding confirmation of the hostages' release until the swearing-in ceremony had been completed and he was no longer in office.

The damage to American prestige and self-confidence is difficult to quantify and the impact of the crisis continues some thirty years on. However, events in the region meant that Iran was not to go unpunished for long. By early 1981 the first few months of the Iran–Iraq War had only served to harden Iran's contemptuous view of the West. This initially stemmed from the outcome of a meeting of the UN's Security Council within days of the invasion. Instead of condemning Iraqi aggression and demanding that they withdraw their forces (as happened later following the invasion of Kuwait), the Security Council simply called for a ceasefire on both sides. Iran's leadership was incensed at this failure to take any meaningful action or even attribute responsibility for the conflict, which was viewed by them as another illustration of the West's arrogance and hypocrisy and also proof of Western involvement in the invasion. While the latter claim is wide of the mark, Saddam's actions were not entirely unhelpful to the West as it was in their perceived interests to see Iran's energies focused on the war. This was largely due to the view held in many Western capitals that the conflict would help contain Khomeini's ability to fulfil his stated aim of exporting the Iranian revolution to the wider Middle East. However, as events in Lebanon in the early 1980s dramatically demonstrated, containment of Khomeini's revolutionary spirit would prove to be an almost impossible task.

During the years that followed and in spite of the growing human cost of the war there was a tendency in the West to support Saddam through the sale of arms and other forms of assistance as a means of continuing to apply pressure to the Iranian regime, whose behaviour was seen as a greater threat to the West's security and interests. Iran naturally sought to secure its own military supplies to help match the military advantage which the West's support gave Saddam but this proved impossible for two reasons. First, US sanctions following the hostage crisis meant that Iran was unable to purchase the types of arms it required. Second, Iran's economy was very hard hit by the sanctions, particularly the US ban on Iranian oil export sales. Consequently Iran simply did not have the funds needed to purchase the military assets it needed.

By 1988 the war had ground to a bloody stalemate despite Saddam's willingness to use any means, including chemical weapons, to gain an advantage. Hashemi Rafsanjani, then speaker of the majlis and a close, trusted aid of Khomeini, had responsibility for the war effort, and he had come to the view that victory was impossible because of the effect that sanctions were having on Iran's ability to procure arms and finance the war. Accordingly Rafsanjani believed that accepting a UN-backed ceasefire was the best way to bring an end to the conflict. The problem which he faced, however, was persuading Khomeini of this. Rafsanjani shrewdly decided to suggest to Khomeini that he announce the news himself, thereby allowing Khomeini to divert the blame onto him. While Khomeini ultimately accepted Rafsanjani's assessment of the likely outcome of the war, he refused to allow him to take the blame on the grounds that the predicament Iran faced was not of his making. Instead on 20 August 1988 he announced the decision himself, likening it to 'drinking a chalice of poison'. If this was propaganda, it was good propaganda.

Perhaps the most significant and lasting result of the Iran–Iraq War was the reinforcement of the Iranian people's belief in their own destiny and resilience – that they could prevail in spite of tremendous external pressure and in the face of enormous hardship. The legacy of this mindset remains tangible almost twenty-five years on as Iran continues to remain defiant in the face of international criticism of its nuclear programme and as an ever stricter sanctions programme continues to bite. (It would be a brave man who would bet against the stubbornness and resolve of such a mindset.)

Less than a year after the end of the war Khomeini was hospitalized. On 3 June 1989 he died aged eighty-six. A fact often overlooked, in part reflecting the length of his successor's tenure, is that the events which led to his eventual elevation took place in the aftermath of a bitter and very public falling-out between Khomeini and his anointed successor, Hussein Ali Montazeri. Montazeri was reported to have disagreed with Khomeini's interpretation of *velayat e-faqih*, upon which the role of the supreme leader was based. An irreconcilable rift developed between the two men whose close relationship had been so instrumental in creating the revolution.

One source of tension related to foreign policy. Montazeri was implacably opposed to Iran having any dealings with the US, which he viewed, in keeping with Iran's post-revolution mantra, as the 'great Satan'. When he discovered through his own channels that covert discussions were taking place between Iran and the US over arms supplies in exchange for the release of American hostages in Lebanon, he was furious and made public the existence of such discussions via a Lebanese magazine in what became known as the Iran–Contra affair. Revealing these contacts invoked the not inconsiderable wrath of Khomeini, and the source of the leak, a close ally of Montazeri, was sentenced to death and executed before he was able to intervene. Montazeri retired from frontline politics although he continued to speak his mind until he died in Qom in 2009.

On 3 June, within hours of Khomeini's death, the Assembly of Experts met to discuss who should be appointed Iran's new supreme leader. The ensuing political theatre was filmed at the time but not released for over two decades. It apparently makes for interesting viewing though I must confess to not having seen it myself (life being much too short). Initially the view prevailed that no single candidate was sufficiently qualified to be given the title of *faqih* (leading jurist) and accordingly, as set out in the constitution, a council of leadership comprising three members should perform the role. This may have reflected a desire to dilute and distribute the power and responsibilities of the role of supreme leader. However, the idea was eventually rejected, and in what very much appears to have been a planned manoeuvre Hashemi Rafsanjani made the case for Ali Khamenei, then president, to succeed to the role. Rafsanjani went so far as to make direct references to Khomeini being in favour of

Khamenei's candidacy, something that no one was able to refute. In an act of self-effacing modesty (and grand theatre), Khamenei stated that he had no interest in the post but later managed to overcome his reservations and was appointed by a two-thirds majority to the position he continues to hold with a vice-like grip today. Interestingly, a change was made to the constitution at the time which designated the role and its incumbent as absolute. While this was done ostensibly to entrench the position of the new supreme leader – who lacked the clerical credentials of his predecessor – the legacy of this change has been more profound than its proponents probably realized at the time.

The Stolen Election of 2009

At the heart of Iran's Islamic Republic sits an almost unique contradiction which implies the compatibility of Islamism with republicanism. On the one hand the principle of *velayat e-faqih* continues to guarantee the office and authority of the supreme leader and the country's corresponding revolutionary bodies, underpinned by the 'religious purity' of the revolution. On the other hand are the functional organs of the state encompassing the executive and legislature, both grounded in the concept of a public mandate. The ability of the Iranian state to function is therefore determined by the degree to which these often opposing, and sometimes completely contradictory, sides of the same coin are able and willing to work together.

Under Khomeini the tensions and contradictions of this architecture were largely suppressed by his charismatic leadership and the impact of the Iran–Iraq War. It was not until Khamenei's succession that the strains became more palpable and the inevitable divisions emerged. Consequently the country's body politic can be divided, somewhat crudely, into two camps – reformist and traditionalist. As Professor Ali Ansari, director of St Andrews University's Institute of Iranian Studies, whom I have known for some years, has observed, many within the former group are intellectually rooted in the Constitutional Revolution of 1906 and stress the importance of constitutional constraints and limits on the power of Iran's leadership. For the latter group the concept of democracy is at best anathema, and to some heretical, and they instead emphasize the inalienable and absolute nature of the principle of *velayat e-faqih* as embodied in the supreme leader. How much of this emphasis relates to belief in the Twelfth 'hidden' Imam, whose return his followers believe will bring an end to tyranny and falsehood and restore justice, and how much is calculated political expediency is highly debatable.

The Iranian electorate for its part seems to have accepted that elections are not entirely free and fair and that a degree of state-sponsored vote rigging is an inevitability. As Ansari put it to me, 'Iranians discussed the imperfections of their "democracy" as if a modest amount of corruption was reassuringly Iranian.' The unspoken bargain appears to be that the governing elite will not overdo this in a way that is too obvious or crude, given the insult this would be to the intelligence of the voters.

And so Iran's president and parliament are the result of what can most charitably be described as a managed democratic process. Under this system there is, however, a substantial difference between the authority which a position of high office confers on its holder and the wielding of real political power. In 1989, as Iran's newly installed supreme leader, Ali Khamenei's authority might have been self-evident but his ability to wield political power was not. Certainly, during Hashemi Rafsanjani's two terms as president between 1989 and 1997, he proved highly adept at centralizing power around an executive-style presidency more in keeping with the scope of the role in other countries. Under his successor Muhammad Khatami, who held the post from 1997 to 2005, however, the limitations of the new president's personal power base became clear as attempts at reform and reconciliation with the West, for which Khatami appears to have been genuinely enthusiastic, were undermined and curtailed at the direction of Khamenei and others. A question mark remains over whether Khatami fully appreciated the inevitability of the defeat of his programme and simply wanted the public to lay the blame on the ruling elite, or whether he actually believed that his electoral popularity would be sufficient to win the day. (Sadly we will never know if he would have been able to change the course of collision with the rest of the world on which Khamenei seems increasingly set.)

The 2005 election saw the emergence, on the international stage at least, of the colourful populist firebrand Mahmoud Ahmadinejad, then mayor of Tehran. While the level of support he received directly from Khamenei is unclear, few believe he would have succeeded without the supreme leader's acceptance of his candidacy. Certainly it was in Khamenei's interest to see Ahmadinejad triumph over Rafsanjani, a seasoned political operator, in the final round of the election. In contrast with the managed election of 2005, the 2009 election opened a veritable Pandora's box and stands as a powerful testament to the limits of the Iranian people to tolerate injustice at the hands of their country's leadership. The crisis went well beyond the casting of ballots and electoral procedures and revealed a deep chasm within Iranian society which raised deep and contentious questions about the very foundations of the Islamic Republic.

Long before polling day arrived on 12 June its outcome had been preordained by the regime's elite – an emphatic re-election victory for Ahmadinejad. The problem with this was that a late surge in support for Mir-Hossein Mousavi, a former prime minister and pro-reform candidate, meant this was by no means the certainty they wanted, and so direct intervention was required. What was so remarkable was the scale of the Ahmadinejad 'victory', which saw him poll the largest number of votes in the history of the Islamic Republic, an outcome which Khamenei went as far as to call a 'divine assessment'. Many others had a very different term for it. It was not even intelligently done, but a clumsy, obvious and clearly ridiculous piece of electoral theft akin to a burglar ringing the doorbell of the house he has just broken into to alert its owners.

Unsurprisingly, many pro-Mousavi voters were unwilling to accept the result and infuriated that they were clearly expected to acquiesce in what was a clear breach of the understanding that had previously existed around the limits of electoral cheating. As a result, an estimated three million people took to the streets of Tehran in a protest rally for Mousavi on 15 June, making any suggestion of an inherent and deep-rooted sense of Iranian political solidarity nonsensical and, worse in the eyes of the ruling elite, highly visible to the rest of the world. In the days that followed a well-orchestrated crackdown on foreign media coverage ensued in an attempt to hide the scenes of turmoil from the wider world. Mobile phone networks were turned off and access to the Internet and satellite television blocked in a full-scale dress rehearsal for the years ahead.

Responding to the protests, Khamenei ordered the Interior Ministry to conduct a review of the election. This of course simply endorsed the official result, much to the fury of the protesters. On 19 June Khamenei declared the demonstrations illegal, although this did little to quell the unrest, and the following day, in one of the most tragic images of the protests, twenty-six-year-old Neda Agha-Soltan was filmed dying after being shot in the heart by security forces. Her death shocked viewers everywhere, and there was a growing expectation from the people on the streets of Tehran that their plight and sense of justified outrage might at last be heard around the globe.

It is worth noting the leading role that women played in the protests – brave and unwilling to bow to antiquated ideas about their role in Iranian society. The flame of their desire for justice has not been extinguished and offers Iran hope for the future.

While the international community reacted by condemning the excesses of the military and security forces, it did nothing to encourage or support the demonstrators. This stands in stark contrast to the tangible support provided to the later Arab Spring uprisings and is regarded as a betrayal by many in what became the Green Movement in Iran. They wonder why the voices of so many other revolts against tyranny have provoked the West to action but the Iranians were ignored. It reinforces the historical perception of many Iranians, with clear echoes from the Constitutional Revolution over a century before, that the Western powers remain at best indifferent to the plight of the Iranian people. Change will come at some point, and this view does not bode well for Iran's future relationship with the West.

I still feel angry about what I see as the West's abandonment of the democracy movement in Iran, not only because we failed to give support to those who needed it but because we failed to reinforce the universal nature of the values we hold and missed a historic opportunity to show that our quarrel is not with the people of Iran but with the leadership of the regime. It stands in stark contrast to the leadership we showed in the years of the Cold War, particularly in the latter years, against the forces of communist oppression. When the Solidarity labour union was founded in 1980, with its membership eventually swelling to almost one third of the working Polish population, highly vocal political support and encouragement echoed from Ronald Reagan's White House, Margaret Thatcher's Downing Street and the Vatican of Pope John Paul II. This moral support, played out on the world stage, was instrumental in enabling Lech Walesa and his supporters to stand firm against the government of

General Jaruzelski even during the years of martial law and political repression. The United States even provided covert financial support for Solidarity, estimated at as much as $50 million. Thus Western policy was able to combine internal dissent against the regime with the external pressure being applied by military and economic means to the Soviet bloc. It is worth reminding ourselves that the Cold War did not end; it was won, with the result that millions of people today enjoy liberty and democracy who would otherwise be denied them. If the victory of Solidarity represented the moral high point of Western democratic society, then the abandonment of the pro-democracy movement in Iran in 2009 represents one of its lows.

What is striking about the election and its aftermath is what they tell us about the contempt in which the ruling elite hold ordinary Iranians and their willingness to resort to violence to put down any dissent – in every way similar to the latter days of the shah. Mousavi and his supporters were not seeking to overthrow the regime and replace the revolution; they simply wanted changes in the style of governance, mainly related to efficiency and transparency as enshrined in Iran's 1906 constitution. The force with which the regime responded sent a shock wave throughout Iran, the likes of which had not been felt since 1979. It saw the children of loyal Iranians arrested and savagely beaten and in some cases far worse. The fact that the regime deemed this response to be necessary tells us a great deal about profound fears regarding its own fragility.

As Ali Ansari notes, 'If a measure of calm has been restored, history suggests that this is little more than a lull while people rest, reflect and reassess the objectives of a movement that at first sought political change but is increasingly seeking a profound structural readjustment to the constitution of the Islamic Republic.' How events will play out is of course unknown, but I think we can say with confidence that the 1979 revolution is a rolling one whose destination is not yet determined. The struggle within the regime between the clerics and what appears to be an ever more centralized and military-dominated state still has some way to run, and a key element in both current and future events is the role of the Revolutionary Guards (IRGC), or to give them their full title, the Army of the Guardians of the Islamic Revolution.

The history of the IRGC mirrors that of Khomeini's revolution. It was established with the role of entrenching the revolution and protecting its Islamic legacy – particularly important in its infancy when the threat of counter-revolution was highest. While this fundamental purpose remains, as a result of its extensive growth and expansion the IRGC has emerged as one of the most powerful organs of the Iranian state. While military in nature, the IRGC remains separate and distinct from the conventional armed forces in keeping with its revolutionary identity. Its leader is appointed by and reports personally to the supreme leader. Estimates of its size suggest some 125,000 personnel (according to the International Institute for Strategic Studies in 2007), and it consists of ground, naval and air arms as well as a special forces formation, the Qods Force. This latter group is known to have been actively involved in the arming and training of Shia militias in Iraq following the 2003 invasion and to have established links to numerous militant armed groups across the Middle East, particularly Hezbollah in both Lebanon and Syria. In addition, there is evidence of a central role in developing military and financial links with both Venezuela and Ecuador. The IRGC also has responsibility for Iran's paramilitary *Basij* forces, a home guard estimated to have one million semi-trained members. Its most significant role is the oversight it has over Iran's strategic missiles, the capabilities of which are an essential component of a nuclear weapons programme.

A source of contention, particularly among the clerical establishment, is the question of the limits to the IRGC's powers within

Iran's theocratic construct. The origins of these tensions are long established and can be traced back to the early years of the revolution. Khomeini himself understood only too well the importance of establishing and protecting clear divisions between military and political responsibilities and went as far as to re-emphasize these in his 'Political and Divine Testament':

> My emphatic counsel to the armed forces is to observe [and] abide by the military rule of non-involvement in politics. Do not join any political party or faction. No military man, security policeman, no Revolutionary Guard, or *Basij* may enter into politics . . . And, as the revolution belongs to all the nation, its preservation is also the duty of all. Therefore, the government, the nation, the Defence Council, and the Islamic Consultative Assembly are all charged with the religious and national responsibility to oppose, from the very beginning, any interference in politics or any action against the interests of Islam and the country by the armed forces, regardless of category, class, branch, and rank. Such involvement will surely corrupt and pervert them.

The fact that Khomeini's will has not been adhered to is in itself an illustration of the changes in the political landscape which have taken place since his death in 1989. From its limited beginnings, over the course of the last two decades the IRGC's economic power base has evolved to encompass all manner of construction projects, defence-related industries, the consumer goods and telecoms sectors and the highly lucrative and strategic oil and gas industries. Its tentacles also extend into the country's extensive black market in, among other things, alcohol, directly at odds with its founding principles.

To an outsider the extent of this metamorphosis is astonishing –

just how could the role of a military body change to the point that it manages the Iranian equivalents of Balfour Beatty, John Lewis and BP while at the same time playing a dominant role in the black market? The answer is that this expansion, at least initially, was seen as in the interests of Iran's leadership, both politically and in the maintenance of their privileged lifestyles. While the process was initiated by Rafsanjani during his time as president, it has been Khamenei who has benefited most: he has used his extensive powers of patronage within the IRGC to both consolidate and maintain his personal authority. There is also a credible view that the pace of the IRGC's expansionism has taken on a momentum of its own. The result is a massive paradigm shift in Iran's power structure and the emergence of a strong political voice to match the IRGC's economic importance.

President Mahmoud Ahmadinejad's time in office saw a marked expansion of the IRGC's political footprint, further altering Iran's political landscape. Ahmadinejad traces his revolutionary credentials back to his involvement in the student group responsible for the assault on the US embassy, which eventually led to his IRGC membership in 1985. Unlike his two direct predecessors, he had no clerical qualification, which although not a requirement for the post, did represent change. Prior to 2005 former IRGC officers held senior political positions including cabinet posts, but under Ahmadinejad the extent of their representation in senior roles expanded. At one point this saw them occupy almost half the cabinet posts including key ministries such as justice, defence and petroleum. He also oversaw a purge of Iran's provincial governors and their deputies, replacing them with hand-picked IRGC loyalists. This process culminated in the parliamentary election of 2008, in which the promotion of IRGC-linked candidates ahead of both rivals and incumbents was further evidence of Khamenei's continued support for, and political use of, IRGC expansionism.

Today, the exact role and nature of the IRGC is a key element in understanding the direction of travel of both the rolling revolution and Iran itself. How unified and stable is the IRGC's leadership given the inevitability of internal power struggles? How much of its zeal is driven by dedication to the revolutionary cause and how much is political expediency reflecting the group's symbolic relationship with the regime itself? Interestingly this latter point seems to transcend the issue of the role of the supreme leader and chimes with the argument that Iran is increasingly an Islamic Republic in name only. If this is correct – that behind Iran's Shiite theocratic facade an incremental but comprehensive erosion of clerical authority is nearing completion and slowly but surely transferring authority to the military – it will have important consequences for any assessment of Iran's intentions, not least its nuclear ambitions.

Green (Shoots) Movement 2013?

The bloody and chaotic aftermath of the 2009 presidential election meant that the build-up to the 2013 poll began earlier and in an atmosphere of some trepidation. As the outside world looked on, the list of possible successors to President Ahmadinejad was whittled down by the Guardian Council, the body assessing the 'suitability' of candidates, to a shortlist of just seven. Most noteworthy of the excluded candidates were Hashemi Rafsanjani and Ahmadinejad's self-appointed successor, Esfandiar Mashaei.

For the sake of clarity it was explained that the former president had been excluded on the grounds of the demands of the office relative to his age rather than his lack of suitable revolutionary credentials. Critics have suggested that the real reason was the potential electoral appeal of Rafsanjani's modernizing credentials combined with his technocratic record of economic management, which stood in stark contrast to the widely held perception of economic mismanagement in the Ahmadinejad years. As for Mashaei, in spite of attempts by Ahmadinejad to appeal, the decision stood, which many have interpreted as evidence of the transitory nature of Ahmadinejad's power base.

Three rather theatrical television debates followed with the selected candidates jockeying for position on the topics of the day. Two clear, unsurprising and closely linked topics emerged as the key electoral issues – the economy and the nuclear programme. Among the vetted candidates were two figures very familiar with the nuclear issue as they had both served as Iran's chief nuclear negotiator. One was the current occupant, Saeed Jalili, and the other Hassan Rouhani. Jalili has been responsible for the country's increasingly strident tone at negotiations with the international community since 2007. Rouhani, in contrast, held the post from 2003 during President Khatami's time, when relations with the West were significantly less adversarial. He stood down following Ahmadinejad's election in 2005.

While the terms 'moderate' and 'pro-reform' have a limited meaning in Iran's political lexicon, Rouhani's electoral message, which included strong support for political freedoms and for improving relations with the West, put him squarely at odds with Iran's hard-line conservative leadership. His campaign gathered momentum, and as polling day on 14 June grew closer, the other reformist candidate, Muhammad Aref, withdrew to avoid splitting the vote. This coincided with former presidents Rafsanjani and Khatami publicly endorsing Rouhani's candidacy, maximizing his electoral momentum in the last few crucial days of campaigning. Predictions for turnout were high, in part reflecting Khamenei's personal intervention encouraging all eligible Iranians to vote to emphasize the participatory nature of Iran's democracy. While the pundits' forecasts for turnout proved to be sound, the result was quite another matter. Rouhani romped to victory with over 50 per cent of the vote, a feat few dreamed possible given that the 2009 reformist leaders Mehdi Karroubi and Mir-Hossein Mousavi continue to languish under house arrest.

Two obvious questions spring to mind following this result. What will change in the presidency mean for ordinary Iranians? How will relations with the international community be affected? The answers are not yet clear, but the election of a reformist should be met with some optimism, albeit with caveats.

Rouhani comes to the office of president with significant experience of operating at very senior levels within the country's regime. Most significantly, he spent sixteen years serving as secretary to the National Security Council, the last two of which encompassed the nuclear portfolio. While he is certainly of the regime, a necessity to have any chance of reaching high office, all eyes will now be on whether he is able to deliver on the moderate position he adopted in his election campaign. While his reference to 'national reconciliation' at the press conference following his victory is probably significant, the international sanctions resulting from Iran's persistence with its nuclear programme mean that progress on the economic front will remain difficult at best. While responsibility for that issue sits firmly in the hands of Ali Khamenei, the ability of the new president to influence wider events will be strictly limited.

Ali Ansari put to me some months ago a very interesting assessment of the predicament in which Khamenei increasingly finds himself. As the stand-off on the nuclear issue with the West continues, its cost to the country and its population grows daily. The Iranian people were willing to bear a tremendous amount, in both financial and human terms, in response to Iraq's invasion, but when it became clear that Iran was unable to defeat Saddam, Ayatollah Khamenei accepted a ceasefire. Ansari suggested that perhaps Khamenei is approaching his own 'cup of poison moment' whereby he accepts a compromise agreement which protects Iran's entitlement to enrich uranium but with heavy external oversight from the UN's nuclear watchdog, the IAEA. Some may claim that this assessment is over-optimistic, that it fundamentally underestimates the Iranian people's determination not to capitulate to external pressure. I keep coming back to what stands out for me from Iran's long and remarkable history – that the ability of its leaders to underestimate their own people is matched only by the determination of the Iranians to stand up to and outwit their leaders. Khamenei, subconsciously at least, must hope that the sum of his legacy will not be to have been the second and last supreme leader of Iran's Islamic Republic.

Atomic Ayatollhs: Going Nuclear

The origins of Iran's nuclear programme predate not only the presidency of Mahmoud Ahmadinejad, with whom it has become closely associated, but also the Islamic Republic itself. The project was in fact initiated by Muhammad Pahlavi Shah in the 1950s with the direct assistance of the US as part of its Atoms for Peace initiative, which through an ironic twist of fate saw work begin on reactors in both Iran and Pakistan. The initiative, launched by President Eisenhower at the UN in 1953, was to a large extent a PR stunt designed to keep US public opinion on board with the nuclear weapons research and armament programmes of the Cold War by promoting the peaceful potential of uranium as the fuel for a new type of power generation. With images of the aftermath of both Hiroshima and Nagasaki still fresh in the public's mind, it concentrated on the positive potential of the new technology.

The foundations of Iran's programme were laid on 5 March 1957, when a 'proposed agreement for cooperation in research in the peaceful uses of atomic energy' was announced under Eisenhower's initiative. In 1967 Iran took its first steps into the nuclear age with the establishment of the Tehran Nuclear Research Centre (TNRC) under the auspices of the Atomic Energy Organization of Iran (AEOI). The TNRC was equipped with a five-megawatt research reactor provided by the US. Iran was among the first nations to sign the newly created Non-Proliferation Treaty (NPT) in 1968, which it ratified in 1970. The treaty's aims were to prevent the spread of nuclear weapons and weapons technology and promote the peaceful use of nuclear technologies.

Even before the revolution there were international anxieties about Iran's real intentions. The United States was concerned about its interest in reprocessing and the ability of the IAEA to properly safeguard any reprocessing facility, and these proved major hurdles in US–Iranian negotiations to sell nuclear reactors to Tehran. The rhetoric of the shah was also less than reassuring. In June 1974 he said that 'without a doubt and sooner than one would think' Iran would get nuclear weapons, and although there was considerable backtracking afterwards, in February 1975 he again said that while Iran had no intention of acquiring nuclear weapons 'if small states began building them, Iran might have to reconsider its policy'.

It was not until the late 1980s that Iran's nuclear programme emerged from its enforced hibernation. Hashemi Rafsanjani publicly called for the development of nuclear and other non-conventional weapons as a result of Iran's experience in the Iran–Iraq War, and in 1987 Iran received, from what the IAEA described as 'a clandestine supply network', technical drawings for a P-1 centrifuge and centrifuge components. The source was almost certainly the A.Q. Khan network, and Iran told the IAEA that gas centrifuge testing began at TNRC in 1988, continuing there until 1995, when the facility was re-sited. Between 1994 and 1999 it is thought that there were more than a dozen contacts between the A.Q. Khan network and Iran. The

Institute for Science and International Security (ISIS) in Washington DC additionally reported that in 1991 Iran secretly imported one metric ton of uranium hexafluoride from China. Neither country reported the transfer to the IAEA. China was technically not obliged to as it was not yet a member of the NPT, but Iran was, under its IAEA and safeguards agreement.

In January 1995 Russia signed an agreement with Iran to complete, under IAEA safeguards, the Bushehr I reactor, which, along with the rest of the site, had been badly damaged in a series of attacks during the Iran–Iraq War. Although initial estimates suggested that the work would take only three years, it was not until 2009 that the power plant became operational. It was seven years earlier, in autumn 2002, that Iran's alleged nuclear weapons programme had been thrust into the light of day. The National Council of Resistance of Iran, a dissident group which opposes the Islamic Republic, revealed the existence of two clandestine nuclear sites under construction: one was a uranium enrichment facility in Natanz, which was partially subterranean, the other a heavy-water facility in Arak.

Iran had not disclosed the existence of the sites and suspicions about their real intentions were immediately aroused among the international community. The facilities were a clear breach of the spirit, if not the letter, of their obligations under the NPT. Iran had not withdrawn from the treaty following the revolution – Khomeini appeared more anti-nuclear than the shah at the time – so it was still bound by its terms and had a duty to share information and to cooperate with the IAEA. Iran responded by inviting IAEA inspectors to the sites in early 2003 in an effort to allay international anxieties, and the coming months would see a flurry of diplomatic activity attempting to find a mutually satisfactory resolution to the situation. Initially this took the form of the Tehran Joint Statement of November that year, in which Iran agreed to temporarily suspend uranium enrichment and sign an additional protocol to the NPT in return for recognition of the country's entitlement to undertake enrichment activities. This in turn led to the Paris Agreement of the following November, but substantive progress was slow in coming.

Mahmoud Ahmadinejad was elected Iran's president in June 2005. This ushered in a new populism and a more confrontational diplomatic posture over the nuclear issue which, within weeks, saw the removal of the IAEA's seals on the centrifuge banks at one of the Iranian enrichment facilities. In April 2007 President Ahmadinejad announced that Iran had begun enriching uranium using 3,000 centrifuges and declared, 'Today our dear country has joined the nuclear club of nations and can produce nuclear fuel on an industrial scale.' When in November 2009 the IAEA Board of Governors demanded that Iran stop building its newly revealed nuclear facility and freeze uranium enrichment, the Iranian government responded by authorizing the construction of ten more uranium enrichment plants. In January 2013 the Institute for Science and International Security in its report 'US Nonproliferation Strategy for the Changing Middle East' claimed that Iran would be able to produce enough weapons-grade uranium for one or more nuclear bombs by the middle of 2014. The report challenged the Obama administration by stating, 'the President should explicitly declare that he will use military force to destroy Iran's nuclear programme if Iran takes additional decisive steps toward producing a bomb'.

At the heart of the nuclear stand-off is mutual distrust. Iran continues to feel that it is being singled out for disproportionate and unjust scrutiny and punishment, motivated by the West's continued desire to subjugate the Iranian people and interfere in its internal affairs. Ali Saeedi, the supreme leader's personal representative to the IRGC, said recently that 'the Iranian nation is committed to resist arrogant powers, including the United States'. Meanwhile, the international community continues to regard Iran's concealment of its programme, along with its unwillingness to comply with its IAEA obligations, as raising questions about the underlying motives of the programme. At a Senate Armed Services Committee meeting in March 2013, the head of US Central Command (CENTCOM), General James Mattis, claimed that Iran had accelerated its nuclear programme in the preceding year despite diplomatic and economic pressure. Suggesting that Iran was using negotiations to play for time, he maintained that Iran was 'enriching uranium beyond any plausible peaceful purpose'. The main international response to Iran's intransigence has been a series of Security Council resolutions and, with them, increasingly restrictive sanctions, the most significant of which has been the implementation of a European embargo on Iranian oil exports, which came into force in the summer of 2012.

How successful have the sanctions been?

They have certainly not precipitated any crisis that threatens the internal overthrow of the regime or a change in the nuclear programme. The *Washington Post* suggested recently that 'the economy appears to have settled into a slow, downward glide, haemorrhaging jobs and hard currency but appearing to be in no immediate danger of collapse . . . Though weakened, Iran has resisted Western pressure by a combination of clever tactics, political repression and sheer stubbornness.' Under the sanctions Iran's oil exports, its chief source of hard currency, have fallen from more than 2.4 million barrels per day to around one million. While the impact has been felt most harshly by the middle and working classes, who have seen both their savings and purchasing power diminished, enough oil has been sold inside and outside the sanctions regime to maintain basic services and the functions of the state and, more importantly, to preserve the affluent lifestyle of the ruling class and business elite. While since 2012 Iran's inflation has exceeded 100 per cent with food prices in particular soaring, and unemployment is estimated to be as high as 35 per cent in some areas, the self-styled guardians of the revolution have continued to live lifestyles largely unaffected by the hardships which their policies have brought upon the heads of many ordinary Iranians.

Iran has, moreover, been able to adapt to sanctions to minimize economic damage. For example, countries that still import Iranian oil may be asked to pay in goods rather than hard currency, despite the fact that Iran desperately needs to increase its foreign currency stocks. This practice counteracts high inflation at home and the imports help Iran conserve cash, which it is then able to use to pay salaries and continue the subsidy of consumer prices which is one of the regime's main methods of suppressing popular unrest. Weaknesses in the current sanctions regime include the continued willingness of countries and individuals to purposely evade them and the official exemptions granted to some of Iran's top customers including China and India.

There may, however, be security implications to sanctions. Bryan Prior, a political-military analyst at CENTCOM who focuses on Iran, has suggested that the erosion of Iran's non-nuclear national security capabilities is an important by-product. Certainly, an acknowledgement by President Ahmadinejad that parts of the Iranian budget had been cut due to financial pressures seems to have been reflected in the fact that Iran's often ostentatious military exercises have been notably curtailed in recent years. Coupled with a lack of announcements on military projects and capabilities, this is likely to reflect cuts to defence programmes. It is also argued that sanctions have diminished Iran's 'soft' power as it has become increasingly reliant on the smaller number of countries who continue to buy its oil. For example, it is maintained that Iran has been powerless to affect Turkish policy in the current civil war in Syria or to alter its decision to accept NATO Patriot missile batteries. Prior argues that a further tightening of sanctions should be sought not only to delay the possibility of a nuclear Iran but also to help curb its other activities. He argues that there are three reasons for a more aggressive sanctions policy: 'to ensure an ongoing sanctions regime against Iran even in the event that it acquires a weapon (economic); preventing the enhancement of Iran's conventional capabilities (military); and further isolating Iran as a pariah state (political)'. This, it is argued, will help reassure the West's Arab allies in the Gulf about the security of their own energy infrastructure as well as demonstrating to any other nations who may seek nuclear weapons that the cost will be high.

If we assume for the sake of argument that Iran's intentions are to develop a nuclear weapons capability, which is my view, what does this tell us about the thought processes and public justifications of Iran's current leaders? Iran and its few remaining allies have sought, with little success, to persuade international opinion that they do not seek nuclear weapons as all weapons of mass destruction are forbidden under Islam. To support their case they refer to the much-lauded fatwa issued against nuclear weapons by Ali Khamenei in 2003. Unsurprisingly, this has not been taken as the credible and final statement on the issue that Iran clearly hoped it would be. The first problem with it is that it does not appear to have been written down; it also appears to be limited only to the 'use' of such weapons. The more serious problem with it is that, like all fatwas, it can be revised. As such, it is likely to be no more than an unconvincing attempt to provide a smokescreen for the regime's true intentions. For those who feel it is premature to discount the authenticity of Khamenei's statement given its religious foundations, the words of Ayatollah Khomeini in 1988 should act as a wake-up call.

A year before his death Khomeini made clear in letters to Khamenei and the Guardian Council the 'unlimited' lengths to which, in his mind, they were entitled to go to in order to defend the revolution and ensure its continuity. He went as far as to state that it was permissible to destroy a mosque or suspend observance of the five pillars of Islam (the confession of faith, prayer, the observance of Ramadan, giving alms and the pilgrimage to Mecca) if such measures were rendered necessary by 'expediency' or the 'interests' of the regime. Khomeini's clear assertion of the supremacy of expediency is not without a religious context. On the contrary, it is in keeping with the established and uniquely Shia principle of *taqiyya* (which equates to 'caution' or 'avoidance'), under which, if a Muslim or his community is at risk, it is permissible to lie or deny one's faith in order to avoid harm. Khomeini's interpretation of this principle appears to conclude that the inclusion of the entire Islamic Republic in the concept of community is permissible in order to protect it. This in effect rules nothing out, including the acquisition of weapons of mass destruction.

Donald Rumsfeld told me,

Rogue states have to be identified and tackled earlier, in order to allow economic measures to be effective and to stave off the pursuit of military agendas. While recent economic sanctions have certainly had a measurable impact upon Iran's economy, and there remains a chance of preventing Iran from becoming a nuclear-armed state, it is less likely because of the delays before reaching a sanction regime tough enough to have an impact. Ultimately, if Iran cannot be made to understand that its integration into the global economy and community hinge upon its ability to demonstrate beyond reasonable doubt it is not pursuing a nuclear weapons programme, then the West will need to very seriously consider broadening its nuclear umbrella in order to prevent a nuclear arms race in the Middle East and the very real concerns to global security this would pose.

The international community – the United States and Europe in particular – should not allow Iran to dictate how the current stand-off progresses and eventually concludes. The political mistakes and miscalculations that have allowed North Korea to acquire nuclear weapons should serve as a stern rebuke to any suggestion that the strategy of containment is not a benign one. We did not fight and win the Cold War in order to allow a period of nuclear expansionism to develop, bringing with it new dangers to future generations. We must be quite clear that if Iran becomes a nuclear-armed state it is likely to be followed in short order by other countries in the region, notably Saudi Arabia, Egypt and Turkey. Do we want to see a nuclear arms race in one of the world's most unstable regions, where the likelihood of the use of such weapons is probably greatest? That is the real issue that the world has to confront, and it can only be answered with a simple yes or no.

What are we to make of Iran's recent manoeuvres in relation to sanctions on its nuclear progamme? Will the Glasgow-educated President Rohani make a material difference, and will the effect of sanctions finally persuade the supreme leader that to continue Iran's nuclear programme in the face of international opposition can only lead to economic ruin and social unrest? I fully understand the reasons why the international community sought to relax sanctions, as a means of encouraging Iran to engage at the negotiating table. But if it were the sanctions that brought the change, then, for many of us, it would seem logical to relax them only after genuine talks, timetables and concessions had been established, rather than on the basis of hope. In any case, whether the appearance of progress turns out to be real or illusory, it is essential that we give peace a chance, both for domestic and international political reasons. If peace in the region slips away, it must be seen to be due to Iranians in transit rather than an unwillingness on the part of the international community to give it a real chance.

The Tentacles of the State

The IRGC supports Hezbollah operations in Lebanon, Iraqi Kurdistan, Jordan and Palestine as well as the Islamic jihad in Egypt, Turkey and the Caucasus. The IRGC was designated a terrorist organization by the United States Senate in September 2007. Secretary of State Condoleezza Rice stated, 'Iran has been the country that has been in many ways a kind of central banker for terrorism in important regions like Lebanon through Hezbollah in the Middle East, in the Palestinian territories, and we have deep concerns about what Iran is doing in the south of Iraq.'

In July 2012 the US State Department provided an update on terrorism around the globe and claimed that Iran not only remained an active state sponsor of terrorism but had increased its terrorist-related activities: 'Iran also continued to provide financial, material, and logistical support for terrorist and militant groups throughout the Middle East and Central Asia.' It maintained that Iran furnished 'lethal support, including weapons, training, funding and guidance, to Iraqi Shia militant groups targeting US and Iraqi forces as well as civilians'. It also accused Iran, through the IRGC's elite Qods Force, of providing training to the Taliban in Afghanistan in the use of small arms, explosives and indirect-fire weapons such as mortars, artillery and rockets. Certainly, whether mediated through the IRGC or otherwise, Iran has been involved in a number of international terrorist incidents.

Iran's main proxy is Hezbollah, which was implicated in the 1982 and 1983 bombings of the Israeli headquarters in Tyre and the explosive attacks on the US embassy in Beirut in 1983 in which 58 Americans and Lebanese were killed, as will be discussed in the next chapter. They were also implicated in the 1983 Beirut barracks bombing of the US Marines and French paratroops in which 241 Americans were killed along with 58 French peacekeepers, the bombing of a Jewish community centre in Argentina in 1994 in which ninety-five people were killed, and the attack on the Khobar Towers complex in Dhahran, Saudi Arabia, when nineteen US service personnel were killed in 1996. Both outgoing president Ahmadinejad and the supreme leader Ali Khamenei appear to have given their support to the activities of Hezbollah in support of Iran's foreign policy objectives. Recent activities have included an explosion in New Delhi in India in February 2012, when an Israeli diplomat was targeted, and there are suggestions that the IRGC may have been involved in targeting other Israeli interests around the world.

The United States has accused Iran of supporting groups such as that of Muqtada al-Sadr in Iraq and has cited the finding of weapons including rockets and mortars bearing Iranian markings. In June 2012 two IRGC members believed to have been plotting to attack American, Israeli, British or Saudi targets were intercepted and arrested in Kenya. Ethiopia and Uganda have also expressed their fears about the willingness of Iran through its intermediaries to extend terrorist activity more widely in Africa.

Despite deep religious differences between the Shia Iranians and Sunni al-Qaeda, there continue to be accusations of Iranian support for this terrorist organization. The official United States 9/11 report stated that between eight and ten of the nineteen hijackers had passed through Iran and that their transit had been facilitated by Iranian border guards. Further, a federal district court in Manhattan ruled that Iran had given material support to the 9/11 plotters by using front companies to obtain flight simulators on which the terrorists could train. The US Treasury reported that Iran has allowed al-Qaeda to channel money through the country and that terrorist recruits have travelled into Iran from other parts of the Middle East and then on to Pakistan. Most recently, the Iranian government has been accused of supporting cyber attacks against oil and gas companies in the Gulf.

One of the more worrying developments in recent years has been the apparent willingness of the Iranians, through Hezbollah, to extend their activities to the western hemisphere. It has been suggested that Hezbollah has substantial connections with the violent Mexican drug cartel Los Zetas, which has itself carried out a number of barbaric terrorist attacks. It is relatively well known that Hezbollah has been involved in Latin America since the mid-1980s, when it first entered the drug trade, primarily in the lawless tri-border area where Brazil, Argentina and Paraguay meet. One of the worries for security forces in the region is that if Hezbollah and Los Zetas are cooperating on drugs then it is likely they are cooperating on weapons.

In October 2011 the US made it known that there had been an attempt to assassinate the Saudi ambassador in the United States. Assistant Secretary of State Roger Noriega stated, 'I believe there will be an attack on US personnel, installations or interests in the Americas as soon as Hezbollah operatives believe that they are capable of such an operation without implicating their Iranian sponsors in the crime.' Although it is acknowledged that Hezbollah has a large operational network in the tri-border area, many believe that its real mission is to plan attacks but lie dormant, awaiting instructions from abroad – i.e. Tehran. Hezbollah operatives have already been arrested in a number of countries for conducting surveillance on US embassies, from Cyprus to Russia to Spain, and they have carried out other surveillance operations in Singapore, Argentina and Germany. Whatever the reason for their presence in some of the world's security hot spots, we can be certain that it is not sightseeing and our intelligence services need to be constantly vigilant.

The Sunni–Shia Divide

As if the tensions between Iran and most of the international community were not sufficient, it also finds itself on one side of the great Sunni–Shia schism within Islam. While it is difficult to give absolute numbers, it is generally accepted that around 80–90 per cent of the world's Muslims are Sunni, and 10–20 per cent are Shia. Majority Shia populations exist in Iran, Iraq, Lebanon, Bahrain and Azerbaijan. Although only 10–15 per cent of Pakistan's Muslims are Shia, they constitute the second-largest Shia population in the world with around twenty-five million souls.

The differences between the two groups date back to the succession to the Prophet Muhammad as leader of the Muslim community. Sunnis believe that the father of Muhammad's wife, Aisha, was the rightful successor while Shiites believe that Muhammad's cousin, adopted son and son-in-law Ali was the First Imam and that his direct descendants were Muhammad's successors. Shias believe that Ali and the other imams have special spiritual qualities. The most prominent and numerous group within Shia Islam – the Twelvers – believe that the imams can understand and interpret the meanings contained within the teachings of Islam. Where Sunnis have a rigid adherence to the concept of sharia law, the Shia view is supplemented by *ijtihad* – research – in the light of the teachings of the Koran.

Until the rise of the Safavid empire, Sunnism was the dominant form of Islam across the Arab world including most of what is now Iran, although a substantial number of Twelvers were scattered across Persia. The Safavid dynasty, which ruled Persia from 1501 to 1722, firmly established the Twelver school of Shia Islam there, one of the great landmarks in Muslim history. Twelvers believe in twelve divinely ordained leaders – the twelve imams – and that the Mahdi (the guided one), the prophesied redeemer who will rule before the day of judgement, will return. They believe that Jesus Christ (Isa) will return to aid the Mahdi against Masih al-Dajjal (the false one) and his followers. According to the Koran, the appearance of Isa shall be a sign for the coming of the day of judgement. Around 85 per cent of today's Shias are Twelvers.

Following the establishment of Safavid authority, the subjects of Shah Ismail either converted, or pretended to convert, to Shia beliefs, the alternative being execution. During this era an increasing number of scholars within Shiism were drawn to Iran, away from its traditional centre of Najaf in Iraq. Today, there remains a tension between the religious centres of Qom in Iran and Najaf in Iraq around where the true spiritual home of Shia religious tradition resides.

Shireen Hunter, Director of the Carnegie Project on Reformist Islam at the Prince Alwaleed Bin Talal Centre for Muslim–Christian Understanding at Georgetown University in Washington DC maintains that there are no parallels in Sunni–Shia history to the Thirty Years' War between Roman Catholicism and Protestantism. Although there was rivalry between the Sunni Ottoman Turks and Safavid Persia, this subsided towards the end of the seventeenth century, and relations between the two empires (and later between Iran and the Republic of Turkey) were largely peaceful. According to Hunter, writing in a paper on Sunni and Shia tensions:

The gradual rise in sectarian tensions which had begun in the early 1970s and escalated following the Iranian revolution and the Afghan War, had to do with politics and competition for influence and power, notably between Iran and the Arab countries, especially Iraq and Saudi Arabia. This competition contributed to a sharp rise in sectarian tensions, especially in

Pakistan and Afghanistan, as both sides tried to use religion as
an instrument of policy.

Some attribute the relatively harmonious relations between
traditionalist Sunni and Shia Muslims in the period between
the collapse of the Ottoman empire and the decline of Arab
nationalism to a joint commitment to see off the secularist threat.
With the Islamic revival, and as colonial influences waned and
Arab nationalism lost its way, the blossoming of fundamentalism
reasserted the differences and potential conflicts between the two
movements, exacerbated by the teachings of extreme scholars such
as Ibn Taymiyyah – a thirteenth-century theologian beloved of al-
Qaeda. According to academics such as Olivier Roy of the French
National Centre for Scientific Research, the Iranian revolution
give rise to an awakening within Shiism, which was then used
as a political instrument by the leaders of the new regime. This
stimulated a very violent Sunni reaction, which began in Pakistan
before spreading to other parts of the Muslim world. According
to Roy, two events created a sea change in the balance of power
between Shia and Sunni – the revolution in Iran in 1979 and the
American military intervention in Iraq in 2003.

Whatever the predisposing causes, recent years have seen
increasing tensions between the two groups across the Muslim world.
In Iraq, following the 1991 Gulf War, Shias, who make up the majority
of the population, openly revolted against the regime of Saddam
Hussein. This resulted in their bloody suppression by Saddam's forces
with deaths estimated as high as 100,000. The succeeding years have
seen a hideous cycle of tit-for-tat killings on both sides. Estimates
suggest that over a thousand Muslim suicide bombers, mostly Sunnis,
have blown themselves up attacking mosques, hospitals, weddings,
funerals and shrines. They were urged on by fanatics such as Abu

Musab al-Zarqawi and by al-Qaeda, which called for a full-scale war on all Shias in Iraq 'whenever and wherever they are found'. Frequent attacks on Iraqi Shias resulted in their senior clerics declaring suicide bombings *haram* – in Islamic jurisprudence an act forbidden by God. For their part, Shia death squads stalked Iraq, murdering hundreds if not thousands of Sunnis in response.

Although only 10–15 per cent of Pakistan's population is Shia, it is numerically larger than the Shia majority in Iraq. Since the late 1980s it is estimated that well over 4,000 people have died in sectarian fighting in Pakistan with most violence occurring in the Punjab and Karachi. While much of the blame for the contemporary violence is attached to al-Qaeda and its affiliates, some see the arrest, trial and execution of Prime Minister Ali Bhutto in 1979 by General Zia ul-Haq as a flashpoint. Bhutto was a Shia, Zia a Sunni fundamentalist, and it was the latter's Islamization under the tutelage of Abdul Ala Maududi that saw the introduction of increasingly repressive laws and regulations based on strict Sunni interpretations. Today, anti-Shia groups inside Pakistan, such as the various offshoots of Jamiat Ulema-e-Islam, demand the expulsion of Pakistani Shias and have been responsible for hundreds of deaths as Pakistan spins in ever deceasing circles towards greater religious intolerance and hatred.

Inside Iran Sunnis complain that there is no Sunni mosque in the capital, Tehran, despite the fact that over one million of them live there, and their complaints have been backed up by UN human rights reports, which suggest that freedom of religion is not respected with regard to the Sunni minority. It is certainly true that, unlike the leadership under Ayatollah Khomeini, who made overtures to the Sunni population in the name of Islamic unity, the recent regime has been much more committed to core Shia values. Anyway Khomeini's attempts to cast himself as the single voice representing all Muslims came apart as a result of the conflict in Syria. His failure to support the Sunni Muslim Brotherhood against the secular Baathists earned their contempt, proving in their eyes that sectarian loyalty trumped his devotion to Islamic solidarity.

Saudi Arabia also has internal problems relating to its religious make-up, with Shia making up 10–15 per cent of the population, largely in the eastern province of Hasa, the centre of the oil industry. Despite attempts by King Abdullah to defuse the tension between the Wahhabi Sunni regime and its Shia subjects, there continue to be accusations of discrimination in employment as well as limitations on religious practices. Iran, of course, does not hold back from attacking the leadership of its pro-Western neighbour. Broadcasts from the Islamic Revolutionary Organization have attacked the concept of monarchy, which it claims is rejected by Islam.

So, on the one hand we have a rigid and fundamentalist Sunni ideology (which is not to suggest all Sunnis are fundamentalists) spread in a range of ways, including violent jihadist methods, and there are also violent Shia groups with overt and covert Iranian support. Which of these threatens us more in the West? We probably need to understand that the Iranians' activities are not primarily an expression of religious fervour but tools by which the regime seeks to increase its influence as part of its campaign to achieve regional hegemony. Fundamentalist Sunni extremists have different motivations. It is useful to compare and contrast them.

The Global Threat of Islamic Fundamentalism

The current campaign of violence being waged by Islamic fundamentalists (a term I will use for the sake of consistency and simplicity) around the world is a toxic phenomenon fed by increased personal mobility, the rapid improvement in communications (particularly the Internet) and a grotesquely distorted and simplified view of history. It threatens both Muslim and non-Muslim states alike, and eats away at concepts of equality, democracy and pluralism. It is a blasphemous interpretation of Islam which sanctions or even encourages the killing of citizens of all nations and religions, even those moderate and orthodox Muslims who do not agree with the radicalization of their religion.

In their exceptional book *Winning the Long War*, one of the best, most read and most frequently quoted books in my library, James Jay Carafano and Paul Rosenzweig state,

> Radical Islam is not terrorism in the name of religion; it is terrorism hiding behind a mask of religion. The main perpetrators of anti-American and anti-Western jihad today are the radical Wahhabi-Salafi sects and twentieth-century mutations: the Muslim Brotherhood [founded in 1929 by an Egyptian, Hassan al-Banna] and Jamaat i-Islami [started by Abdul Ala Maududi in Pakistan in 1941]. They go on to quote Angelo Codevilla, professor of international relations at Boston University: Murderous heresies arise as revolutionary movements. They take one, or more, of the faith's central tenets and twist it into a warrant for overthrowing the norms and practices first of the ordinary faithful, then of mankind. This kind of heresy sets itself apart by entitling the heretics to do whatever they want. The heretics . . . slip the bounds of orthodoxy and endow themselves with boundless revolutionary discretion.

Today, this boundless discretion not only justifies the murder and maiming of innocent civilians but glorifies atrocities such as suicide bombings. Fanatics deluding themselves that they are divine instruments have tried to obtain weapons of mass destruction and will undoubtedly use them if they do. They do not lack the will to kill us – if necessary all of us – merely the capability to do so. That is what we must deny them. From Bali to Madrid to Manhattan, this particularly venomous threat is probably the world's first truly global terror phenomenon and will require prolonged international cooperation if we are to have any chance of containing or defeating it. Meanwhile, the inability, or unwillingness, of certain political elements in the West to understand the uncompromising and fanatical nature of this threat has made it more difficult to deal with.

What are the goals of these people and where did they come from? Their prime objective is the establishment of a caliphate – a global Islamic state strictly governed by sharia law (more accurately, the fundamentalists' interpretation of sharia law). The purpose of such a Muslim superstate is to convert the rest of the world to Islam, if necessary by violence. One of the inspirations behind contemporary extremist Islam is Sayyid Qutb, executed for his part in plotting to overthrow President Nasser in 1966. Qutb's extreme views took fundamentalism a stage further than before in proclaiming that not only infidels but also 'not sufficiently Islamic' Arab rulers should be killed. Qutb's ideology, more recently echoed by Maududi, has encouraged the terrorists to see all Westerners, including innocent civilians, as combatants and therefore legitimate targets.

Carafano and Rosenzweig's analysis suggests that the particular brand of fundamentalist terrorism represented by Osama bin Laden and the al-Qaeda network has deep ideological roots, particularly in Wahhabism, the most fundamentalist interpretation of Sunni Islam. The origins of Wahhabi ideas can be traced back to the earliest stages of Islamic history and the Khariji sect of the seventh century AD. This movement was responsible for creating the original Sunni–Shia split within Islam by the killing of Ali (to Sunnis the fourth caliph and to Shias the First Imam), who, as we saw earlier, was the

Prophet Muhammad's cousin, adopted son and son-in-law. Khariji Islam and the teachings of the fourteenth-century fundamentalist Muslim scholar Ibn Taymiyya were taken up by Muhammad ibn Abd al-Wahhab in the eighteenth century and Wahhabism became the dominant form of Islam in Arabia and later the creed of the royal house of Saud. In the course of the nineteenth and twentieth centuries the peninsula was almost entirely cleared of non-Wahhabi Muslims with the doctrine supplanting what had been traditional respect for 'people of the book' – Jews and Christians. Jihad was declared against them, resulting in their expulsion.

According to Carafano and Rosenzweig,

In the 1970s and 1980s, boosted by oil wealth and a tactical alliance with Washington, Wahhabism launched a global challenge to mainstream Islam and to the Soviet domination of Afghanistan, attempting to spearhead jihad against the Soviets in that country, which in fact was fought by traditional Sunni Afghans. With complacent and non-comprehending US administrations, Wahhabism went on to spawn global terrorist movements backed by oil power and oil money.

Fundamentalist Muslims begin by defining themselves as different (and better) than their co-religionists, who are then labelled unbelievers and thereby targeted for conversion or death. They then look outwards and divide the world into two – the land of Islam (*dar al-Islam*) and the land of war (*dar al-harb*), which ultimately, of course, needs to be converted and subjugated or destroyed. Today, groups influenced by these ideas have a growing global presence and include groups such as Hamas, Palestinian Islamic Jihad, Pakistan-based organizations, some Chechen and Uzbek groupings and Jemaah Islamiyah in Indonesia, led by Abu Bakar Ba'asyir.

Not only do these groups unflinchingly attempt to subvert and destroy moderate Muslim states but they have become adept at using the legal systems and liberal sensitivities of the West to give themselves maximum room to manoeuvre. It has been said that Western legal systems fail to see that, for terrorists, first comes the jihad of the tongue, then that of the purse, and finally that of the sword, which is supreme. We cannot say that we have not been warned. The question is whether we have the political and moral courage to pick up the gauntlet that has been thrown down to us.

Chapter Four

TERROR IN OUR TIME

Terror is a word that seems to have invaded our daily existence. From TV news coverage to train station luggage warnings to the intrusive security we face with every flight we take, we're constantly reminded of its presence.

What do we mean by it? Terror is a natural phenomenon – the overwhelming emotional response felt when we are potentially in mortal danger. Terrorism is simply the conscious exploitation and manipulation of this feeling and is a particularly human thing – a violent manifestation of anger in response to a real or perceived slight. It may be the expression of a frustrated political or religious ideology or merely a disguise used by brute criminality. Terrorism has probably always been with us and probably always will be – a sad but warped testament to our inability to deal with our differences in a peaceful and civilized fashion.

Is it a new phenomenon? Absolutely not. It is at least as old as humans are as a species. Moreover, the story of what we commonly refer to as terrorism is probably much more of a continuum than we might imagine. It is a reflection of culture, religion, politics and the resentments and conflicts they can produce. Events that seem at first unconnected may on closer examination be intricately linked. Resentment can echo down the years nursed in the wrath of folklore or selective memory. Events and causes are rewritten, embossed, glorified or even embellished with virtues that never really existed. The accidental or wilful distortion of historical events can provide a fertile ground in which to grow deeply held grudges and foster hatred.

Sometimes one series of events triggers another, like a row of dominoes falling one against another, moving further and further away from the original force. In recent times, for example, the Russian invasion of Afghanistan gave birth to the Arab mujahideen and their training camps there. The fall of the Soviet Union preceded the break-up of Yugoslavia, and the subsequent war in Bosnia was provoked by generations of resentments. The radicalization of young Muslims in that conflict took them to Chechnya, to the camps in Afghanistan, now controlled by al-Qaeda, and ultimately to terror on the streets of the West. These events may be separated by time and geography, but they are linked by the rainbow influences of shared experience and human interaction. Very little in our world happens in isolation, and in the future there will be less still. Human actions have human consequences, for better or for worse.

I have never really liked the term 'war on terror'; it implies military concepts of identifiable enemies and a definable conflict. A quick look at history tells us that what some call today the war on terror cannot and will not be a discrete time-limited entity. It will not end with a victory or defeat on a battlefield. Terrorism learns to mutate. It will change its manifestations according to time and technology. Just as war was different after the invention of the gun and gunpowder, terrorism changed after the invention of dynamite, and cyber, nuclear or chemical terrorism will be the technological children of their ages. The tools of terror are usually created by science and industry for peaceful purposes, but are then used for more malevolent ends by those of a different intent. The current war on terror to defeat al-Qaeda and the scourge of radical Islamist violence will eventually morph into new conflicts. The predominant social, political and economic factors of the day will conspire to produce new grudges and new hatreds with a new supply of the violently disaffected.

So, terrorism is neither new nor homogeneous. It manifests itself in many different ways, from intimidation to the remote killing of innocents to the sacrifice of a suicide bomber. Yet despite the impact they can have, we seem all too easily to forget many of the individual events that make up the narrative of terror that scars our history – even our recent history. I have often wondered why that is. Is it because we want to believe such an event can never (or is unlikely to) happen to us or those we love? Perhaps, like medical staff who regularly deal with human trauma, we learn to compartmentalize as a psychological defence mechanism. Maybe we tend to forget because we want to – who knows? Maybe we have just learned to live with it because, frankly, there is no choice.

History's Bitter Lessons

Our ability to cut ourselves off from a turbulent past is considerable. In Britain and the United States how many people now remember the extraordinary levels of violence and insecurity that stalked Europe in the 1970s and 1980s? How much has seeped into our collective consciousness? How many of us would pass the exam question? My guess is very few.

The facts would shock many of us. In Italy between 1969 and 1987 there were 14,591 terrorist attacks; 1,182 people were wounded and 419 killed. Some 193 of these deaths were caused by neo-fascist terrorists, 143 by the extreme left, and 63 by the various Middle Eastern terrorist groups operating in Italy. In 1979, while Britain struggled with trade union unrest in the winter of discontent and the constant threat of IRA violence, and while the United States focused on the Iran hostage crisis, Italy suffered from no less than 2,513 terrorist events. Some may remember the kidnapping and murder of former prime minister Aldo Moro, or the horror of the Bologna railway bombing, but the scale of the terrorist violence inflicted on the Italian people will come as a surprise to most. Outside the United Kingdom (and to a surprising extent inside too) who really remembers the scale and frequency of the IRA attacks on both civilian and military targets in the last quarter of the twentieth century?

I tried an experiment by giving colleagues a list of 'IRA atrocities' and asking them to state which ones were real and which I had invented. In fact every event had actually happened. Most of those I asked were able to recall about half of the events but no one came close to remembering them all. How can it be that so many of us have already forgotten those killed in September 1975 in the bombing at the Hilton in Park Lane or in December 1983 in Harrods? How many remember the eight soldiers and their horses killed in the Hyde Park and Regent's Park bombings of 1982 or the ten young soldiers killed at the Marine School of Music in Deal in September 1989? Can we really have forgotten the Christmas bombs in Manchester in 1992 which injured sixty-five people or the ten people killed in McGurk's bar in Belfast in 1971? Perhaps we recall the sheer barbarity of the Enniskillen bomb at the Remembrance Day service in 1987, when eleven people were killed and sixty-three injured, but how many remember the soldiers and children killed in the coach bombing on the M62 in February 1974 or the February 1996 bus bombing near the Strand in London which killed three and injured many more? It is a long and bloody list with each atrocity a life-changing event for the families of the victims and the survivors themselves.

'What makes them tick?' is a question we often ask ourselves. For most of us, it is virtually impossible to understand the mindset of those who indiscriminately kill or maim the innocent. The motivation behind terrorism has been endlessly discussed and written about by historians, politicians and psychologists, with the full spectrum of human behaviour invoked from religious fanaticism to political idealism to frank criminality. Yet whatever the reasoning or excuses given, the effect is always the same. Michael Burleigh's book *Blood and Rage: a cultural history of terrorism* remains for me one of the best and most accessible historical narratives of terrorist acts, which he combines with intuitive insights into the psychology of those who carry out such atrocities. It dispassionately describes and analyses the sorts of individuals and organizations who have carried the terrorist label over time. I have liberally dipped into his research throughout this book, for which I hope he will forgive me. His point about the victims of terrorism is particularly excellent and worth repeating. It should be on the desk of every politician, security officer and journalist.

> Their victims usually have one thing in common regardless of their social class, politics or religious faith. That is a desire to live unexceptional lives settled with their families and friends, without some resentful radical loser – who can be a millionaire loser harbouring delusions of victimhood – wishing to destroy and maim them so as to realize a world that almost nobody wants . . . They all bleed and grieve in the same way.

Before anyone tries to explain – or even excuse – the actions of terrorists they should look at pictures of the remains of those whose lives were brought to an untimely end, from the frail elderly doing their best just to bring the shopping home, to toddlers in shorts who never made it to their day at the beach, or the body parts the experts were unable to match to a living, breathing individual whose loss destroyed the lives of those who loved them. If I mention victims throughout, it is to remind ourselves constantly that this savagery has a very human price. Terrorists are not heroes; they kill and maim and hurt and destroy. They are the worst of our kind.

One thing that, by definition, unites all terrorist groups is the desire to produce widespread fear, either targeted at specific groups or indiscriminately across whole populations. They may want to overthrow a whole system of governance and achieve revolution or simply alter the behaviour of a particular regime. They may want to weaken those in authority to induce a sense of chaos, paralysis or powerlessness. They may want to provoke those in power to overreact and implement oppressive measures in the hope that they will produce a counter-reaction leading to greater violence and instability. They may have a specific aim in mind such as the freeing of prisoners or wish to extort money, resources or weapons. Their targets will range from individuals through physical infrastructure in order to disrupt economic activity to communications. With the explosion of opportunities for publicity made available by satellite TV, the Internet and social media, they may see acts of violence as a way of obtaining wider recognition for their cause – a not unreasonable view to take, given the events spanning the years from the Munich Olympics to 9/11.

As Burleigh puts it, 'The milieu of terrorists is invariably morally squalid, when it is not merely criminal . . . and as endless studies of terrorists' psychology reveal, they are morally insane, without being clinically psychotic.'

The Long British Tussle with Terror

Britain, with its long history of civil war, nationalist tensions and colonial legacies, has seen most, if not all, of the terrorist aims and means discussed above.

Perhaps the most famous example of an attempt to murder the entire governing class came with the Gunpowder Plot of November 1605, when Guy Fawkes and his fellow conspirators planned to blow up King James I at the state opening of Parliament. This would have removed the monarch, the bishops of the Church of England, members of the House of Lords and House of Commons and the senior judges of the English legal system at a stroke. Motivated by religious fervour and resentment and wishing to replace the Protestant James with his Catholic daughter Princess Elizabeth, the attempt merely resulted in the relatively tolerant king embarking on a much more repressive religious policy and the execution of the conspirators. The attempted killings of Elizabeth I of England and Alexander II had similar effects.

Although the plot was led by Robert Catesby, it is Guy Fawkes who is best remembered, and his effigy is burned to this day in bonfires on 5 November. Ironically, although he was physically torn and broken by his torture on the rack, Fawkes escaped the full horrors of being hung, drawn and quartered – the fate of many of his co-conspirators – by throwing himself from the gallows and breaking his neck. If people are surprised by this last detail, this is not unusual – popular history often overlooks such inconvenient facts.

Almost 320 years later, on 12 October 1984, the IRA made its own attempt to murder the British government, this time the Conservative administration led by Margaret Thatcher as it met during the party's annual conference. The time bomb placed by Patrick Magee behind a panel in a bathroom exploded in the early hours of the morning, injuring thirty-one people and killing five, though none of them were government ministers. I remember this event particularly vividly as it was one of the few conferences that I missed (following a back injury as a junior doctor). I watched with horror from home as the story unfolded, thinking that if I had been fit, I would probably have been in the Grand Hotel bar with many of my friends. The bomb went off in the bathroom of Donald and Muriel Maclean, whom I knew very well. It was only when I visited Donald in hospital afterwards that I realized how dreadful were the injuries he had sustained, although, like so many victims, he underplayed his own suffering. Pictures of the shattered hotel were beamed around the world and the chilling propaganda message of the IRA was repeated by the national and international media: 'Today we were unlucky. But remember we only have to be lucky once. You will have to be lucky always.'

Unlike the gunpowder conspirators who were executed for treason, Patrick Magee was released in 1999 as part of the Good Friday agreement having served only fourteen years in prison.

During its campaign of terror the IRA made two attacks on Parliament. On 17 June 1974 a bomb went off in Westminster Hall, the oldest part (built in 1098) of the complex, fracturing a gas main and setting off a fierce fire, and on 30 March 1979 Conservative Northern Ireland spokesman Airey Neave was murdered when a tilt bomb exploded under his car as he left the House of Commons car park. Thus we are no strangers either to the concept of political assassination. Assassinations may be carried out to remove individuals because they are particularly hated, powerful or both, to send a signal to others in authority about what may befall them if there is no change in behaviour or to feed the cycle of violence in the hope that reprisals will stimulate repression and revolution.

I find it interesting how similar, or indeed identical, targets can be chosen by different terrorist groups for different reasons with lengthy time intervals separating the events. For example when Islamist bombers struck the London Underground in 2005 most Londoners would not have been aware of an earlier and not dissimilar campaign.

In 1841 William Mackey Lomasney was born in Ohio, the son of Irish immigrants. His life of violent Irish nationalism culminated in a bombing campaign against the London underground railways in November 1883. From the first-class carriages at the front of trains he and his accomplices dropped bombs onto the trackside which exploded as the passengers in second class passed – they certainly had no qualms about hurting ordinary people. The first attack occurred on a Metropolitan Line train, injuring seventy-two people. Less than half an hour later another bomb exploded beyond Charing Cross underground station as a District Line train left. On 2 January 1885 the Metropolitan Line was again targeted when a bomb exploded as a train approached Goodge Street station. The 7/7 suicide bombers were certainly not the first to see the London Underground as a high-profile or totemic target.

The IRA attack on Westminster Hall and the murder of Airey Neave also had antecedents. In 1884 an Irish-American called John Daly was arrested before carrying out a plan to throw dynamite bombs from the Strangers' Gallery onto the floor of the House of Commons in a plot designed to kill both government and opposition MPs. On 24 January 1885 Henry Burton, another Irish-American terrorist, tried to explode a bomb in the chapel of St Mary Undercroft in the crypt under Westminster Hall, while an associate again prepared to drop a bomb into the chamber of the House of Commons.

Public transport and government buildings have been regular targets for acts of terror across the globe.

The Pain of Italy and Spain

Why is it that railways have been such frequent targets? The answer probably lies in their relative ease of access, their economic and social value and sometimes their national symbolism. Attackers often achieve similarly destructive and murderous outcomes, but their motives and consequences have been dramatically different.

Early on 2 August 1980 a bomb ripped through the waiting room of Bologna central station in Italy, killing 85 people and wounding more than 200. In the warmth of the Italian summer many were families with children heading for a day out by the seaside. The Italian government, which initially believed that it was an accident, quickly came to the same conclusion as the Italian political left – that the atrocity was the work of some new fascist militant group. Two weeks later the Bologna prosecutor issued twenty-eight arrest warrants against members of the Nuclei Armati Rivoluzionari. Despite numerous trials, appeals and judgments which continued until 1995, it is not clear to this day who exactly was responsible for these senseless murders or what their true motives were. In classic conspiracy fashion, however, military leaders, security services and even Masonic lodges came under suspicion as their respective enemies tried to implicate them. Francesco Cossiga, who was prime minister and later became president of Italy, repeatedly proclaimed his belief that the attack was the work of Palestinian groups operating in Italy. Interestingly, Cossiga maintained that the bombings could not be the work of the Italian left because 'unlike leftist terrorism, which strikes at the heart of the state through its representatives, black terrorism prefers the massacre because it promotes panic and impulsive reactions'. This analysis has mirrored much later thinking about the difference between terrorism inspired by political ideology and that derived from religious fanaticism. This analysis had an immediate attraction but was always much too simplistic and is likely to lead to the wrong conclusions.

On 11 March 2004, three days before the Spanish general election, ten separate explosions tore through four trains in rush-hour Madrid. They killed 191 people and wounded 1,800. The victims came from Europe, Africa, Asia and South America with the majority of the dead – 142 – from Spain itself. In Atocha station three bombs exploded within four seconds of each other. In Santa Eugenia station a bomb exploded at exactly the same moment, coinciding with two more in El Pozo del Tio Raimundo station. At Calle Tellez, around half a mile from Atocha station, four more bombs exploded within the next minute.

Again, it is unclear which organization carried out the bombings. While al-Qaeda associates claimed responsibility, US intelligence services were sceptical. There did appear, however, to be a link to Moroccan terrorist groups and there was initial speculation that the bombs used were typical of Morocco's radical Islamist Combat Group. Twenty-nine suspects were charged on 11 April 2006 and Judge Juan del Olmo concluded that 'local cells of Islamic extremists inspired through the Internet' were responsible for the attacks. On 31 October 2007 twenty-one of the defendants were found guilty on a range of charges.

In most countries terrorist atrocities of the scale of those in Madrid would create an environment of political solidarity, with parties from across the political spectrum coming together in a spirit of national solidarity, anger and mourning. This was not the case in Spain in March 2004, with the bombings coming within seventy-two hours of a general election. The reaction of the government was controversial at best, knee-jerk and inept at worst. Leaders of the governing Partido Popular were quick to lay the blame at the feet of the Basque separatist organization ETA, the traditional enemy of the Spanish state. There was a strong reason to make ETA the scapegoat: the unpopularity of Spain's involvement in the Iraq War and the belief that any al-Qaeda link to the bombings would suggest that ordinary people were being punished for the government's pro-war policy. In the event it became clear that the attacks were the work of Islamist militants of some form, and the government lost the election.

Political commentators have tended to believe that the PP lost as a result of its mishandling of the situation rather than because of the bombings. There is, however, a widespread view that had there been no attacks the government would have been re-elected. Directly or indirectly the terrorist attack changed not only the government of a Western democracy, but the new administration swiftly withdrew Spanish troops from Iraq. By design or default the terrorists success-fully achieved a change in policy. Who knows what encouragement has been given to jihadist leaders or the conclusions they have drawn from this episode? The implications could be profound indeed.

Although there was no direct evidence of an al-Qaeda link to the Madrid bombers, there was a great deal of speculation that the terrorists were motivated by a general jihadist call to reconquer previous Islamic territory as part of the eventual creation of a global caliphate. Whether this is true or not, it is clear that second- or third-generation immigrants to Western countries can be influenced by extremist propaganda and that 'home-grown' terrorism is a real threat now and in the future, which will require sensitive but urgent handling. The London bombings of July 2005 made it very clear that even those who appear on the surface to have integrated socially and culturally may provide a lethal threat if contaminated by violent fundamentalist ideology.

A rough rule of thumb among many commentators on terrorist violence has been that secular terrorism tends to attack iconic or infrastructure targets with human death and injury regarded as unavoidable collateral damage, while religious fanatics seek to cause maximum death and destruction. This is a variant of the distinction made by Cossiga noted above.

Following the London bombings on 7 July 2005 videotapes made by two of the bombers were discovered. In one of them, bomber Muhammad Sidique Khan set out the reasons for his actions:

> I and thousands like me are forsaking everything for what we believe. Our drive and motivation doesn't come from tangible commodities that this world has to offer. Our religion is Islam, obedience to the one true God and following the footsteps of the final Prophet messenger. Your democratically elected governments continuously perpetuate atrocities against my people all over the world. And your support of them makes you directly responsible, just as I am directly responsible for protecting and avenging my Muslim brothers and sisters . . . We are at war and I am a soldier.

This was not rhetoric from a man known to the security forces as a potential threat or a political activist. Khan, aged thirty, worked as a learning mentor with children at a primary school near Leeds. His suicide left behind a wife and a young child.

Germany Staggers

Germany in the 1960s was still in a state of flux and the Cold War was at its frostiest. On 13 August 1961, only sixteen years after the end of the Second World War (and less than a month before my own birth), construction began on the Berlin Wall – designed to isolate capitalist West Berlin from Soviet-dominated, east-European communism. Later that decade a grand coalition was formed between West Germany's two main parties, the CDU and the SPD. This was seen by many on the left as a sell-out by the social-democratic SPD to pro-NATO pro-capitalist forces and it exacerbated political tensions. Leftists feared a return of the German right, not least because the new chancellor Kurt Georg Kiesinger had been a Nazi. Such worries might appear almost absurd today with a stable unified Germany at the heart of the European Union, but this future was far from an inevitability in the divided Europe of the Cold War, flower power and student protest.

In his book *The Baader Meinhof Complex* Stephan Aust wrote:

> We were the first generation since the war, and we are asking our parents questions. Due to the Nazi past, everything bad was compared to the Third Reich. If you heard about police brutality, that was said to be just like the SS. The moment you see your own country as the continuation of a fascist state, you give yourself permission to do almost anything against it. You see your action as the resistance that your parents did not put up.

One of the events that was to become seminal for the radicalized new left came on 2 June 1967, during a visit by the shah of Iran to West Berlin. As demonstrators outside the opera house were dispersed, a twenty-six-year-old student called Benno Ohnesorg, who was attending his first ever political rally, was chased, beaten and 'accidentally' shot in the head by a plain-clothes policeman. The death of Ohnesorg became a cause célèbre, inspiring some of those who would go on to form the Red Army Faction, whose terrorist activities plagued Germany for the next two decades. The policeman, who was acquitted at a subsequent trial, is now known to have worked for the Stasi, having been a member of the East German Communist Party.

The Red Army Faction (RAF) had three iterations. The first primarily consisted of the Baader–Meinhof Gang and its associates and ended with the apparent suicide in prison of Baader on 18 October 1977, along with most of his remaining convicted accomplices. The second, which overlapped in terms of time, running from the mid- to late 1970s, involved the Socialist Patients Collective (SPK) and other groups sympathetic to the original protagonists, including the Movement 2 June, named after the date of Ohnesorg's death. The third RAF period ran from the early 1980s to 20 April 1998, when the group declared itself dissolved.

The Baader–Meinhof story could not be invented by a Hollywood script writer yet it did actually happen in Germany less than five decades ago.

Andreas Baader was a strong-willed narcissist whose various careers had come to nothing. An expert car thief, he was drawn to violence and prone to provoking fights in bars, often as the result of an inability to control his famously violent temper. Although he strenuously asserted his heterosexuality, he was widely known to greatly admire his uncle, Michael Kroecher, a gay ballet dancer, and was happy enough to be photographed naked for a gay pornographic magazine. What really matters about this side of Baader's personality is that, whatever his sexual inclinations, it is clear that he was just as willing to use his sexuality as a tool as he was violence and psychological intimidation, in order to achieve what he wanted.

Ulrike Meinhof was brought up by her widowed mother during the war and became a strong opponent of nuclear weapons and German rearmament. In 1962 she married the influential editor of the pro-communist newspaper she worked for and, with him, had twin girls. Her divorce six years later was acrimonious, and with thirty of her radical friends she trashed the former family home. They finished by collectively urinating and defecating on her marital bed. It was when she moved with her girls to a large apartment on Krufsteinerstrasse that she met the wayward but manipulative Baader and his student companion Gudrun Ensslin. While Baader and Ensslin were somewhat in awe of the radical columnist, both Meinhof and Ensslin were enthralled by the vulgar, violent and sexual Baader. It was the ménage à trois from hell.

On 2 April 1968, the three set fire to a number of department stores in Frankfurt, accompanied by Thorwald Proll and Horst Sohnlein, and were subsequently convicted for arson and endangering human life. Their three-year sentences in prison were curtailed by a political amnesty in 1969, soon reversed by the Federal Constitutional Court, which meant they should have gone back to jail. Unsurprisingly, they did not. Along with their personal psychological and political baggage, Baader, Ensslin and Proll went on the run, initially to France, where they stayed with, among others, the revolutionary-chic friend of Che Guevara, Régis Debray, which no doubt boosted Baader's already overblown heroic self-image. After a detour through Italy, they returned to West Germany and the Red Army Faction was formed.

Arrested again in the spring of 1970, Baader was freed by Meinhof and others in the most audacious fashion. After shooting an elderly doorman, they escaped in a stolen car. It was not of course a car chosen to maximize anonymity but an Alfa Romeo – stolen up-market cars were Baader's favourite form of transport. It was at this point that they headed for the Middle East and trained in the West Bank and Gaza with the Popular Front for the Liberation of Palestine and Palestinian Liberation Organization guerrillas.

In retrospect it is interesting how much popular sympathy the group inspired among guilt-ridden West Germans, especially the left-leaning liberal elite, despite the deaths of thirty-four innocent victims. According to Stephan Aust, when the gang started robbing banks,

Baader, the charismatic spoiled psychopath, indulged in the imagery of the romanticized outlaw, telling people that his favourite movie was *Bonnie and Clyde*.

Baader, Meinhof, Ensslin and two other gang members, Holger Meins and Jan-Carl Raspe, were arrested in June 1972. Holger Meins died on hunger strike on 9 November 1974. Meinhof would hang herself in her cell on 9 May 1976, during the trial. Baader and Raspe were to die of gunshots to the head and Ensslin by hanging in her cell on the night of 18 October 1977. Another gang member, Irmgard Möller, who had several stab wounds in the chest, survived and was released from prison in 1994.

'Crazies to Arms'

It was during the incarceration of Baader and his comrades that the second generation of the Red Army Faction came to prominence. In 1971 Baader and Ensslin had teamed up with a group of psychiatric patients in Heidelberg known as the Socialist Patients Collective, who joined the organization under the initial slogan 'Crazies to arms!' Hanna-Elise Krabbe and her sister Friederike, both members of the SPK, were involved in the kidnap and murder of Hans Martin Schleyer, president of the German Employers' Association and one of the most powerful men in Germany. On 5 September 1977 he was abducted in an operation in which his driver and three policemen were killed. Chancellor Schmidt refused to comply with the kidnappers' demands and the crisis dragged on until 18 October, when the RAF announced that Schleyer had been executed en route to France, where his body was discovered in the boot of a green Audi. This was the same day that the Lufthansa hijack ended in Somalia. This hijack was designed to secure the release of the RAF leaders being held in prison, but it ended in failure and resulted in the suicide of the leaders in prison.

Following the murder of Schleyer, Krabbe fled to Baghdad. She disappeared and remains unaccounted for.

After the demise of the Baader–Meinhof Gang and the SPK, the third iteration of the Red Army Faction continued its programme of violent terrorism for almost twenty years, including attacks on industrial and political figures, US and NATO bases and the attempted assassination of Al Haig, at the time supreme commander of NATO and later US secretary of state.

The involvement of the mentally ill in the SPK and subsequently the Red Army Faction invites the questions of whether terrorists are in general more likely to suffer from mental illness, and whether the disturbed are more easily recruited by terrorist organizations. In his book *The Sociology and Psychology of Terrorism: who becomes a terrorist and why?* Rex Hudson looked at the dynamics of these groups and individuals in an effort to understand their motivations. He quotes psychiatrist W. Rasch, who in the late 1970s interviewed a number of the West German terrorists and subsequently stated, 'No conclusive evidence has been found for the assumption that a significant number of them are disturbed or abnormal.' Psychologist Ken Hesken, who studied the behavioural patterns of terrorists in Northern Ireland, came to a similar conclusion: 'In fact, there is no psychological evidence that terrorists are diagnosably psychopathic or otherwise clinically disturbed.'

Although those who carry out acts of terrorism may be extremely alienated from the societies – national or, increasingly, global – in which they live, this does not imply that they are mentally ill. Professor Scott Atran of the National Centre for Scientific Research in Paris thinks radicalization is a social rather than a mental health problem, echoing a general consensus. Professor Atran maintains that 'militant terrorism is born in the streets, schools, cafes and barbershops . . . Rather than plotting in cells, plans for bombings were hatched at weddings and festivals.' He also warns about the potential of the Internet to bring individuals together, suggesting that it is an ideal medium for terrorism: 'Men bond very fast over the Internet. It dispenses with the need to be the alpha male you get when two men meet in person.' Women, too, can get more easily involved over the Internet.

Psychologists point to a number of differences that separate the psychopath from the political terrorist, although the experience of the SPK suggests that they can never be mutually exclusive. One difference is the psychopath's inability to profit from experience, another that the motivation for a psychopath's actions is likely to be largely personal. Given the complexity of terrorist plots, those in charge are unlikely to choose psychopaths, whose reliability or controllability are suspect. This goes some way to explaining why the ordinary citizen who blends in with society is a much better candidate for terrorist activity. Yet while it partly explains why Muhammad Sadique Khan, the 7/7 bomber, a quiet primary school mentor with his own young child, might not have been such an unsurprising suicide bomber, it raises further disturbing issues.

The Suicide Tendency

If mental instability is not contributory to involvement in terrorism, how do we explain the phenomenon of the suicide bomber? Most people think it axiomatic that if you kill yourself and innocent people around you then something must be amiss in your cognitive processes. They would be wrong. The use of suicide in terror attacks is by no means a recent phenomenon. While we have come to think of suicide attacks as being synonymous with bombings, they have a long pedigree.

One of the earliest documented instances dates back to the Jewish zealots of the first century AD, who sought to destabilize and demoralize their Roman occupiers and stir their fellow countrymen to rebellion. The attackers used *sicaras* (derived from the Latin *sica*, meaning a short sword or sabre), which were easily hidden under their garments, to cut the throats of Roman soldiers, often in the most savage way and in the most public circumstances. The attacks took place in the full knowledge that the retaliation of nearby soldiers would result in the certain death of the zealot. While not suicide by their own hand, it was certainly suicide by their own intent.

Throughout history this pattern has been repeated, notably by a secret order linked to a Shia sect, the Nizari Ismailis, who lived in Syria and Persia from the eleventh to the thirteenth centuries. To eliminate rivals and prominent political or military opponents, highly trained figures known as *fida'i* (self-sacrificing agents) were dispatched from a number of mountain castles which the order occupied. Brutally successful, the reputation of the order spread far and wide, reaching the ears of both the crusaders and Marco Polo, whose misinterpretation of the word *hashishi* wrongly gave rise to the term 'assassins' for the group. The agents, the lowest level of their order, accepted near-certain death in carrying out their missions – what we today might characterize as virtual suicide.

Even in these very early examples which, if not strictly speaking suicide, resulted in the death of the attacker at the hands of others, a number of common factors can be identified. The first is the acceptance by the attacker that their own death is an acceptable price for the success of the attack. The second is the attacker's possession of deeply held personal motivations, an ideology usually based on religious or political foundations or a combination of the two. The third is the careful planning of the attack and the deliberate selection of highly visible, valuable or symbolic targets.

None of this implies that the attackers themselves were regarded as valueless, although they were almost by definition dispensable. For example, the *fida'i* had a great deal of time and resources put into their training by their superiors. Although young, they tended to be both physically strong and intelligent. They were expected to have not only the necessary physical prowess, but also a detailed knowledge of their enemy, their enemy's culture and even their language. They were trained as stealth killers, to be what were later seen as archetypal assassins, rather than full-frontal attackers.

Two decades of work at Turin University in the 1840s produced an innovation that, while having enormous peaceful benefits, was to prove an unexpected windfall for the forces of terror. In introducing his new type of explosive, Alfred Nobel could not possibly have anticipated how quickly it would be used by suicide attackers. Previously, all that had been available to the terrorist was either gunpowder (which required enormous quantities to achieve the desired effect and was therefore easily detectable, as Guy Fawkes and his friends discovered) or nitroglycerine, whose inherent instability made it dangerous to handle and thus limited its potential (as Razmi Yousef, the original shoe bomber, and his associates would realize too late 150 years later). Sadly, dynamite arrived in the nick of time for the period of enormous political instability and social unrest that was to characterize Europe in the second half of the nineteenth century.

If it is possible to determine the exact date of the birth of the suicide bomber, then history tends to point to a cold March morning in 1881 in the Russian city of St Petersburg. It was then that a far-left anarchist group, People's Will, succeeded in assassinating Tsar Alexander II, having failed on a previous attempt. The tsar and his attacker died within hours of one another. The historian Benedict Anderson notes that, with this event, 'Nobel's invention had now arrived politically.'

The story then moves on, away from individual assassins, to over half a century later, towards the end of the Second World War. The combination of impending military defeat and their own warrior heritage was to produce the Japanese kamikaze phenomenon. The ritual of seppuku already existed in the Japanese tradition – suicide rather than capture and shame was part of the samurai code, bushido – but the deployment of suicide as a tool of war was unprecedented. It was not unknown for pilots of damaged aircraft – of any nation – to choose to crash them into enemy assets when safe return to base was impossible, but the kamikaze took the concept to new and horrifying levels.

The deployment of kamikaze began at the Battle of Leyte Gulf in October 1944, and by the end of the war almost 4,000 pilots had killed themselves in this way, damaging around 300 warships and sinking an estimated 57 vessels. For Allied servicemen the tactic was shocking and terrifying, but for the Japanese it was an effective, if brutal, use of diminishing human and material assets at a time when defeat was looking more and more like the dishonourable outcome they so dreaded. Notwithstanding the effectiveness of the initial campaign, however, a full range of countermeasures was soon deployed, as is inevitably the case in response to new terror strategies.

We see a more familiar manifestation of the suicide attack if we roll forward to the early 1980s, when the Middle East was convulsed by the continuing Israeli–Palestinian struggle, the aftermath of the Iranian revolution of 1979 and the bloody Iran–Iraq War. In what was to become a depressingly familiar pattern, sixty-one people were killed and over a hundred injured when a car filled with explosives was driven into the Iraqi embassy in Beirut in December 1981. It remains unclear who the perpetrators were on this occasion, although a number of opposition groups to Saddam Hussein's regime claimed responsibility. The following year, in an attempt to deny the PLO territory from which to attack targets in Israel, the armed forces of Israel invaded southern Lebanon. The months and years that followed saw not only the complete expulsion of the PLO from Lebanon but the emergence of a radical Shia movement in the country whose most enduring embodiment has been Hezbollah, whose paymasters, Iran and Syria, have been only too happy to see chronic instability on the borders of Israel.

Four further suicide bombings led to mass casualties between November 1982 and October 1983. In Tyre, Lebanon's fourth-largest city, 89 died when a truck bomb was driven into Israeli military headquarters. The following spring 63 were killed in a car bomb targeted at the US embassy. In the most bloody of the attacks, Islamic Jihad orchestrated dual truck bomb strikes on a US Marine barracks and the French paratrooper headquarters, killing 273 and 58 respectively. Just as the killing of the unprotected Tsar Alexander II in 1881 had shaken Russia, so the attacks on what were seen as 'protected' targets in 1983 showed that the determined suicide attacker could cause massive casualties and damage to a seemingly greatly superior military power.

It was consequently no time at all before the know-how of the suicide bomber was for sale and available for export. It was on the tropical island paradise of Sri Lanka where this deadly commodity was to find its most bloody export market. The Liberation Tigers of Tamil Eelam (LTTE) were a terrorist separatist organization who waged a civil war against the government of Sri Lanka for almost three decades until their eventual military defeat in 2009. The group demanded the creation of a separate Tamil state on the island to reflect the cultural and religious divisions between the majority Sinhalese, who account for around 75 per cent of the population in Sri Lanka, and the Tamils, accounting for around 10 per cent. Tension between these two groups had grown since Ceylon, as it was, gained independence from Britain in 1948. Post-independence ethnic tensions were exacerbated by the introduction of legislation such as the Sinhala Only Act, which recognized Sinhala as the sole official language of government.

My friend Lakshman Kadirgamar, a Tamil, was murdered by the LTTE in his own back garden. The two of us often talked late into the evening about our hopes for peace in Sri Lanka and we shared the view that peace is not simply the absence of war. A genuine peace requires positive attributes. It requires freedom from fear and freedom of expression, including a free press and broadcast media and the right to dissent within the law. It requires an inclusive political solution that addresses the underlying causes of the conflict and takes into account the legitimate grievances and aspirations of all the people of a land. Until the rights, identities and hopes of all Sri Lankans, whatever their ethnic origins or religion, are treated as equal, peace and reconciliation will not be achieved.

The failure to create a genuinely united Sri Lanka able to take advantage of a well-educated population, abundant natural resources and a beneficial geography is a source of considerable personal sadness to me. This is not only because of my own political involvement since 1996, when I negotiated what became known as the Fox Agreement, an early attempt to create a political mechanism that might have helped bring an end to the conflict, but also the frustrating experience of watching so many lives lost or disrupted by needless violence and the continuing haemorrhaging of hope.

It was in an increasingly fractious political atmosphere that the LTTE was formed in the late 1970s. The first major attack on the Sri Lankan state came in 1983, when fifteen members of a military patrol were killed in Jaffna, at the northern end of the island. The ramifications of this event were enormous and led directly to what became known as Black July. Anti-Tamil pogroms across the country saw the torching of an estimated 18,000 businesses and homes and resulted in the deaths of over 300 Tamils, although non-government estimates put this figure considerably higher. The dual effect of these events was the flight of Tamils abroad (an estimated 150,000 emigrated) and the hardening of attitudes among a generation of young Tamils. The stage was thus set for a civil war, the true cost of which – in terms of both loss of life and damage to physical and social infrastructure – is still being calculated today.

Over the following years the LTTE earned its reputation as one of the most ruthless and violent terrorist groups in history. One reason for this was the creation in 1987 of the Black Tigers suicide bomber unit. This group attacked civilian and official targets indiscriminately. According to the LTTE's own figures, it undertook 378 suicide missions, 104 of which were carried out by female attackers. A video, still available on YouTube, shows graphically the horror of the suicide bomb, when on 20 November 2007 a young woman blew herself up in the Social Services and Social Welfare Ministry in Colombo in what appears to have been a failed attempt to assassinate Minister Douglas Devananda. No amount of time passing diminishes for me the sense of anger, frustration and horror I feel when I see it – such a waste, so callous and so pointless.

The strategy of the LTTE in targeting high-profile public figures was from their point of view highly successful, killing thirty-seven members of parliament, including ten party leaders and seven cabinet ministers. The most audacious attacks claimed the lives of Indian Prime Minister Rajiv Gandhi in 1991 and Sri Lankan President Ranasinghe Premadasa in 1993, the political fallout from both being enormous.

As with most states under attack from terrorism, technological advances – in this case in armoured car design and security systems – meant that the Sri Lankan government developed an increasing ability to thwart the LTTE's campaign of high-value assassinations.

By 2008 this had undermined the LTTE's most effective propaganda claim – that no one was safe from their suicide attacks. Ultimately, significant increases in the defence budget combined with more effective deployment of the armed forces meant the Sri Lankan government was able to establish and maintain military superiority. The asymmetry, which had assisted the LTTE in the earlier years, ultimately proved no match for an overwhelming military force and led to their defeat.

The emergence of the female suicide bomber is worth considering. In her book *Dying to Kill: the allure of suicide terror*, Mia Bloom, assistant professor of international affairs at the University of Georgia, points out that since the first recorded female suicide bomber, a seventeen-year-old Lebanese girl who killed five Israeli soldiers in 1985, of the approximately seventeen groups that have used suicide bombing, women have been operatives in more than half of them. Professor Bloom notes,

> Their participation in suicide bombings starkly contradicts the theory that women are more likely to choose peaceful mechanisms for conflict resolution than men are – that women are inherently more disposed towards moderation, compromise and tolerance in their attitudes toward international conflict. Complicating these notions of femininity further is the fact that the IED is often disguised under a woman's clothing to make her appear pregnant, and so beyond suspicion or reproach.

It is clear that the motives of the female bomber are as varied as those of the male and may be revenge or escape or be derived from religion or a political ideology. Bloom suggests, however, that in many instances women are drawn to suicide bombing for personal reasons of revenge rather than ideology. She cites the example of Chechnya, where female bombers are called the Black Widows because many are the sisters, mothers or wives of Chechen men killed in battles with Russian troops. Zarema Muzhikhoyeva was one such widow. On 10 July 2003 she was arrested carrying a home-made bomb in Moscow. She admitted to having been recruited by Chechen rebels as a suicide bomber, in exchange for $1,000 paid to her relatives to compensate them for jewellery she had stolen from them. When the rebels sent her to Moscow to carry out her mission, however, she changed her mind and got herself arrested by police. Muzhikhoyeva was the first bomber to be captured alive. When the court sentenced her to the maximum of twenty years, despite the fact that she had opted not to explode her cargo, she shouted, 'Now I know why everyone hates the Russians!' adding that she would return and 'blow you all up'.

I think one of the most interesting of Mia Bloom's observations is that the involvement of women suicide bombers does not in any way represent an extension of gender equality in their societies. In fact, many of the women who take part in suicide bombings are among the most vulnerable members of those societies, including rape victims and widows. There are even recorded instances of women raped or sexually abused by insurgents so that they are stigmatized and become easier to exploit. Left-leaning females who sympathize with groups such as Hamas or Hezbollah should give Professor Bloom a read.

Following the lead of the LTTE, numerous other terrorist organizations have adopted suicide bombing. These include the Kurdish Workers Party, the Ba'ath Party, the Syrian Social Nationalist Party and, as has been mentioned, Chechen separatists. It is Palestinian terrorist groups, however, such as Hamas, Islamic Jihad and the al-Aqsa Martyrs Brigade, who have been most frequently associated with this tactic. The most spectacular suicide attacks came, of course, on 11 September 2001, when large passenger jets were deliberately flown into the World Trade Center in New York City and into the

Pentagon. Following the US-led invasion of Iraq in 2003, suicide bombings became a staple feature of the news from that country with both military and civilian targets being attacked, including mosques and shrines. Pakistan and Afghanistan have also seen frequent use of suicide bombing, with twenty-eight attacks, killing 471 people in the first eight months of 2008 in Pakistan alone.

In Afghanistan and more widely suicide bombing has become the archetype of Islamist violence – not only against Westerners or outsiders but against other Muslims. Perhaps the most extreme attack of this kind was when a suicide bomber in Lashkar Gar, the capital of Helmand province, killed fellow Muslims, including women, applying to go on pilgrimage to Mecca. There can be no clearer example of how religious dedication is little more than a disposable excuse for terrorism.

All the types of behaviour discussed here fit with the three motives for martyrdom set out by Karl Menninger in his book *Man Against Himself*, published a year before the outbreak of the Second World War. He described the self-punitive (suicidal), the aggressive (homicidal) and the erotic (sexual) motives. J. Reid Meloy, commenting on this typology, says that in our time martyrdom has taken on a much more directly aggressive aspect: the intentional killing of others as well as the self. Reflecting on the sexual motive, which is characterized by the attacker renouncing actual sexuality, and his moral masochism – 'the eagerness with which he would directly seek suffering and death' – Meloy comments, 'There appears to be a fourth aspect of the erotic or sexual component of martyrdom, and that is the idealisation of sexuality in fantasy . . . with the young Islamic martyr promised hope . . . of dozens of black-eyed virgins in his afterlife.' He may be disappointed.

America: the Long Road to 9/11

There are no geographical boundaries to terrorism. There never have been. Modern communications and transportation may have speeded up the tactics of global terror and provided new targets and opportunities, but it is not a difference in essence, only degree.

Just after midday on 16 September 1920 a bomb in a horse-drawn cart exploded across the street from the J.P. Morgan bank on Wall Street. Thirty-eight people were killed and over 140 injured as over forty-five kilos of dynamite blasted cast-iron weights acting as shrapnel through the air. The Bureau of Investigation, part of the Justice Department, was unable to determine who carried out the bombing or what their motives were. Its successor body, the FBI, carried out a subsequent investigation and – excluding the usual suspects such as Russian-inspired communists – concluded that the most likely explanation was that 'the explosion was the work of either Italian anarchists or Italian terrorists'. While it is certainly true that Italian anarchists had carried out a series of bombings the previous year, the Wall Street bomb was of a scale and design to cause a level of death and injury that would not be repeated in the United States until the Oklahoma bomb planted by Timothy McVeigh on 19 April 1995, which would claim 168 lives. Whoever carried it out, the Wall Street attack of 1920 had very different historical antecedents to the bombings of the early twenty-first century, coming as it did before the convulsions of the Second World War, Western decolonization, the Cold War and the collapse of communism and the eventual emergence of a multipolar world with freedom of expression supercharged by the information revolution. A number of these strands were brought together in the most appalling terrorist attack in living memory, the events of 11 September 2001 – 9/11.

Yet the story of 9/11 did not begin in Manhattan in 2001 but with earlier, preparatory attacks, a reminder of how seemingly unconnected episodes can with hindsight prove part of the same spider's web. The first of these was on 26 February 1993, when a bomb detonated below the North Tower of the World Trade Center, and the second was an intended three-pronged operation aimed at killing Pope John Paul II, blowing up eleven airliners across the globe and crashing an aircraft into the CIA headquarters in Virginia.

At 12.17 p.m. on 26 February 1993 a truck parked by the plot's mastermind Ramzi Yousef and a Jordanian accomplice exploded at the WTC, killing six people and injuring more than a thousand. The dead included a 35-year-old secretary, Monica Smith, who was seven months pregnant, and her unborn child. Also killed was a 45-year-old dental products salesman, John di Giovanni, who happened to be parking in the underground garage. Among the terrified injured were seventeen children from a kindergarten who were trapped in a lift for five hours between the thirty-fifth and thirty-sixth floors of the South Tower when power was cut off. For the terrorists, who cared nothing for their victims, the plan was at least a partial failure as they had intended to knock the North Tower into the South Tower and bring both of them down, killing thousands of people. Yousef had received funding for this particular atrocity from his uncle Khaled Sheikh Muhammad, who would go on to mastermind the 9/11 attacks in which his objective would be realized.

Yousef had arrived illegally in the United States in 1992 and tried to claim political asylum. While awaiting a hearing he made contact with Omar Abdel Rahman, a blind cleric who had been given a visa by the US embassy in Sudan and now preached controversial sermons in Brooklyn. Repeated requests by the Egyptian authorities for his extradition had been rejected and he was able to remain at liberty in the US. Hours after the bombing Yousef escaped back to

Pakistan while another conspirator, Abdul Yasin, who was taken to the FBI's Newark field office, was soon released and immediately flew back to Iraq. Yasin has never been caught. These were among the many security failures identified after the events of 9/11 and which produced much-needed changes in the American security architecture. Omar Abdel Rahman was, however, subsequently arrested and is still in a US prison.

Yousef next appears in the story in January 1995 in the Philippines, chosen as the operating base for the three-pronged Operation Bojinka, the name of which comes from a word that Khaled Sheikh Muhammad heard during a visit to Afghanistan whose meaning is obscure if it has any at all. Yousef had arrived in Manila from Singapore in the autumn of 1994, where it was suggested to him by Osama bin Laden that he might try to shoot down Air Force One with a Stinger missile during President Clinton's visit to the Philippines. In fact, he ended up taking a short break from his bomb-making activities when one of his ingredients blew up in his face, forcing him to make a short hospital stay followed by a recuperating trip to Bangkok. Instead of behaving like a regular tourist to the city, visiting palaces and temples, Yousef tried to blow up the Israeli embassy. He followed this with a more deadly attack on a Shia shrine in Iran at the height of the Ashura festival, killing twenty-six pilgrims and injuring around 200 more.

Back in Manila, when it became clear that the security arrangements around the American president would make killing him impractical, it was decided instead to assassinate Pope John Paul II on his forthcoming visit to celebrate World Youth Day. A suicide bomber dressed as a priest would get as close as possible to the Pope during his motorcade and detonate the bomb. In the apartments rented by Yousef and his accomplices the police later found street maps of Manila showing the route of the papal motorcade, Bibles, crucifixes and a rosary. The apartments themselves were 200 yards away from the embassy of the Holy See in Manila, and one of the windows directly overlooked the path that the Pope would take. The plot was financed by Osama bin Laden and Islamic extremists in the region including Wali Khan Amin Shah, who laundered money via women in Manila go-go and karaoke bars with a religious devotion reminiscent of the Taliban, who during their control of Afghanistan made an estimated US$20 million per year from opium production in Helmand province.

The second part of Bojinka was designed to murder thousands of airline passengers over the Pacific utilizing a new type of bomb that Yousef had perfected using nitroglycerine disguised as contact-lens solution and a timer made from a Casio watch which could be set up to twelve months in advance. Yousef first tested the bomb in a generator room in a mall in Cebu City, followed by an explosion under a seat in a Manila theatre. On 11 December 1994 he tested another bomb which was to have only a fraction of the power of his later efforts. He boarded Philippine Airlines Flight 434 in Manila bound for Tokyo's Narita airport but got off the plane during its stopover at Cebu. Yousef had managed to get the batteries for the bomb past security by hiding them in the hollowed-out heel of one of his shoes. Before leaving the aircraft he assembled his bomb in the lavatory and placed it inside the lifejacket under his seat. This was the blueprint for the British Muslim shoe bomber Richard Reid, who tried to bring down an airliner over Detroit on Christmas Day 2002.

At around 11.43 a.m., two hours before the plane was due to land in Tokyo, the bomb under seat 26K exploded, tearing 24-year-old businessman Haruki Ikegami in half. The lower part of his body fell through a two-foot-square hole in the cabin floor into the cargo hold. Fortunately, the fuselage remained intact, and the crew managed to land the aircraft in Okinawa, saving the lives of the other 272 passengers. It was a very lucky escape indeed.

Yousef and his co-conspirators planned to repeat this horrendous exercise on eleven US-bound airliners. Each flight had two legs, allowing the bombers to leave and plant bombs on a second batch of aircraft. It has been estimated that, had this atrocity occurred, some 4,000 people would have lost their lives over the Pacific Ocean and the South China Sea, a death toll greater than that of 9/11 itself.

The third phase of the operation would involve Yousef's co-conspirator Abdul Hakim Murad flying an aircraft into the CIA headquarters in Langley, Virginia. Murad trained as a pilot in North Carolina and was prepared to die. A plan to hijack aircraft and fly them into the World Trade Center in New York, the Pentagon, the US Capitol building, the White House, Sears Tower in Chicago and the US Bank Tower in Los Angeles was abandoned due to lack of trained personnel.

Operation Bojinka collapsed after a fire at the apartments in Manila and the discovery by police of chemicals and other suspicious materials. Cooperation between law enforcement agencies across the world eventually resulted in the arrest of Yousef in Islamabad in February 1995. He is currently serving a life sentence, without any chance of parole, in solitary confinement in a maximum security establishment in Colorado. As a consequence of the failure of Bojinka, Khalid Sheikh Muhammad decided not to use explosives smuggled aboard aircraft for his next plot. Instead, he would use aircraft as the explosives themselves and thus was the road to 9/11 truly embarked upon.

This road brought together travellers from a number of routes. During the early stages of the break-up of Yugoslavia the inactivity of the international community allowed inter-ethnic violence to flare out of control with the appalling spectacle of 'ethnic cleansing' on European soil and the massacre of some 8,000 Bosnian Muslims by Christian Orthodox Serbs at Srebrenica. This was the starting pistol that many believe prompted a stream of young Muslim men to seek to defend their 'brothers and sisters' against 'infidel oppressors'.

I asked both Sir John Major and Sir Malcolm Rifkind why the intervention in the Balkans was so delayed and whether they thought the claims of radicalization were correct. According to Malcolm Rifkind,

> We asked, is this a civil war or isn't it? If it is, does it destabilize the countries around it? There were two kinds of crisis. The first was ethnic cleansing, with people being driven out of their homes. It was horrendous but, early on, was not about the loss of life, though food and medical supplies were woefully short. The next stage was a split within NATO between the US and Europe. The US wanted a 'lift and strike' policy – lifting the arms embargo and striking the enemy forces by air. This could only work with a dual-key policy, including the agreement of the UN troops on the ground, to avoid fatalities on our side.

John Major reflected on the difficulties that faced the decision makers at the time:

> The humanitarian crisis and the threat of ethnic cleansing became intolerable. It was also developing into a full-scale war on the very edge of the European Union. The West – the United States, the EU – all of us, wanted to keep Yugoslavia together. Milosovic wanted a greater Serbia. After Slovenia and Croatia declared independence, all the ingredients were drawn into hell's kitchen. It was the most complex situation that I've seen in my entire political life. We were all focused on the collapse of the Soviet Union – the Balkans really crept in by the back door.

But had it contributed to radicalization in the way that some have suggested? 'I don't think it was a significant factor in radicalization. The UK and France had been providing significant humanitarian aid to Bosnia. Young [Muslim] men may well have said that the West took four years to act but I think the overall effect was small.'

The overall effect may well have been small, but there is no doubt that some of those who fought on the Muslim side in Bosnia took their radicalization with them to the camps in Afghanistan, where, under the tutelage of Osama bin Laden and hosted by the Taliban, they trained for jihad. Two of the 9/11 terrorists, Khalid al-Mihdar and Nawaf al-Hazmi, fell into this group, but as both failed their pilot training they were retained purely for brawn. Each had had communications picked up in 1999 by the US National Security Agency and each was on the FBI's wanted list at the time of the attack – another security failure that would subsequently bring big changes to the relationship between law enforcement and intelligence services. Both were killed when American Airlines Flight 77 smashed into the Pentagon.

Of the nineteen hijackers of 9/11, fifteen were citizens of Saudi Arabia along with one Egyptian, one Lebanese and two citizens of the UAE. Osama bin Laden provided financial support for the plot, selected some of the participants and gave ideological leadership. He was supported by his deputy Muhammad Atef, who helped organize travel for the hijackers and was involved in the target selection. Atef, religious by nature, had been radicalized during his time in Hamburg and formed a terrorist cell in Germany which tried to reach the fighting in Chechnya but ended up in al-Qaeda training camps in Afghanistan. Initially Khalid Sheikh Muhammad's idea, Osama bin Laden gave his support to the plot somewhere around the end of 1998.

What happened on that terrible day has been described in exhaustive detail and examined officially and unofficially so often that it does not require re-examination here. As Donald Rumsfeld put it, 'within the seventeen minutes between the first and second plane crashes, the world passed from one period of history into another'. As he walked away from the burning section of the Pentagon, he recalled in his book *Known and Unknown*,

> I turned back towards my office to gather what additional information I could. On my way I picked up a small, twisted piece of metal from whatever had hit the Pentagon. Minutes later, I would learn from an army officer that he had seen the unmistakable body of a silver American Airlines plane crash into the Pentagon. That piece of the aircraft has served me as a reminder of the day our building became a battleground – of the loss of life, of our country's vulnerability to terrorists, and of our duty to try to prevent more attacks of that kind.

It is, however, worth restating some of the basic, terrible and tragic statistics of that day. At 8.46 a.m. American Airlines Flight 11 slammed into the North Tower of the World Trade Center with 11 crew, 76 passengers and 5 hijackers on board. At 9.03 a.m. United Airlines Flight 175 crashed into the South Tower with a crew of 9, 51 passengers and 5 hijackers. At 9.37 a.m. American Airlines Flight 77 flew into the Pentagon with 6 crew, 53 passengers and 5 hijackers. At 10.03 a.m. the heroic efforts of passengers on board prevented United Airlines Flight 93 from reaching its desired target and it crashed into the ground in Pennsylvania with its crew of 7, 33 passengers and 4 hijackers.

I remember the events of that day, as many will, with incredible clarity and as though it was yesterday. As a regular traveller to New York and Washington, I could see in my mind's eye not only the targets themselves but could imagine the localities and the sights and sounds of normal life there. I find it difficult to describe my feelings – disbelief turned to numbed shock and eventually to anger and fury. As I watched events unfold alongside colleagues in my office at the House of Commons, however, it became clear that things were never going to be the same again.

A total of 2,996 people perished in the attacks, including the 19 murderers: 246 on board the aircraft, 2,606 in the Twin Towers of the World Trade Center or their immediate vicinity and 125 at the Pentagon. Such was the violence of the explosions, the raging fires and the collapse of the buildings that fewer than 1,700 victims have ever been identified. Over 10,000 unidentified bone tissue fragments have been identified that cannot be matched to the list of the dead. The agony for relatives was exacerbated by phone calls from the doomed planes, desperate last messages from those trapped in the towers to their families and the sight of over 200 victims leaping or falling to their deaths from the blazing buildings. The New York Fire Department lost 340 firefighters and the police departments of New York City and the port authority lost 60 officers. Over 3,000 children lost a parent in the attacks, with the pain and loss to be carried for the rest of their lives and into the next generation.

More than 90 per cent of those who died in the towers had been at or above the point of impact. Some in each building made their way towards the roof in the desperate hope that they might be rescued by helicopter. They found the doors locked, partly in response to the first World Trade Center bombing, although it is likely that the intense smoke and heat as well as obstacles on the roofs would have made rescue by this means difficult if not impossible.

From later interviews with Khalid Sheikh Muhammad it appears that the destination of United Airlines Flight 93 was the Capitol building. It is likely that the immediate aims of the bin Laden plot were to create death and destruction on United States soil to the greatest possible degree and to disrupt the American system of government. His reasons for wishing to do so have been discussed in our look at the rise of the jihadists, but his deeper objectives – to whip up support for jihad and to turn 'the clash of cultures' into a broader war between the West and the Islamic world – have echoes of earlier revolutionary and terrorist movements. In the case of 9/11, however, the impact was magnified by technology both in its scale and its message.

An initial reaction in Washington was to look for the involvement of Saddam Hussein's Iraq, but attention quickly switched to the activities of the Taliban government in Kabul.

The Taliban (Pashto for 'students') emerged from the ranks of madrasa students and the mujahideen fighting the Russian occupation of Afghanistan. Following the Soviet withdrawal in 1989, the Taliban – with help from Pakistan and Saudi Arabia – eventually gained control in 1996, imposing medieval restrictions on basic rights of speech, education and movement. Particularly harsh were the indefensible restrictions on women, which amounted to nothing less than institutionalized brutality. Sharing many of their religious and ideological roots with Saudi-born Osama bin Laden, the Taliban provided a safe haven for his training camps on Afghan soil, which were used to radicalize and indoctrinate in violence young men from across the Islamic world.

With Afghanistan identified as the source of the attackers' inspiration, training and funding, the United States government demanded that the Taliban hand over Osama bin Laden. They unsurprisingly refused to do so, and little over a month after the atrocities in Manhattan and Washington, the US began bombing Afghanistan on 7 October 2001. By December it was all over for the Taliban as the government of the country, but it was the beginning of what has come to be known as the war in Afghanistan, in which they would regroup and create a formidable insurgency. Meanwhile the

North Atlantic Council had invoked Article 5 of the NATO charter – that an attack on one member is an attack on all. This provided the military basis for joint action against the Taliban government and ultimately gave rise to ISAF, the International Security and Assistance Force, the coalition of over forty countries which has remained in Afghanistan for over a decade.

The economic costs of 9/11 highlighted the asymmetric nature of the attack and showed how a security incident in one part of the world can quickly create contagious instability in the global economy. A relatively low-cost operation for the terrorists had a significant direct impact on stock markets and New York City itself. It also had longer-term consequences for the United States and its allies, not least the costs of the war in Afghanistan. There was naturally a great deal of anxiety in global financial centres in the days after 11 September, and when the markets reopened in New York on 17 September the Dow Jones industrial average fell by 7.1 per cent. By the end of the week its losses had reached 14.3 per cent or some $1.4 trillion – a record at that time. The GDP of New York City is estimated to have fallen by $27.3 billion in the last three months of 2001 and the whole of 2002, with the federal government providing over $20 billion in aid. What the total bill will be for the war in Afghanistan is currently unknown but is likely to run into several trillion dollars, and that is before long-term support for the country is taken into account.

Politically, the most important and enduring legacies of the 9/11 attacks on American life are arguably the 2001 (USA) Patriot Act (Uniting and Strengthening America by Providing Appropriate Tools Required to Intercept and Obstruct Terrorism) and the Homeland Security Act of 2002. The latter created the Department of Homeland Security in a colossal and expensive restructuring of the US government, but it is the Patriot Act which provides the controversial centrepiece to the debate around liberty and security.

Opposition to the act has come mainly from libertarians, who have objected to the extension of FBI powers to search email, telephone and financial records without a court order and the enhanced access of law enforcement agencies to business and financial records. The indefinite detention of immigrants has also been a controversial point, and a number of the provisions of the act have been ruled unconstitutional by federal courts. However, despite the original intention to 'sunset' a number of the provisions, a reauthorization bill was signed into law by President George W. Bush on 10 March 2006 following the failure of the Senate and the House of Representatives to reach a consensual agreement, and in spite of Democratic Party opposition to elements of the act President Barack Obama signed a four-year extension of three key provisions on 26 May 2011.

Opinion on the legislation is still divided among the American public. According to polling by the Pew Research Centre, the proportion of Americans who believe that the Patriot Act is a necessary tool that helps government find terrorists has risen from 33 per cent in December 2004 to 42 per cent in February 2011, while those who believe that it goes too far and poses a threat to civil liberties has fallen from 39 to 34 per cent. Interestingly, support for the legislation has fallen among Republicans from 65 per cent in 2006 to 57 per cent in 2011. Over the same period the number of Democrats, who initially opposed many of the proposals, who believe it is a necessary tool has risen from 25 to 35 per cent.

The Department of Justice has been robust in its defence of the Patriot Act and willing to cite in support senior figures in the Obama administration. For example, it is quick to highlight the contribution of Senator, now Vice President, Joe Biden, who said during the passage of the act, 'The FBI could get a wiretap to investigate the Mafia but they could not get one to investigate terrorists. To put it bluntly, that was crazy. What's good for the mob should be good for the terrorists.'

The department has emphasized that 'the act removed the major legal barriers that prevented law enforcement, intelligence, and national defence communities from taking and coordinating the work to protect the American people and our national security'. These were major concerns highlighted in the investigations into the failure of the security apparatus of the United States to prevent the 9/11 attacks. The Department of Justice also maintains that 'the act brought us more up-to-date with current technology so we no longer have to fight a digital age battle with antique weapons – legal authorities left over from the era of rotary telephones'.

It is this test – whether those given the task of protecting our security will be as agile in using developing technology as the terrorists – which will become of increasing importance. Just as terror on underground railways moved on from the London bombs of 1893 to the horrors of the sarin attack in Tokyo in March 1995, terrorism moves with the technology of the times. It was not just the mechanics of the attacks on 9/11 that shocked, but the real-time imagery beamed around the world. A colossal and murderous attack on a city that many of us knew was beamed directly into our homes and offices. It was a lesson in the communications aspect of the propaganda war that is not lost on the contemporary terrorist.

Single White Male

Political and media attention has understandably concentrated on the threat from Islamist terrorism in recent times. From immigration to integration to passenger profiling, the assumption has been that the greatest threat to life and limb will come from Islamic fundamentalists, either imported or home-grown, yet two of the greatest atrocities in recent years have come from a completely different source – the single white male – first in Oklahoma, then in Oslo. On the surface both men were unremarkable but each harboured violent feelings of resentment and frustration. Could they have been identified in advance and stopped? The evidence suggests probably not. It may well be that 'behavioural outliers' in our society look too much like the rest of us to be spotted.

Oklahoma City, 1995

In downtown Oklahoma City on 19 April 1995 America saw its greatest terrorist attack since the 1920 bombing on Wall Street. A huge blast, with an effect equivalent to that of over 2,300 kilos of TNT, destroyed or damaged 324 buildings within a 16-block radius, killing 168 people, including 19 children under the age of six. More than 680 people were injured. The bomb was estimated to have caused damage costing at least $650 million. It was planted by Timothy McVeigh, four days short of his twenty-seventh birthday, in front of the Alfred P. Murrah Federal Building, which housed fourteen federal agencies including the Drug Enforcement Agency, the Social Security Administration and recruiting offices for the US Army and Marine Corps. The same building had been targeted in 1983 by a white supremacist group, the Covenant, the Sword and the Arm of the Lord, led among others by one Richard Snell. In a complete coincidence, Snell was executed for two unrelated murders on the same day as the bombing. The building was demolished on 23 May 1995, five weeks after the attack.

McVeigh had originally planned only to destroy a federal building but subsequently decided that his political point would be better made if many employees died. It is said that he ruled out the destruction of a forty-storey government building in Little Rock, Arkansas, because there was a florist's shop on the ground floor and, did not want its staff killed or injured. It seems highly unlikely, however, that McVeigh would not have known that the Murrah building housed the America's Kids Daycare Centre, given his detailed planning and reconnaissance. He later said, 'I didn't define the rules of engagement in this conflict. The rules, if not written down, are defined by the aggressor. It was brutal, no holds barred. Women and kids were killed at Waco and Ruby Ridge. You put back in the government's faces exactly what they're giving out.' Hardly the words of someone who had taken all possible measures to prevent 'civilian' casualties.

The bomb exploded at 9.02 a.m. local time, destroying a third of the building and creating a thirty-foot-wide crater in Northwest Fifth Street. Flying glass accounted for 5 per cent of the death toll and 69 per cent of the injuries, and around 86 cars in the vicinity were destroyed by fire or blast. Most of the deaths, however, resulted from the collapse of the building following the explosion, rather than the blast itself. The youngest victim was three months old, the oldest 73 years. The death list also included three pregnant women, and 99 of those who died worked for the federal government. A 15-year-old girl was the last survivor, dragged from underneath the collapsed building about 10 hours after the blast.

Timothy McVeigh was stopped by an Oklahoma state trooper, Charlie Hanger, less than an hour and a half after the explosion, pulled over for driving without a licence plate. He was then arrested for having a concealed weapon and incriminated by a business card that he tried to hide in the police car. On the back of the card, from a military surplus store, McVeigh had written, 'TNT at five dollars a stick. Need more.'

McVeigh and his chief accomplice, Terry Nichols, had met during basic army training at Fort Benning seven years earlier. They shared an interest in opposing any form of gun control and in the militia movement. Both had been enormously angered by FBI actions, particularly the fifty-one-day stand-off at Waco with the Branch

Dravidian cult, which culminated in a gunfight ending with the burning of David Koresh and over eighty other people. McVeigh was hugely affected by his visits to Waco during the siege and afterwards. This seems to have been the point at which he decided that bombing a federal building was a suitable way to express his hostility to the FBI and what he perceived as the oppressive nature of the US Government towards its citizens.

As McVeigh parked his truck outside the Murrah building he wore a T-shirt displaying the call shouted by John Wilkes Booth following his murder of Abraham Lincoln (also the motto of the Commonwealth of Virginia), *Sic Semper tyrannis* – 'Thus always to tyrants.' McVeigh had a history of displaying his prejudices on his back, and had been reprimanded during his military service for sporting a white power T-shirt as part of a Ku Klux Klan protest against the alleged wearing of black power T-shirts on military premises. He also carried with him to the bombing a range of anti-government slogans and materials contained in an envelope, including a Thomas Jefferson bumper sticker proclaiming, 'When the government fears the people, there is liberty. When the people fear the government, there is tyranny.' McVeigh had added his own comment to that of the great American statesman: 'Maybe now, there will be liberty!'

McVeigh did not exhibit any of the characteristics of the psychopath discussed earlier. His motivations do not appear to have concerned himself but he seems to have believed that he was acting in a political cause. He was fuelled by his ideology; he knew what he was doing and was clear about the consequences. He also showed a complete lack of empathy with the victims of the bombing. In one of his statements he said, 'Think about the people as if they were the storm troopers in *Star Wars*. They may be individually innocent, but they are guilty because they work for the Evil Empire.' American outrage at the calculated, mechanical ruthlessness of McVeigh's actions was given a clear voice in President Clinton's speech to the nation when he said, 'The bombing in Oklahoma City was an attack on innocent children and defenceless citizens. It was an act of cowardice and it was evil. The United States will not tolerate it, and I will not allow the people of this country to be intimidated by evil cowards.'

Oslo, 2011

Separated by 4,076 miles and sixteen years, another brutal and grotesque manifestation of terrorist hatred would be perpetrated by a blue-eyed, blond-haired Scandinavian – another single white male. Anyone who has visited Oslo and its surrounding area or who has travelled in Norway and understands its people will readily and painfully comprehend why 22 July 2011 will be etched on their minds for ever.

Just after 3.25 in the afternoon, outside the building which houses the office of the prime minister of Norway, a white Volkswagen van exploded. The driver had left the car some nine minutes earlier before switching to a pre-positioned getaway car. An alert receptionist who became suspicious of the van was killed while calling security guards. The driver, dressed as a police officer, was seen getting into the getaway vehicle by a member of the public, who reported its number to the police. A failure of communication meant that the licence plate was not transmitted for more than two hours over the police radio network. Six people died immediately from the blast; two others died soon afterwards from their wounds. Over 200 people received blast and debris injuries. The prime minister, who was not in his office but at his official residence, was unhurt. In typical Norwegian fashion, people remained calm, and public transportation continued to function. The police later revealed that the explosive was a mixture of fertilizer and fuel oil similar to that which had been used in the Oklahoma City bombing.

Some twenty-five miles away from Oslo at Utøykaia, and around ninety minutes later, the same man in a police uniform boarded a ferry, MS *Thørbjorn*, heading for the island of Utøya. Utøya is owned by the Workers' Youth League, the youth wing of the Norwegian Labour Party, which holds an annual summer camp there. Arriving on the island, the apparent police officer told people he was there because of the events in Oslo but then started shooting. Like so many other terrorist atrocities, this was no random act by a psychopathic killer. Motivated by a toxic political ideology, Breivik is reported to have shouted, 'You're going to die today, Marxists,' as he shot the young campers with an accuracy that he later put down to having practised at length on video games, particularly Call of Duty: Modern Warfare 2.

The death toll would have been higher but for the bravery of both the young people themselves and those who quickly answered the distress calls. When confronted with a pointed gun, the eleven-year-old son of Trond Berntsen, the security chief who had been Breivik's second victim, told the killer that he was too young to die. Remarkably, he relented and allowed the boy to live. Local residents responded to the situation with tremendous heroism, pulling cold, terrified and often bleeding teenagers who had swum away from the island from the water. Holidaymakers with boats made several trips to rescue those in the water. A German staying at a nearby camping resort on the mainland, Marcel Gleffe, is credited with saving up to thirty lives by taking his boat repeatedly into the dangerous waters around the island, throwing lifejackets to all he could find and picking up as many as he could manage.

The gunman, 32-year-old Anders Behring Breivik, laid down his weapons shortly after 6.25 p.m. by which time 69 young people had met a brutal and untimely end. Of the 517 survivors, 66 had been shot, half of them more than once. Of the 69 dead, 15 were under the age of 18, and 57 were killed by one or more shots to the head. Breivik fired at least 186 shots and was far from out of ammunition when he surrendered to the police. The sheer scale of the attack shocked the entire Norwegian nation. Those who died came from 18 of Norway's 19 counties, and it is estimated that a quarter of the population of Norway knew someone affected by the events in Oslo and on Utøya.

With a mindset that would not have been alien to Timothy McVeigh, Breivik admitted that he was responsible for both the bombing and shootings but denied culpability, saying that his actions had been 'atrocious but necessary'. Breivik's mental health was to become a major issue ahead of his trial. Initially, he was diagnosed with paranoid schizophrenia by forensic psychiatrists appointed by the court. However, following further examinations and the complex interaction of medical and political considerations, he was declared sane in April 2012. Like McVeigh, Breivik had migrated to the fringe of politics and become obsessively ideological. Around 90 minutes before the car bomb exploded in Oslo, Breivik emailed a document entitled '2083: A European Declaration of Independence' to 1,003 addresses. His Islamophobic rants quoted the Unabomber Ted Kaczynski, who planted and posted bombs in the US from 1978 to 1985, along with a number of neoconservative writers, bloggers and fringe figures as well as respected figures ranging from Thomas Jefferson and Edmund Burke to Bernard Lewis and Mahatma Gandhi. Although primarily Norwegian-xenophobic, Breivik's tract calls, among other things, for Indian Hindus to drive Muslims from their country. Breivik wanted all Muslims expelled from Europe by the year 2083 through a process of repatriation, the annihilation of what he and others have called Eurabia (a conspiracy by the European Union to Islamise Europe) and the elimination of multiculturalism in order to preserve a Christian Europe. Interestingly, Breivik never saw himself as religiously, but rather culturally, Christian. A further insight into his frame of mind can be gained from his denunciation of feminism for what he sees as the erosion of the fabric of European society.

Breivik used his trial to repeatedly set out and justify his extremist ideology, much to the outrage of the families of the victims, who regularly complained that he was insulting the memories of the children they had lost. On 24 August 2012 Breivik was sentenced to twenty-one years in prison, which can be repeatedly extended by five years as long as he is considered a threat to society – the maximum sentence allowed by Norwegian law.

Looking for Clues

So what turns young men into monsters, the boy next door into a frenzied killer seemingly stripped of empathy and guilt? Is there anything in the background of either McVeigh or Breivik that can give us pointers for the future?

McVeigh was a middle child, with an older and younger sister. His parents divorced when he was ten years old. Raised by his father in New York, he described how he had been bullied at school and how eventually he substituted the American government for the school bullies as his enemy. He appears to have had trouble, or at least little success, with the opposite sex. His biography goes as far as saying, 'his only sustaining relief from his unsatisfied sex drive was his even stronger desire to die'. McVeigh's time in the military, during which he graduated from the US Army Combat Engineer School and served as a gunner in the Gulf War of 1990–1, gave him ample scope to study his favourite subjects, which of course included explosives and firearms. He aspired to join the United States Army Special Forces but was turned down for the training programme as his psychological profile was deemed unacceptable. Disillusioned, he decided to quit the army and was discharged on New Year's Eve 1991.

McVeigh then drifted around the United States, ever more aggressively critical of the size and role of the US government. Unable to repay his gambling debts, he was infuriated when he was informed that he had been overpaid while in the army and would have to give back over $1,000. He wrote back: 'Go ahead, take everything I own; take my dignity. Feel good as you grow fat and rich at my expense; sucking my tax dollars and property.' It was another step on his journey from respectable and respected member of the armed forces to disgruntled transient to angry and violent rebel. Moving from his 'propaganda phase' to his 'action phase', McVeigh claimed he considered assassinating those he deemed responsible for the Waco deaths and the Ruby Ridge incident in Idaho in 1992. The cycle of hatred and increasingly violent reactions to what he perceived to be an authoritarian US government would end with the appalling loss of life in Oklahoma City.

What did the psychiatrists make of McVeigh? Dr John R. Smith spent more than twenty hours talking to him after his arrest. In an interview with the BBC he said McVeigh was in many ways surprisingly normal, of above-average intelligence and with good social skills. However, 'He's a young man capable of feeling great anger particularly at people or institutions that he considers to be bullies.' Dr Smith also described McVeigh's reaction to his killing of Iraqi soldiers during the Gulf War: 'They later went over and of course he saw the Iraqis he had killed and it was very moving for him . . . Other Iraqis were coming out and surrendering. He went back to his armoured vehicle, sat alone and started crying.' But McVeigh also admitted to Dr Smith that he knew there were children in the building. He viewed the dead toddlers as collateral damage.

During his trial McVeigh showed no remorse and continued, as Breivik would do in Norway, to claim that it had been his duty to do what he had done. An oppressive state in McVeigh's eyes justified and indeed demanded a violent response. This echoed Aust's analysis of the thinking behind the Baader–Meinhof outrages: 'the moment you see your country as a continuation of a fascist state, you give yourself permission to do almost anything against it'.

As he awaited execution on what was known as bombers' row at ADX Florence, a federal maximum-security facility in Colorado, McVeigh met one of our earlier protagonists, the first World Trade Center and shoe bomber, Ramzi Yousef, who had been given over two centuries in jail following his failed attempt to murder more than 4,000 airline passengers over the Pacific Ocean. Yousef made regular but unsurprisingly unsuccessful attempts to convert McVeigh to Islam. McVeigh was denied a request for a nationally televised execution, eventually dropped further appeals and was executed by lethal injection at 7.14 a.m. on 11 June 2001, the first federal prisoner to be put to death by the United States federal government since 1963.

It is hard to derive any real lesson from the life and actions of McVeigh. He was an increasingly angry, bitter and estranged young man who gradually shed those around him who might have given him support, abandoned any hope of physical or emotional partnership and ultimately lacked any sense of empathy, or at least learned to override it. Perhaps that is what some people mean by evil. Understandably, the families of those who died, including the parents of the little innocents at the kindergarten, will have their own views. I think the concept of what is evil and what is not is best left to theologians.

Anders Breivik's story has some similarities to McVeigh's, though none which show as a pattern that might have predicted his actions. Breivik was deemed 'unfit for service' by the Norwegian Defence Security Department and exempted from service in the Norwegian army. He began his own computer programming business although it was later declared bankrupt. Throughout, Breivik appears to have been bright with a strong entrepreneurial spirit and a forward-looking mentality. He claimed that as far back as 2002 he began planning a campaign to finance what would eventually become the 2011 attacks. In May 2009 he set up a farming company called Breivik Geofarm, and in June 2011 moved to a rural part of Hedmark county, the site of his farm. This allowed him to obtain large amounts of artificial fertilizer and the other chemical elements that he needed for a bomb. An indication of how methodical he was is the fact that just a month before the attacks he paid off the outstanding sums on his credit cards to ensure that he would have access to funds during his final preparations.

As a doctor as well as a politician, I find the elements around the psychiatric evaluation of Breivik fascinating, controversial and confusing. Having initially diagnosed him as suffering from paranoid schizophrenia, psychiatrists found him to be criminally insane. According to the initial report he displayed inappropriate and blunted affect and a severe lack of empathy, something almost certainly shared by McVeigh. The report claimed that he acted in a compulsive way and inhabited a universe of bizarre, grandiose and delusional thoughts, describing himself at one point as 'Europe's most perfect knight since World War II'. On hearing the diagnosis, Breivik was quoted as saying, 'I must admit this is the worst thing that could have happened to me as it is the ultimate humiliation. To send a political activist to a mental hospital is more sadistic and evil than to kill him! It is a fate worse than death.' In an echo of the German terrorist Andreas Baader, who famously complained about his prison conditions and ultimately was indulged by the German authorities to the point of having the wall to the adjacent cell demolished. Breivik has grumbled that he has to wear too many clothes to keep warm, that his cell has no view and that it is poorly decorated. He has also complained that in the morning he is too rushed to be able to shave and brush his teeth properly.

It is this complete lack of empathy in favour of their own concerns which seems to connect many of the terrorists considered in this book. Why they are driven to their extreme ideologies is difficult to grasp – the answer may lie in their personalities, their upbringing or their experiences – but those ideologies negate any appreciation of the pain caused by their actions and substitute a world of abstraction. Perhaps, as we develop a greater understanding of the workings of the human mind, we will find out why some of our fellow citizens embark on such violent paths. Maybe they are simply outliers on the fringes of human behaviour, those who have always behaved in a way that is morally reprehensible, destructive of life and hope and ultimately self-defeating, albeit exacting an enormous human price along the way. Until we do know more, we will need to learn the skills necessary to protect our societies, which are justifiably proud of the rule of law and liberty, from their horrific excesses.

Terror in the Globalized Age

In January 2013 al-Qaeda launched an attack on the Tigantourine gas plant in southern Algeria which caused the deaths of dozens of international hostages including British citizens, yet another reminder of the reach and permanent threat that transnational terrorism poses. One of the interesting elements about the crisis in southern Algeria was the inability of the international media to get real-time pictures and commentary. There was widespread criticism of both the Algerian and European governments about the 'lack of information' given to the press. While this might have been a result of the geographical isolation of the gas plant and the unwillingness, or inability, of the Algerian government to provide information, there are sound reasons why the media should not expect to have the free access to information that they might have taken for granted in the past.

In retrospect, the 2008 Mumbai attacks may prove to have been a turning point in how terrorist events are covered by the media. The attacks began on 26 November 2008 and continued until 29 November. A total of 164 people were killed and over 310 wounded. The ten terrorists, members of the militant group Lashkar-e-Taiba, came ashore at two locations in inflatable speedboats, but the suspicions of local fishermen went largely unheeded by the police. There were four main focuses of attack: the Chhatrapati Shivaji Terminus railway station, the Taj Mahal Palace and Oberoi Trident hotels, the Leopold Cafe and the Nariman House Jewish centre.

Many of those who have visited Mumbai as tourists will have had a beer at the Leopold Cafe on Colaba Causeway, a place popular with both Indians and tourists. It was here on the evening of 26 November that two of the gunmen walked in and indiscriminately opened fire on those having a casual drink or eating with friends, killing ten people and injuring many more. It was murder without pity or reason.

At the Chhatrapati Shivaji Terminus (CST), the iconic railway station which serves as the headquarters of the Central Railways in Mumbai, two men entered the passenger hall at around 9.30 p.m. Armed with AK-47 rifles they sprayed the waiting passengers with a hail of bullets, killing 58 people and injuring another 104 in an hour and fifteen minutes of sustained slaughter. Eyewitnesses described the killers as apparently amiable and smiling as they gunned down their victims. Following the arrival of security forces, the gunmen tried to flee, killing a number of police officers and civilians before eventually running into a roadblock at which one of the terrorists was killed and the other, Ajmal Kasab, was wounded and captured. Fortunately they never made it inside the Cama Hospital, their intended next target, where they planned to shoot patients in their beds.

Six explosions ripped through the Taj Mahal Palace and one was reported at the Oberoi Trident. I remember finding this particularly shocking as my wife and I spent the first night of our honeymoon at the Taj and I soon discovered that a number of members of the European Parliament were present during the attack including my friend Syed Kamall. Both hotels were surrounded by Indian commandos and on the morning of 29 November the buildings were stormed and all the attackers killed. One of the most disturbing elements of the attack on the hotels was the realization that the attackers were watching live television coverage, helping them respond to events and find potential victims. When this emerged, feeds to the hotels were blocked.

The fourth target was Nariman House, a type of Jewish centre, where two gunmen held several residents hostage. Nine were rescued from the first floor on the first day by Indian commandos and on the second day both terrorists were killed when the building was stormed – but not before Rabbi Gavriel Holtzberg, his six-month-pregnant wife Rifka and four other hostages were murdered. It is said that the Pakistani handlers of the Mumbai terrorists told them that 'the lives of Jews were worth fifty times those of non-Jews'.

The most chilling aspects of the Mumbai killings were how the terrorists used modern technology to plan, monitor and carry out their killings and how they may represent the first terrorists culturally attuned to the truly globalized environment. VoIP (voice over Internet Protocol) phones for the terrorists were acquired in Spain by a Pakistani national. Two others Pakistanis were arrested outside Milan on 21 November 2009 and accused of providing logistical support to the terrorists, transferring money to Internet accounts. The attackers' SIM cards were bought in different international locations. Blood tests later showed that these devout Muslims had taken cocaine, LSD and steroids during the attacks to increase their alertness.

The ease by which the terrorists were able to navigate the streets of Mumbai was explained by the surviving gunman, who said that they had used Google Earth to familiarize themselves with the locations of buildings used in the attacks. He described how the terrorists were armed with standard AK-47s, explosives and hand grenades, but used modern information and communications technologies, including smartphones, satellite imagery and night-vision goggles to locate additional victims and kill them. 'Moreover,' he says,

> the terrorists created their own operations centre across the border in Pakistan, where they monitored global news broadcasts, online reporting and social media in real time, leveraging the public's photos, videos and social network updates to kill more people. The terrorists in the Mumbai incident even used search engines during their attack to identify individual hostages and to determine, based upon their backgrounds, who should live and who should die. These innovations gave terrorists unprecedented situational awareness and tactical advantage over the police and the government.

The implications of the Mumbai attacks and relations between India and Pakistan are considered elsewhere, but the one surviving killer, Ajmal Kasab, who was hanged and buried at Yerwada Jail in Pune on 21 November 2012, claimed under interrogation that they were conducted with the support of Pakistan's ISI. In January 2013 a court in Chicago sentenced a fifty-two-year-old Pakistani-American, David Coleman Headley, to thirty-five years in prison for carrying out a three-day surveillance operation for the terrorists prior to the Mumbai attacks. The investigation into his involvement again raised serious questions about the role of the ISI. US prosecutors have indicted Sajid Mir, a Lashkar-e-Taiba chief and the man accused of being the lead planner of the Mumbai atrocities. Yet, despite overwhelming evidence including telephone intercepts that actually recorded Mir directing the slaughter, Pakistani authorities have not pursued him. Why not? Some believe he was, or is still, an officer of the ISI. A former French intelligence operative is reported as having claimed that Mir is 'untouchable in Pakistan'.

According to ProPublica, a New-York-based news source, in the months after Mumbai, Mir worked on further plots against India and sent Headley to carry out reconnaissance for an attack on the Danish newspaper that had published cartoons of the Prophet Muhammad. Despite his wanted status, Mir was sufficiently confident about his invulnerability in Pakistan to make a number of prison visits to other Lashkar chiefs. Investigators say Mir remains operational today and that his whereabouts are known to the Pakistani security services, yet they do nothing. This only adds to the widespread impression that while the government of Pakistan may be serious about cracking down on the many terrorist groups who operate from within its borders, the ISI all too often turns a blind eye, leaving Pakistan's international partners to wonder whether it is a real ally in the battle against transnational terrorism or whether religious, ethnic and tribal considerations will cause them always to face both ways at once.

The Dirty Bomb

When people think about the nature of the threats we face, it is not unusual to hear them remark that, with so much nuclear technology around, it's amazing we have never had any sort of nuclear terrorist attack. In this context I often ask people this question: according to our security advisers, how long is it likely to be before a major Western city experiences some sort of nuclear terrorist incident?

Will it be a year, three years or five? There is usually a sharp intake of breath with most guesses being earlier rather than later. It is of course a trick question as there have already been at least two such incidents. The first came in November 1995 in Moscow, when Chechen rebels contacted a Russian television station and boasted of their ability to build a radioactive bomb. The press were directed to a location in Ismailovsky Park, where they found a partially buried container of caesium-137. There was no actual bomb and neither the Chechens who put it there nor the original source of the caesium were ever discovered, but the message was clear – the Chechens had nuclear material and could easily have created a so-called dirty bomb. The second episode also involved Chechen terrorists. A container filled with radioactive materials and attached to an explosive mine was found in a suburb ten miles to the east of Grozny, the Chechen capital. Again there was no explosion but the implication was all too obvious.

A dirty bomb combines radioactive material with conventional explosives and aims to contaminate the area around the explosion with radioactivity. The levels of radioactivity likely to be possible with such a device are relatively low, so while a dirty bomb does not qualify as a weapon of mass destruction, it almost certainly qualifies as a weapon of mass disruption. Public fear plus the time and expense required to clean up would probably cause considerable disruption and adverse economic effects. After 9/11 there was a great anxiety that terrorists might target the United States with some kind of dirty bomb, with New York seen as particularly vulnerable. It was assessed that the economic costs of such a device might be greater than even the 9/11 attacks themselves. Even if the radiation levels were not so high as to require abandonment of a section of the city, contaminated buildings would have to be torn down and soil removed in a time-consuming and expensive operation. Economic activity would be interrupted, working time lost and there might be residual public fear about inhabiting such a place again – and not much hope for the recovery of tourism.

Nuclear material, even relatively small amounts, is hugely damaging to the human body, although this of course applies just as much to any would-be terrorist handling it. In early 1998 two Brazilians broke into an abandoned radiotherapy clinic in the hope of scavenging metal and removed a capsule containing powdered caesium-137. Within a day, having tried to take it apart and sell it as scrap, both men were showing signs of radiation sickness. The real problem began when, having punctured the capsule, they released the powder. Noticing that it glowed in the dark, they took it home to show their family and friends. After two weeks 249 people were contaminated: 151 showed both internal and external contamination, of whom 20 were seriously unwell and five died. The same sort of contamination caused the death in 2006 of the former KGB agent Alexander Litvinenko who, in some form or another, ingested polonium-120. He was almost certainly murdered in London by Russian agents in a despicable crime that continues to sour relations between London and Moscow.

Russia's Soviet-era nuclear lighthouses have been responsible for several incidents. In December 2001 three Georgian woodcutters came across a generator used for a beacon in such a lighthouse, which emits strontium-90 rays. Within a few short hours they exhibited signs of acute radiation sickness and were estimated to have been exposed to the equivalent of the radiation initially released in the Chernobyl accident. Earlier the same year, in June, two people in Kandalashka, in Russia's Murmansk region, were also hospitalized after plundering one of the 132 similar lighthouses dotted along Russia's north coast. A programme has now been put in place to replace the energy sources in all these lighthouses.

So small amounts of nuclear material are not hard to come by and in fact regularly go missing. Only around seven reactor-produced isotopes are likely to be suitable for radiological terror purposes, but the US Nuclear Regulatory Commission estimates that a quantity of one of these is lost, abandoned or stolen every day of the year. Inside the European Union around seventy go missing every year and a large number were thought to have disappeared during the break-up of the Soviet Union. In March 1998 nineteen small tubes of caesium went missing from a locked safe in Moses Cone Memorial Hospital in Greensboro, North Carolina. Despite scouring the city with highly sensitive radiation-detection equipment, the caesium was never recovered. The authorities believe that whoever took the material knew how to handle it, as unprotected contact would likely have produced serious injury or death. Its destination remains unknown.

The question that all of this begs is: if such material is so easily available and the terrorist motive is present, why have we not had more such attacks? It is clear that at least one terrorist group may have succeeded in constructing a small dirty bomb, as files, diagrams and computer documents were discovered in the Afghan city of Herat in 2003. The answer probably lies in the nature of the material itself and the problems associated with using it. Terrorists would have to get a considerable amount of nuclear material to generate sufficient radioactivity to cause widespread disruption. (Far more people are likely to be killed by the explosion of a dirty bomb than would be affected by the radioactive material itself.) Then there is the problem of handling the nuclear material, with sufficient shielding to protect the carrier but not so much that it will be too heavy to move. This is difficult but not impossible, and if terrorists are willing to kill themselves and thousands of others by flying aircraft into office buildings, why would they worry about potentially fatal doses of radiation?

Graham Allison is a nuclear terrorism expert and was assistant secretary of defense under President Clinton. Imagining a situation in which Yousef, the first World Trade Center bomber, had used a nuclear device instead of fertilizer-based explosive, he said, 'you would have seen not just the World Trade Center crumble but the whole southern tip of Manhattan disappear. You wouldn't have seen anything there; it would have vaporized. And you would have seen buildings up to Gramercy Park – that is, up to thirty streets or so in New York City – looking like the federal office building [in Oklahoma City].' The fear of an actual nuclear bomb falling into the hands of terrorists is the real nightmare for security authorities. While this would be much more difficult to obtain than radioactive material, the threat of global proliferation and the cooperation between nuclear states and terrorist groups are real dangers, as we have seen. These threats are compounded by the potential for chemical or biological attack. From the mustard gas of the First World War through Saddam Hussein's attacks on the Kurds in 1998, in which 5,000 died and around 10,000 lived with blindness, cancer and birth defects, to the sarin attacks on the Tokyo underground, such weapons have already been used.

So, what can be done to help protect us from those who, in our day, want to do us harm?

The United States Department of Defense has its own definition of terrorism: 'the calculated use of unlawful violence or threat of unlawful violence to inculcate fear: intended to coerce or to intimidate governments or societies in the pursuit of goals that are generally political, religious or ideological objectives'. I think this fuller definition is a sound place to start when looking for constructive ways forward in our ability to deal with terrorism. The duty to defend our peoples and territories requires us to do four things. The first is to *know* – to have adequate intelligence about the specific threats that we face. The second is to *understand* – to see threats in their appropriate political, historical and cultural context. The third is to *prepare* so that if required we have the ability to deter or deal with terrorism. The fourth is to *act* – to have the means and will required to pursue to the end the action required to deal with the threat.

Know, Understand, Prepare and Act

It is essential to know what we are up against – its nature, scale and capabilities. Effective intelligence gathering and, equally importantly, effective intelligence sharing, are required to exploit fully both national and international capabilities that allow us to detect, deter or deal with terrorist threats. Stephen Sloan of the Strategic Studies Institute of the US Army War College believes that

> intelligence can be viewed as being on the forefront of counterterrorism warfare. For, once the terrorists go tactical (i.e. initiate operations and move to the target), the authorities are essentially forced into a reactive crisis – emergency management mode with its emphasis on rescue, recovery, damage control, and reconstitution. Therefore intelligence is central in preventing, deterring, and when feasible pre-empting acts of terrorism.

I fully agree with him.

There are a number of ways in which intelligence is gathered. The most widely recognized by the public is probably Humint – human intelligence gathered from a person on the ground – which might be through benign data gathering or espionage or even interrogation. Sigint – signals intelligence – is derived from the interception of communications such as telephone tapping. Geoint – geospatial intelligence – is gained from mapping data, aerial photography or satellites. Masint – measurement and signature intelligence – involves everything from the optical measurement of nuclear explosions to weather and sea data. Osint – open source intelligence; Techint – gathered from the analysis of weapons and equipment used by foreign nations; and Finint – financial intelligence gathered from analysis of monetary transactions – make up the full set.

Back in 1996–7, as a junior minister at the British Foreign and Commonwealth Office, I remember writing a memo to Foreign Secretary Malcolm Rifkind worrying that, if reports were to be believed, then the diminution of our Humint capabilities would mean that we would have a greatly reduced ability over time to interpret international events in their proper cultural and historical context. It was a point that has been echoed on the other side of the Atlantic. In spring 2005 US Senator Saxby Chambliss, in a paper entitled 'We have not correctly framed the debate on intelligence reform', said,

> Americans like technology and we are good at it. Our ability to monitor certain activities via satellites, signals intelligence, or other technical means, while not perfect, is pretty good. Our weak point is Humint, which has atrophied to the point that it must be rebuilt. Human intelligence, relative to the other intelligence disciplines, can tell us what the enemy is thinking. The strength of good Humint is that it can enter this key question: what are the enemy's intentions about when, where, and how to strike?

Despite this warning, we now find ourselves able to read all the car number plates in Iran by Sigint but are often unsure about internal political dynamics or whom exactly we should be talking to. This may represent technological advances but can it really be called progress?

Senator Chambliss was particularly scathing about the American intelligence community's failures in the run-up to the 9/11 attacks. He pointed out that they were the first significant foreign attacks on the US mainland since the War of 1812, yet in the weeks and months leading up to 11 September 2001 the US collectively failed to interpret, analyse and share information gathered. He believes the situation was complicated when

> Subsequently the intelligence community failed the President by presenting an inaccurate analysis of the quantities and capabilities of Saddam Hussein's weapons of mass destruction. While there is no doubt whatsoever that Saddam's intentions were to reconstitute his WMD programs and become a supplier of these weapons to the radical Islamist terrorists who are bent on the destruction of democratic and secular Western societies, the fact remains that the CIA did not have a single agent inside Iraq to verify the true state of these programs before coalition forces, led by the United States, attacked Iraq in 2003.

Understanding comes in a number of forms. We need to understand the context of the threat, its cultural and historical background, where and to whom it is attractive and why. We need to win the war of ideas. We need to comprehend what changes in technology might bring, the asymmetric advantages such changes may confer on the terrorist and how we can respond to restore our advantage. We also need to understand the implications for our own society of the options we choose to pursue in response to these challenges. As George Kennan put it, 'The greatest danger that can befall us . . . is that we shall allow ourselves to become like those with whom we are coping.'

In *Winning the Long War*, which I have already extensively cited, Carafano and Rosenzweig set out to learn how the highly influential so-called Long Telegram sent from Moscow by diplomat George Kennan at the outset of the Cold War could be interpreted in the current security climate. They state,

Winning the long war is all about winning the struggle of ideas, destroying the legitimacy of a competing ideology, and robbing the enemy of the support of the people. Such an effort implies some essential tasks: 1) understanding the enemy; 2) delegitimising its view of the world; 3) offering a credible alternative and 4) demonstrating the will to prevail in the long conflict.

They are clear about the root of the current terrorist threat:

It is a blasphemous interpretation of religion, which sanctions the killings of Americans – and citizens of all nations and religions, even moderate and Orthodox Muslims who do not agree with the radicalisation of their religion. Religious extremists (and the allies they have found among the secular, radical Arab nationalist movements) not only justify the murder and maiming of civilians, they glorify suicide bombings and other terror tactics.

Carafano and Rosenzweig point out that there appears to be no limit to the appetite for violence and the murder of innocents by the extremists, who have tried to obtain and use weapons of mass destruction and will likely continue to do so until they succeed or are neutralized.

Dealing with this threat will require a multi-pronged approach involving unified international condemnation of terrorist acts; support for moderate governments in the Muslim world so that terrorists are deprived of recruiting grounds; refocusing the international community's efforts and resources on the areas most at risk of terrorism; and using modern information and communication technologies to kindle aspirations for freedom in those societies ruled by the sponsors of terror.

The willingness to use new technologies is also essential in dealing with the problems of asymmetry discussed earlier. Asymmetrical warfare aims to exploit vulnerabilities and negate advantages rather than engage in traditional force-on-force engagements. The incentive to use this strategy is usually greater for the weaker party, whose aim is to use the physical environment and military capabilities in a way that is unusual and unanticipated by the conventionally stronger side, thus catching them off balance and unprepared.

As we have repeatedly seen, events often usher in unintended consequences. With the restraints of the Cold War removed, new and significant players entered the international arena, including newly formed countries, rogue states no longer constrained by an artificially chosen side and non-state actors such as terrorist groups. The events of 9/11 showed how a relatively small but well-resourced and careful group could cause immense damage at the heart of the global superpower. The experience of the sarin gas attack in Tokyo and the potential for nuclear terrorism make it very clear how asymmetry can be the terrorist's friend.

Stephen Sloan in a US Army War College publication has two pieces of advice for those facing this problem. The first is that because simplicity is a necessity for the adversary (the terrorist) but much more difficult as a goal for the superior power (the state) then the bureaucratic bloat which so often affects developed governments and prevents both information sharing and response must be dealt with. Second, there needs to be agreement about the essential nature of terrorism itself. In particular, we have to take a clear and consistent view as to whether terrorism is primarily a criminal act, a form of political violence or, ultimately, a form of warfare. The fact that terrorism spans the spectrum of conflict, violence and warfare makes it more difficult to evolve a single doctrine with which to deal with it. He says,

If terrorism is viewed to be primarily a criminal act, it falls under the purview of law enforcement. When the responsibility is placed in the context of democratic law enforcement, counterterrorism measures would focus on prevention and response and only when necessary the utilization of force. In contrast, if terrorism is primarily perceived to be an aspect of warfare, the application of offensive measures combined with the use of maximum force may be viewed as appropriate. Finally, between both polls is the view that terrorism is essentially a form of political violence regarding which a mixture of both diplomacy and force may be employed to achieve strategic objectives.

Whichever definition, or combination of definitions, is chosen, the state has a duty to conduct a properly integrated effort involving police, military and political forces to prevent, detect and respond to the forces of terror. How well have we achieved this in recent years? The answer is probably quite well, but if we are to continue to do so, we need to be willing to invest in the appropriate technologies for emerging risks and not simply for those that provide an immediate threat. We also need to challenge the mindsets of both the military and the public by scrapping some highly visible, even totemic, land, sea or air weapons in order to invest in apparently invisible capabilities in space or cyberspace.

During the Strategic Defence and Security Review carried out in the United Kingdom in 2010 we were confronted with both diminishing financial resources as a result of the general economic situation and the fact that no review had been carried out for more than a decade. It was clear that a number of older and more traditional platforms (ships, tanks and planes) would have to disappear in order to finance investment in the next generation of weapons, and also that we would have to invest more in areas such as cyber defence, where the benefits are not visible on a military parade. One senior participant laughed as he wished me good luck, saying, 'There is only one thing more difficult than getting a new idea into the head of the military – and that is getting an old one out.' Nonetheless, the frequency and seriousness of attacks in the cyber domain are causing those right at the top of military structures to consider seriously whether our balance of forces is correct.

We also need to prepare public opinion for the types of threats that they may face, so that, if the worst happens, their response is appropriate, thus lessening the effectiveness of the terrorists' primary weapon, fear. The public's likely response to a dirty bomb is a case in point. Proper education, in good time, seems to me to be a good investment. There is, however, a constant debate within democratic governments about how much information to give the public and how much to withhold. It boils down to the balance between telling people enough to ensure they are vigilant against threats and well informed in the event of a crisis, and on the other hand frightening them with too much information and doing the terrorists' work for them.

Finally, when confronted with either the threat of terrorism or a terrorist act itself, we must be willing to act in an appropriate manner not simply a politically expedient one. We must act to diminish the source of the threat, at home or abroad, in the physical world and in the mind; we must act to weaken the forces, political or financial, that sustain the threat and we must ultimately act to remove the threat itself.

Much has been written in recent times about the impact of the wars in Iraq and Afghanistan on the willingness of the international community to involve itself in areas of rising tension and imminent risk. With fears in the Gulf region and beyond (not least in Israel) growing about Iran's nuclear programme, this could rapidly become more than an academic discussion. Yet one of the most important factors may not be the military capability of the international community to stop Iran's leaders from developing a nuclear weapon but the willingness of democratic governments, particularly that of the United States, to continue to bear the enormous economic cost of the conflicts in Iraq and Afghanistan. The lack of an appetite among both politicians and voters to do so might easily be seen in Tehran as weakness in the West. If the same view is reached about willingness to tackle global terrorism by non-state actors involved in terrorist planning, then the consequences do not need to be spelled out.

If I have one worry about all of this, it relates not to our capabilities, but to our political will. I vividly remember a conversation I had in the Elysée Palace with a senior member of President Sarkozy's government. I was talking about how we had won the Cold War not just because of our military and economic superiority but because we also had a moral superiority and belief in our own values. I asked why it was that we had been so willing to use the word 'better' then (democracy was better than dictatorship; freedom was better than oppression; capitalism was better than communism) but seemed so afraid to use it now. Surely in relation to fundamentalist Islamist views our ways *are* better – better to have religious tolerance than violently imposed orthodoxy, better to have a concept of universal human rights than not, better to have societies in which women play a full and equal role with men? The answer was depressing: 'I don't think we can really say "better" nowadays, only "different".' If this is what we really believe, we are in deep trouble. Has the concept of moral equivalence become so prevalent that it has diminished our belief in what has made us who we are? If we do not believe that our values are better than the alternatives, and worth defending, then why should anyone else listen to us. Liberty, equality and the rule of law are better than the alternatives. We need more 'better' and less 'different' or we risk losing the battle of ideas and ideals for the future. That would be an unforgivable betrayal of those who sacrificed so much for what we too often seem to take for granted.

Chapter Five

GLOBAL MONEY: TRADE, AID, TAX AND DEBT

Talk to most people about the financial aspects of globalization – the interconnection of capital and currency markets, current account surpluses and deficits, trade balances or financial flows or the origins of the banking or Asian currency crises – and their eyes glaze over. They may think the subject dull and find some concepts difficult to understand. Yet the issues involved – earning, borrowing, spending, taxation and debt – are encountered daily by the vast majority of adults in Western societies. So I will not attempt here to deal with the complexities of the financial world but to set out some of the arguments relating to major global financial issues in a way that is hopefully a little more comprehensible.

Global Imbalances

One of today's most widely discussed financial topics is that of imbalances, seen as one of the major causes of potential instability in the global economy. Put simply, global imbalances occur when some countries have more assets than others. When a state's current account is in balance the inflows and outflows of capital are cancelled by each other and the account has a zero value – not dramatically different from balancing the family budget each month. Countries with a current account surplus are increasing their net foreign assets – their overseas investments. A country with a current account deficit is increasing the assets that foreign investors hold there. Put another way, if a state has a current account deficit it is absorbing more than it is producing. This can only be done if other economies are willing to lend their savings in the form of debt or investment, or if the economy is running down its own foreign assets such as its official foreign currency reserves. Countries with a current account surplus are producing more than they absorb and so are saving and able to invest abroad, creating foreign assets. Since, by definition, all current accounts and the net foreign assets of the states of the world must be zero, then some countries must be indebted to others. Easy!

In recent years the scale of global imbalances has become a significant concern. The US and other developed countries such as the United Kingdom have run long-term deficits (absorbing more than they produce), while in other countries, especially in east Asia and oil-exporting states such as Norway and Saudi Arabia, the opposite has occurred. Although the current period of global imbalances is much longer than has ever occurred before, due to the size of the global economy and its unprecedented openness, periods of imbalance are not unusual. Between the 1870s and the outbreak of the First World War in 1914, for example, another period of financial globalization, countries such as Britain, Germany and France experienced large current account surpluses as massive amounts of capital flowed to countries of recent European settlement, especially the Americas and Australasia. Consequently countries such as Canada, Australia and Argentina ran up current account deficits often exceeding 5 per cent of their GDP. What makes the current period of global imbalances unprecedented is that this time capital is flowing in the opposite direction, from the emerging market economies to the advanced economies. Along with this, foreign asset holdings have become much larger, the degree of capital mobility is the highest for many decades, and financial linkage between economies has increased. The opening-up of financial markets over the last two decades – what might be termed monetary globalization – has been central to the creation of greater international capital flows but has also been a prerequisite of large global imbalances.

The Savings Glut

One of the driving factors of global imbalances in recent years has been a phenomenon known as the savings glut, the enormous amounts of money accumulated in countries with current account surpluses (those creating more wealth than they are absorbing). This is a result of the improved export performance of many of these countries as well as increases in government revenues generated by rises in commodity prices, especially oil.

In the early years of the new millennium a rapid acceleration in global growth was accompanied by sluggish increases in commodity supplies, which inevitably led to a marked rise in the prices of those commodities, which in turn boosted the incomes of commodity exporting countries. And, as was the case with the 1970s and 1980s oil price rises, expenditure inside the commodity exporting countries lagged behind, so they were earning much faster than they were spending, leading to increased saving. This has also happened in some advanced countries such as Germany, Japan and New Zealand, although the rise in saving has tended to be more related to ageing within the population – putting something extra aside for retirement.

For a number of reasons, much of the savings glut, particularly that of east Asian nations and the oil exporters, has been held abroad, particularly in the United States and the United Kingdom, enabling the latter to fund spending which is much higher than their earnings. Poor social security provision is an important factor contributing to high savings in east Asia in particular. In China, for example, private education and health expenditures have increased significantly in recent years, in part because the government has scaled back public sector support in these areas, something that is often seen as counter-intuitive in the high-spending Western nations with their ever hungrier public programmes. Whether this pattern can be sustained as a more vocal and powerful middle class emerges, or whether these countries will be forced to spend more of their money at home, is a key question in determining whether the current imbalances can be sustained.

Another factor may be the slow pace of financial development in many of the east Asian economies, which has led to a short-term dearth of domestic investment opportunities, something unlikely to persist for long given the creativity and entrepreneurship of the region. For the moment investors have sought more advanced markets and financial instruments in places such as London and New York, with money finding its way into sovereign wealth funds, portfolio investments and foreign reserves.

One further factor is the precautionary increases in foreign reserves undertaken as a hedge against a repeat of the Asian currency crisis of the late 1990s. The crisis began on 2 July 1997 when Thailand's central bank floated the national currency, the baht, after failing to protect it from aggressive attacks from speculators, which had become too costly to fend off. The financial and economic collapse that quickly followed spread to neighbouring countries in the region, in turn causing stock market declines, reduced import revenues and even changes in government. As GDP growth rates contracted sharply, companies that had allowed themselves to become overexposed to foreign currency risks were bankrupted.

The Asian crisis ultimately produced essential financial and government reforms in countries like Indonesia, South Korea and Thailand, but left a legacy of caution, even fear, among regional policymakers, which continues to affect their behaviour today. It was a warning of the hazards created by the interwoven nature of markets, particularly in relation to currency trading and national account management, but it was a warning that was not heeded, or not understood, where it mattered.

'Four Generations of Global Imbalances'

The 'four generations' view, first put forward by Ansgar Belke and Gunther Schnable, holds that when Japan liberalized international capital flows in the early 1980s and America pursued monetary tightening, the financial flows which resulted pushed Japan's current account into surplus (increased the country's net overseas assets) and the United States went into a deep deficit. When attempts to deal with this by manipulating currency values failed, the next response set the stage for the Japanese bubble economy. When it burst, as bubble economies always do, it left behind a legacy of over twenty years of economic stagnation and the persistent Japanese current account surplus that we see today. Japan was soon joined by China, Indonesia, Malaysia, Singapore, South Korea, Taiwan, Hong Kong and Thailand, which continue to finance the American current account deficit, creating the second generation of imbalances. Unlike Japan, however, when their turn came, the Chinese allowed a controlled nominal appreciation of their currency, the yuan, a cause of considerable friction with the United States to this day. Since markets saw this as a one-way bet on the future upward movement of the Chinese currency, there was an unprecedented accumulation of foreign reserves by the People's Bank of China as speculators rushed to buy the yuan.

Rapidly rising oil and raw material prices after 2003, as previously mentioned, created the third generation of global imbalances. Increasing net exports and government budgets in the surplus countries were matched by current account deficits rising even further in the United States and a number of south European countries. For other countries, notably in northern Europe and east Asia, the economic impact of rising commodity prices tended to be offset by buoyant exports to many of the oil producing states. With the oil currencies closely tied to the value of the dollar, this time there was no distortion in currency rates or foreign currency reserves accumulated. Rather, the excess money was stored in sovereign wealth funds with differing results. In Norway it has financed stable external investment, while in Russia and Dubai using the funds to finance capital spending or industrial policy has produced its own internal distortions sometimes with direct political consequences.

Europe produced the fourth generation of global imbalances. In the early 2000s countries on the periphery of the continent, notably Spain, Portugal, Greece and Ireland, ran up large current account deficits. At the same time, Germany and a number of the smaller northern European nations (who might at one time have considered themselves candidates for a Deutschmark zone) achieved current account surpluses as a result of both private and public austerity. Inevitably and predictably, diverging labour costs and current account positions plus net international debt led to the repeated crises in the Eurozone, which still continue. The euro was always a flawed project. Intellectually, it was never clear whether it was a political or economic entity, while since its inception rules have been regularly ignored, creating new cracks in its already inherently flawed architecture. Such was the rush to join that no exit mechanism was devised, with the consequence that no one has any idea how to get out in a crisis.

There were two intellectually defensible models for the euro. The first was to say that it was such an important element of the European project that everything possible had to be done to make it succeed. Some saw this as analogous to the American experience after the civil war. With the abolition of the Confederate currency, a hugely difficult operation, the states' debts were consolidated into the federal debt for the first time and free fiscal transfers were enabled between the federal and state governments if required. This process proved impossible in Europe because of the huge disparity between countries' debt levels and the unwillingness of sovereign states to bail out other sovereign states. The second model was a purely economic one. Currency union was to be available to those economically similar nations which could meet strict criteria for entry and maintain sufficient fiscal discipline to be allowed a say in the central bank.

In the end neither model was followed; instead an unstable and unworkable hybrid emerged. Not only were countries who failed to meet the convergence criteria allowed to join anyway, but a lack of fiscal discipline subsequently meant that many countries, including at times France and Germany, broke through the barriers that were supposed to keep the currency on the rails. Little wonder that some states operated in the apparent belief that whatever they did a financial solution would be found for them from outside. Germany more than any other country will probably decide whether this hybrid will be allowed to survive. The German position seems to be, yes, the euro is an indispensable landmark on the road to ever closer European union but, no, Germany will not make the fiscal transfers necessary to make it happen. Worse still, Berlin's stance has been interpreted as, Germany is willing to tolerate any level of austerity in any other country apart from Germany in order to make the project succeed. This is a recipe for instability and the revival of nationalism in Europe. It makes the stability pact potentially a suicide pact. The idea of austerity being forced upon smaller nations by Berlin has too much historical resonance to succeed without fostering potentially dangerous political backlashes on both left and right.

Here I feel some sympathy for the position of Chancellor Merkel. She is undoubtedly right that austerity measures and living within your means are absolute requirements for long-term stable recovery, but the message was delivered too late and will have a financial cost. And that cost will largely have to be carried by Germany, whose own strong economic performance, especially in exports, has been helped by the weakness of the euro. Like it or not, it is in Berlin that the future of the entire single currency project will primarily be decided. If funds are not made available by the richer economies to stabilize the poorer ones, then default in the face of politically undeliverable austerity could result in debts being transferred via banking failures to the latter's sovereign governments.

How will the Eurocrats in Brussels react to events? History suggests that they will first try to do nothing and stick to their path towards ever closer union encompassing as many countries as possible. They will throw European taxpayers' money – current or borrowed – at the problem for as long as they can; after all they are not accountable to those who pay the taxes. When that ceases to be an option they will probably try to do the minimum damage to their political ambitions by pushing for a single – most likely Greek – exit from the euro. This could be the worst option. Once the markets recognize that the principle of membership can be breached, one country after another will be forced to leave under constant bombardment. It will be the ERM writ large. There is a strong body of opinion, which I share, that believes if a number of countries leave simultaneously it will at least send a signal to the markets that the rump currency has a real prospect of maintaining its value.

Throughout this tragic pantomime Britain and the rest of the global financial community will largely only be able to look on, waiting to see how much damage is done to our collective economic prospects before the inevitable reality sets in. It is like an EU horror economic version of the 'Emperor's New Clothes' children's story, in which sooner or later the voice of sanity will be heard but after who knows how much damage has occurred.

The euro crisis continues to be the dominant issue in European politics, and this is unlikely to change any time soon. Despite all evidence to the contrary, European leaders continue to treat the problem as a fiscal issue when in reality it is the fiscal symptom of economic and cultural differences. The underlying truth is that the economies inside the Eurozone are no closer to convergence today than when the currency was created. There is as much chance of realizing the alchemist's dream of turning base metals into gold as there is of turning an economy like that of Greece into one that resembles Germany's.

Of course it is true that the euro did not create the deficits and debt that so bedevil the economies of Europe – we can see how many countries outside the system have the same difficulties – but the fact remains that certain fiscal and economic policies were permitted which widened rather than narrowed the gaps between the member states, ensuring that an unstable structure became even more unsafe. In the end rationality will have to prevail. With unemployment among young people soaring – in Spain it is 52 per cent – it must be hoped that this will be sooner rather than later, if the hopes and dreams of a generation of young Europeans are not to be sacrificed on the altar of the single currency.

The 2007 Crisis – the Alarm Bell Sounds

The 2007 banking crisis has been the most sobering recent event in the increasingly interdependent global economy, and its effects have been profound and long-lasting, both economically and politically.

The Bank of England's third Quarterly Bulletin of 2009, authored by Mark Astley, Julia Giese, Michael Hume and Chris Kubelec, entitled 'Global Imbalances and the Financial Crisis' analyses the causes of the crisis in the second half of 2007. It is an excellent exposition which anyone with an interest in the subject is well advised to read. It suggests that although it was primarily a financial market crisis, global imbalances contributed to the problem.

At the same time as the savings glut was being exported as international capital flows, there was a rapid growth of credit in deficit countries, contributing to the global credit boom. Savings rates were reduced and this was accompanied by strong domestic demand. For example, in the late 1990s in the United States and the United Kingdom domestic demand grew more rapidly than GDP and the entry of low-cost producers such as China into the world trading system resulted in wider current account deficits. Some of the inflowing capital was used to provide loans to businesses and households, but much more flooded into traditionally safe assets such as government bonds, with the result that long-term interest rates were pushed down. In this low interest-rate environment there was strong pressure on asset managers and banks to maintain returns, and this in turn led to an appetite for buying riskier assets. There was thus both less discrimination between assets of differing credit quality but at the same time the creation of increasingly complex financial instruments which employed leverage to produce higher returns. (Leverage is defined as the use of financial instruments or borrowed capital to increase the potential return of an investment. In the personal sector this is usually a mortgage taken out on a home with the expectation of a much higher return later on. The term is also used to describe the amount of debt that is used to finance a company's assets; so a firm with more debt than equity is said to be highly leveraged).

All of this occurred at a time when investors believed that risks in the financial markets had declined. This was in part due to the psychological effect of what has become known as the great moderation – a prolonged period of stability in both macroeconomic and financial variables. The low-inflation environment associated with this period of stability also saw a loosening in global monetary policy following the stock market crash of 2000–1. The net result of all of this was lower credit risk premiums, with the price of risk being set too low by markets which had been lulled into a false sense of security and which therefore tended to take for granted the abundant liquidity in the financial markets that had typified the years preceding the crisis. With hindsight it can be seen that the pre-crisis period was characterized by the serious vulnerability of high leverage in the financial system and the underpricing of both credit and liquidity risk.

Since a great deal of the debt involved in the American and British economies was secured against housing assets there was an inbuilt vulnerability to house price falls. The credit risk associated with securitized assets, including those backed by mortgages, was particularly underpriced. This was especially true for mortgages given to sub-prime borrowers, who did not meet traditional credit standards and whom had always been riskier to lend to. Despite the inherent risk, many mortgage lenders had provided deals with short-term low interest rates, and as these expired many homeowners found it impossible to re-finance at similar rates, and so began a spiral of rising default and falling house prices.

As US mortgages, including sub-prime deals, were the underlying asset in a large proportion of securitized assets, confidence in the markets for securitized assets more generally was undermined when it became increasingly clear that the assumption (either genuine or a convenient self-delusion) that the risk associated with these assets was much higher than that associated with the traditional vehicles of government and corporate bonds. When the extent of credit risk mispricing fully dawned on the financial world, the markets for securitized assets collapsed amid the rush to reprice risk. To make matters worse, the complexity of securitized asset packages meant that investors were in the dark as to which financial institutions were potentially most at risk from falls in their value. This frightening new environment with heightened fears of risk in inter-bank credit markets led to a substantial increase in the cost of inter-bank lending and low transaction volumes – the triggers for the crash.

An article in *The Economist* magazine in 2009 characterized the period with great lucidity.

After the dot-com bust, American firms turned cautious and investment spending was weak. That ruled out a natural home for foreign capital. Faced with strong external demand for Triple-A rated assets, the financial system got creative. Marginal home loans were packaged into supposedly safe securities. That supply of credit lifted house prices and sparked a boom in residential construction which filled the gap in demand left by sluggish business investment. As these loans turned bad and losses mounted, it became clear that banks had set aside too little capital to protect themselves against unexpected losses. That left the banks crippled and the economy on its knees. The villains in the story are the banks for making silly loans and regulators for not insisting on more precautions.

Complex linkages in the international financial system meant that what began as a crisis in the US housing market soon affected financial institutions in a large number of countries – and quickly, just as the Asian currency crisis had spread ten years previously. As the forces of leveraging, the impact on the real international economy and pressures on inter-bank funding markets escalated, the crisis claimed its most high-profile victim in September 2008 with the collapse of Lehman Brothers.

So, how were the previous global imbalances affected by the crisis? To begin with, many financial institutions around the globe started to liquidate assets in order to rebuild their capital positions. In particular, bank lending overseas fell more sharply than domestic lending. In the UK there was a sharp reduction in the amount of credit made available to UK residents by foreign banks – the same banks who had played such a major role in the expansion of lending to British residents in the period leading up to the crisis. With sharp rises in inter-bank interest rates, UK banks' increasing difficulties accessing funds in wholesale markets, and the need for UK banks to rebuild their capital positions, the net result was a reduction in the supply of credit to UK households and businesses; the credit crunch had arrived.

In the short term there were some corrections which reduced the scale of the global imbalances. Demand in deficit countries fell sharply; exchange rates adjusted (there was a 20 per cent depreciation in the effective exchange rate of sterling between August 2007 and June 2009); and commodity prices fell steeply as demand dropped, but these were reactive changes and did not deal with the structural problems present in the economies of the deficit countries. As the Bank of England noted at the time, one lesson from the crisis was that the persistence of global imbalances depended on the ability of deficit countries to supply enough high-quality assets to meet the demands of those investors overseas who were effectively lending their savings.

Expansionary fiscal policies pursued in the deficit countries, including increased supplies of government bonds, have been able to meet the investment demands of surplus countries. However, without the sort of structural reforms that deal with long-term deficit problems it is difficult to see how these investors will be willing to park their money in economies such as the US or UK without tending to raise the cost of borrowing.

In a paper entitled 'Stable Disequilibrium' the CEO of global investment adviser PIMCO, Muhammad A. el-Erian, wrote that while global imbalances may have shrunk somewhat in recent years, this has been the result of a downturn in global activity rather than a change in economic behaviour. There is therefore a risk that politicians from around the world will be lulled into a false sense of security and consequent inaction. While deficit nations will, for a range of reasons, find it difficult to continue to spend vastly greater amounts than they take in, countries with very large surpluses will find that this may undermine their future growth and that as a consequence global financial imbalances will become unsustainable. He points out that geopolitical risks, including those which have pushed oil prices – along with a range of other commodity prices – higher, have increased, and that many US and European politicians are preoccupied with political bickering and point-scoring rather than devising concrete solutions to the structural faults in their economies.

The United States still accounts for a significant chunk of the underlying deficits – one third today compared with one half before the crisis. On the other side, just five countries account for half of the global surplus, similar to the pre-crisis situation. The China–US trade balance deterioration has continued, with the imbalance now greater than it was on average during 2006 to 2008. Meanwhile, the major imbalance between Germany and countries on the periphery of Europe continues to serve as a complicating factor in an already complex and perplexing regional debt crisis.

As many commentators have pointed out, one of the difficulties in reducing or eliminating the imbalances is that everyone has had something to gain from sticking to the status quo. The Chinese might complain about the US deficit and that Americans have insufficient savings, but they would not want Americans to save more and buy less of their exports. Likewise, the Americans might complain about China's failure to revalue its currency and boost domestic demand, but not if that means China is less willing to buy American public debt. I will leave the last warning to *The Economist*, which has commented on the continuing tendency of Britain, the US and other deficit countries to gorge themselves on cheap credit from abroad rather than trying to diminish their own need for that credit: 'Because the structural forces behind the global saving glut are unlikely to abate quickly, there is a real risk that the dangerous imbalance will persist – with America's public sector as the new consumer of last resort. It would be foolish to focus on fixing the financial industry only to find that the public finances are left in ruins.'

The problem has not gone away, and massive credit easing is unlikely to be without serious consequences, as will be discussed later.

The Global People Problem

It is not just money that suffers from a global imbalance; increasingly, this is a human problem too. There is an ageing population in the deficit countries, which needs to produce more wealth (or consume less or both), and a disproportionately large number of young people in the surplus countries, who need to find employment. In a real global market with free movement of labour, population flows would deal with this problem. However, in many of the world's most powerful countries political issues relating to immigration make any solution extremely difficult.

In the United Kingdom immigration is a potentially explosive political issue. The demands of business for new skilled labour clash with issues of racial and cultural balance, and one of the consequences of membership of the European Union – the free movement of EU citizens – adds another complication. Even within the UK attitudes vary enormously. While multicultural cities such as London see the debate from one angle, the issues appear very different in other parts of the south-east of England, the most accessible region for those seeking work from eastern Europe. In the rural shires the perspective is different again.

Immigration is never a simple issue. On the political left the temptation to characterize any meaningful debate about immigration as racist makes any mature debate very difficult and risks fanning the flames of perceived discrimination among racial minorities. On the other hand, elements on the right tend to focus solely on cultural issues, ignoring our deteriorating demographics and the need for a continued supply of appropriate skills if we are to successfully compete in a cut-throat global economy. So, before we deal with the economic arguments relating to immigration, let me put my own cards clearly on the table. I believe that for immigration to be successful, there are two human prerequisites. The first is that there is a willingness among the host population to integrate those coming into the country. The second is that the immigrant population has to be willing to integrate into the legal and cultural systems of the host population. Unwillingness on the part of either group is likely to result in hostility to immigrant groups with an increased likelihood of consequent ghettoization. Ideas of commonality need to be fostered. There has been a tendency – rightly and understandably – to celebrate the cultural diversity of the UK, but if we only cheer diversity and ignore commonality, then we are likely to achieve little more than fragmentation. The United Kingdom has had a history of successfully integrating many different groups over many years, but the rapid increase in immigrant numbers over the past decade or so has made the process more difficult as resistance among the host population has increased and immigrants have increasingly settled in large communities, often remaining separate rather than simply retaining their cultural identity. Sadly, the debate has largely revolved around numbers of immigrants rather than who they are, where they come from and what their relationship with their new home will be – whether they will be contributing to our economic well-being or becoming passengers on the welfare train.

However, if we are to understand fully the political context within which any economically based argument about migration takes place we need to look at the basic statistics. Under the last government Britain's immigration ramped up to previously unknown highs. Moving from a steady average of around 300,000 per year, it quickly escalated to almost double that figure. This meant that there was approximately one new immigrant arriving in Britain for every minute of the Labour government. Although there was only a modest fall in 2011, the new Conservative-led coalition government made it a priority to get immigration back under control. Looking at current projections for UK net migration, the numbers are now (2013) coming back in line with broadly comparable countries, a substantial reduction from previous years.

Other countries see the issue of immigration in a very different light. Countries with relatively small populations such as Qatar, the United Arab Emirates and Singapore continue to have high immigration rates to fuel their rapid economic growth. In 2012, for example, Qatar topped the list of migration destination countries with a rate of 40.62 net migrants per thousand population. Singapore was in fifth place at 15.62. The United Kingdom, with 2.59 migrants per thousand, was in 29th place below Australia, in 17th place at 5.93. Canada was in 18th place at 5.65 and the United States 26th at 3.62. However, this still put the UK well ahead of France, in 51st place with 1.1 net migrants per thousand, and Germany at 0.71 in 59th place. These figures indicate that we are not necessarily in the grave danger that some commentators suggest – at least if we are sensible about which immigrants are allowed to enter our country.

So it is important to look in detail at what level and kind of immigration might be relevant and beneficial to the UK. Evidence suggests that many professional and manual labour immigrants were absorbed by the shortfalls created by people emigrating from the UK. However, there has been a clear trend in recent years for an increasingly large proportion of those coming to the UK to be current or former students. In other words, we are cutting back on professionals while bringing in a larger number of students who may not have the skills that our economy needs. Despite this trend, studies project an increase in the need for both highly skilled and low-skilled labour, so it is important to look at what the country's needs are likely to be.

According to a recent UK government report, the British economy is expected to generate around 1.2 5 million more jobs in the decade ending in 2020. The employment groups expected to show the most significant increases during this period are higher-level occupations: managers, directors and senior officials (around 544,000 more, an 18 per cent increase), the professions (some 869,000 more, a 15 per cent increase), and associated professional and technical occupations (around 551,000 more, a 14 per cent increase). On the other hand, declining requirements are projected for administrative and secretarial occupations, skilled trade occupations, and process plant and machine operatives. Although direct comparisons are difficult, filling these roles from the existing UK population alone, given its demographics and skills base, does not look possible.

Of course getting the right skills from abroad is only one of the options available; the other is an educational system in Britain that does not consistently fail those in the middle and lower social groups. Many of us think it is a national disgrace that education is the third biggest call on government finance yet so many of our young people leave school unable to read, write or count properly. The failure of publicly funded education to equip our children with the skills they require to compete in the global economy, in one of the world's ten richest countries at the beginning of the twenty-first century, is an outrage. Perhaps if more policymakers, educational experts and political commentators – especially those in our capital city – were dependent on the state sector to educate their children, the situation would be different. No one can, or should, blame parents for wanting the best for their children, but when so many of those responsible for the state system choose to opt out of it, what does that tell us?

However, there are complicating factors that we need to take into account. Demographic changes within the UK also need to be addressed, particularly the projected increase in the number of retired citizens in relation to the working population. The UK population is ageing, with the proportion of over 65-year-olds projected to increase from 16 to 24 per cent by 2051. Coupled with projected increases in life expectancy, the age dependency ratio (number of pensioners per 1,000 people of working age) will increase from 300 (which has been a stable average since the 1970s) to almost 500 in 2051.

With an age dependency rate of 370, Japan is already dealing with this issue. It has used technological improvements to increase the efficiency of labourers, and the government is trying to mobilize more of its retired and female population. Although these measures have no doubt helped, they are not enough on their own. The UN has recommended that Japan either raises its retirement age to 77 or allows an additional 40 million immigrants over the next 40 years – equivalent to third of the country's current population. The retirement age is currently being increased from 60 to 65 – a step in the right direction but still not enough to deal with the labour shortfall.

When we look at the situation in the UK, and Europe in general, we can see that we are heading for similarly tough decisions. Currently, for every three workers contributing to National Insurance, there is one person receiving a pension in the UK. In the next forty years this will reduce to two workers for every pensioner. The amount of money required to meet future pension liabilities is frighteningly high, and there is no easy way of finding it. We therefore have a problem based on a structural imbalance which requires a sustainable solution. This is likely to involve similar measures to those taken in Japan, including increasing the retirement age, mobilizing more of our existing population to work, and encouraging more economically beneficial labour into the country. The alternative to a viable place in the global market is managed decline – not an option we should be willing to contemplate.

UK immigration policy needs to be rebalanced so that those who come to our country are usefully economically active. There is neither the public appetite nor an economic case for allowing immigrants to come to the UK who will simply absorb our national wealth rather than helping to create it. Equally, we must develop policy that ensures that we are not turning away workers we need. Many of these will be skilled workers, a group currently in danger of being choked off, but it may ultimately mean unskilled labour too. In short, I believe that we need to have what we might call an 'open and shut' immigration policy. That is, an approach that is open to those who are economically active and have the skills our economy requires but closed to those who will become dependent on the state or who possess skills we do not require for our economic well-being.

How do we construct and sell an economically effective and politically viable immigration policy in a Western country with adverse demographics and the need to produce greater wealth, all set against the background of a potentially incendiary political debate? The key variables we have to keep in mind are the following: first, the impact of immigration on national income and its distribution among non-migrants (including income per capita, economic growth, structural change, inequality, poverty rates); second, the national labour market (including wage levels, unemployment rates, labour market participation rates, labour market segmentation); third, the fiscal balance (including public services, social security, tax revenues, etc.); and fourth, the impact on national identity and the attitudes of the migrant and non-migrant population.

We also need to be aware of the impact on public services. Although getting the right people into the economy as active participants should mean higher growth and tax receipts in the future, we need to be mindful of what our current infrastructure can actually handle. An assessment of capacity will help work out what we need to be providing, and what that means in terms of immigration. One of the problems in recent years has been that an inadequate infrastructure combined with largely uncontrolled immigration has diminished appreciation of the benefits that immigration can bring – one of the reasons Britain has had a generally good record on assimilation and race relations.

The impact of immigration on national identity should not be understated. How much any society will find acceptable depends on the level of cultural diversity which it is willing to tolerate. Nations such as Japan and Korea value a homogeneous culture considerably more than they value immigration and the economic benefits it brings. The US, Australia and Canada, on the other hand, are more receptive, with their history of cultural diversity and dependence on immigration. Britain's more limited tolerance of multiculturalism has been lessened by recent high levels of immigration and cases of immigrants draining rather than increasing the nation's wealth.

A properly balanced approach would ensure that the UK benefited economically from immigration and that it did not adversely affect national security, public order or the social and political stability of the country. Whether or not explicit protection of existing citizens' rights to employment (and other benefits) over those of potential citizens is required or desirable is an issue worthy of debate, a complex and contentious matter involving potentially competing ideas of the free market and national entitlements. The formulation of such policies will never be easy in a political environment which is more often knee-jerk than considered but, if done successfully, the outcomes will be better for all those involved.

It is important to note that not all immigration is viewed the same. The British public tend to be pragmatic and are actually strongly in favour of immigrants they perceive to be socially and economically beneficial. Qualifications are seen as more important than the country or region of origin. Professionals and genuine students are seen positively irrespective of where they come from, while unskilled immigrants are seen negatively. In other words, the British public does not like the concept of immigrants 'coming in to live off the state', an attitude that is very difficult to rationally disagree with. Overall, the British public's view of the cultural impact of immigrants has traditionally been a net positive; it is the economics that concerns them, particularly if they are low skilled or unemployed themselves.

There is considerably less concern about skilled immigrants, almost certainly indicating that not all immigration is seen in the same way.

How are other countries in the global economy managing their immigration policies? It's worth us having a look at four – Australia, Canada, Singapore and Hong Kong.

Australia used to be very open to immigration, providing incentives for certain categories of people to enter the country. However, since around 1970 there has been a fundamental change in policy, with millions more migrants and refugees wanting to enter Australia than the government has been willing to accept. All subsidies have been abolished, and immigration has become progressively more difficult. During the 2001 election campaign, immigration, asylum and border protection became important issues. This was in part due to foreign events such as 9/11, but also national scandals such as the Children Overboard affair. This was a political controversy which involved members of John Howard's Liberal government in the run-up to the election. The allegation that asylum seekers attempting to reach Australia by boat had deliberately thrown children overboard to ensure rescue and thereby entry into Australia caused anger among Australian voters. With public opinion turning against asylum seekers, the so-called Pacific Solution was voted into law by both sides of parliament. Under the legislation all asylum seekers looking to stay in Australia would be kept in detention camps on certain Pacific islands while their cases were being considered. Despite this the actual level of immigration continued to substantially increase. Australia has since moved towards a points-based immigration system. Previously open to over a hundred different skills, the new system homes in on those areas of greatest importance to the country. These include medical, mining and engineering skills, which are particularly vital, given China's insatiable demand for Australia's abundant natural resources.

Canada has always been open to immigration, with over 20 per cent of the county's current population being born abroad, and immigrants accounting for half of the annual population growth. Its immigration policy focuses on 'human capital'. The aim is to encourage immigration by young, bilingual, highly skilled workers in order to rebalance and improve Canada's ageing labour force. In order to attract the right type of migrants, Canada uses certain education and skills criteria that advantage potential migrants who have the experience, higher education and language skills it needs.

In 1967 a points system was introduced to determine immigrant eligibility with preference given to educated French and English speakers of working age, while the Immigration Act of 1976 officially made Canada a destination for migrants from all countries. The new act was constructed around three pillars of admission: independent applicants would be assessed on the basis of points awarded for employment skills, education and language abilities rather than national or racial origin; sponsorship by close family members; and refugee status. The Federal Skilled Worker Program (FSWP) is responsible for over four fifths of all economic migrant admissions and almost half of all admissions. Workers must have at least one year of experience in professional, managerial or skilled trade/technical occupations in order to qualify, and are evaluated based on other points-based criteria such as education, age, proficiency in English or French, and adaptability.

As the country debates the ability of its younger generations to support an ageing population, the size of the labour force and tax base necessary to maintain economic growth, and the population's ideal cultural and linguistic composition, Canadians are re-evaluating the goals of the immigration system and the direction in which they want it to help lead their society.

Singapore has had a pro-immigration stance for most of its short history. It separates potential immigrants into two categories: foreign workers and foreign talents. Foreign workers are unskilled or semi-skilled employees who primarily fill manufacturing, construction and domestic posts. Foreign talents possess professional qualifications and degrees relevant to Singapore's services economy. To attract foreign talents, various policies and incentives are in place. They includes the provision of comfortable yet affordable accommodation and specific programmes to make the process of immigrating easier.

The regulations for foreign workers are considerably stricter. At one point there was talk of all but stopping this stream of immigration, but the idea was rejected in the face of pressure from the companies who needed the labour; instead, the government formulated a new system. The main elements of this were a monthly levy paid by the employer for each foreign worker and a 'dependency ceiling' limiting the proportion of foreign workers employed by each company. Later, a two-tier levy was introduced requiring employers to pay a higher levy for workers whose employment changed the dependency ceiling value of the company. As of last year a new immigration rule means that only foreign workers earning above S$4,000 a month (£2,100) can sponsor their spouses and children to stay in Singapore.

There are three main immigration categories in Hong Kong: capital investment, skilled immigrants and family class. Capital investment immigrants, those from outside Hong Kong who want to invest there, must have net assets of HK$10 million (£850,000) or more throughout the two years before their application. This amount is due to be reviewed later in 2013, as it is reassessed every three years. For skilled immigrants, a quota-based system is used, allowing applicants to apply before entering the country even without having a job offer. Decisions are based on two tests: the Achievement Based Points Test and the General Points Test. Permanent residents of Hong Kong can sponsor related immigrants through a family class application. For this the applicant must be the permanent resident's spouse, or an unmarried dependent child, or a parent over sixty years of age.

The Political Impact of Immigration

There is a political as well as an economic imperative to control immigration. Large population movements can easily be used by those on the political extremes to mobilize feelings of vulnerability and fear. If mainstream political groups do not deal with the immigration issue in a rational and decent way, there are plenty of people on the shadowy fringes of politics waiting to exploit it in an irrational and thoroughly unpleasant way.

Recent experience in Europe has shown how volatile public opinion can be. As with much of Western Europe, France has seen increased immigration in the last ten years, not least from the newer EU member countries. In France's last presidential elections Marine Le Pen, candidate of the right-wing Front National, polled 6.4 million votes, 17.9 per cent of the total. The strenth of Le Pen's challenge posed a dilemma for the centre-right candidate Nicolas Sarkozy. He had to decide whether to move onto some of the territory occupied by the FN to shore up his base vote at the risk of losing the centre ground and more moderate voters to the socialists. Politicians in this predicament risk unwittingly helping the far right through publicly targeting its voters, thereby raising both its profile and apparent importance. In Germany the National Democratic Party (NPD) was founded in the mid-1960s and is the country's largest extreme-right grouping. It is racially nationalistic and has been described as neo-Nazi by the mainstream media. It achieved limited success in recent elections and is represented in two state parliaments in Germany. In Finland the ethnically nationalist True Finns group saw its electoral support rise from 4.1 to 19.1 per cent at the 2011 parliamentary elections. Although TF is not as anti-immigration as other nationalist parties (it speaks more to an anti-Brussels audience), it has attracted similar demographics to groups like the FN in France.

The next question to be faced is whether economic growth in developed economies can provide the extra resources required to extend state services such as health and education to new migrants – assuming they have the same access to such services as long-term citizens. The net fiscal impact of immigration is typically estimated as the difference between the taxes and other contributions that immigrants make and the costs of the public benefits and services they use. This is hard to measure, and will depend on several factors, including the characteristics of particular immigrant groups, their impact on the labour market, and the rules of the welfare system. In theory, young skilled immigrants doing highly paid jobs are likely to make a more positive contribution than those with low skills.

For the UK (and most other countries) the majority of studies show that the overall economic impact of immigration is positive, but small, resulting in a decrease in the dependency ratio in the short to medium term. However, this effect will likely diminish over time, as immigrants who permanently settle in the UK become older and retire themselves.

The Challenge of Aid: When, Why and Where?

Readers might be surprised to see the issue of international aid considered at this point. Inside the tidy administrative structures of Western governments it is often treated as an isolated policy area, a means of demonstrating the largesse of a developed economy towards less fortunate states. In reality, it is one of a number of economic tools that can shape emerging economies, interact with trade and influence patterns of migration.

Aid is an extraordinarily emotive subject, especially in difficult economic times, when aphorisms such as 'Charity begins at home' can take on extra connotations. Coined by Sir Thomas Browne, an English physician of the mid-seventeenth century, the observation originally had a slightly different meaning. In his book *Religio Medici* – an early attempt to fuse religion and science – he questioned how we could be charitable to others when we were uncharitable to ourselves. He wrote, 'Charity begins at home is the voice of the world: yet is every man his greatest enemy, and, as it were, his own executioner.' Think Whitney Houston's 'The Greatest Love of All' (originally recorded by George Benson) for the contemporary mindset. Many literary and biblical quotes can be used to make the case both for and against international aid. The following is my favourite and, I think, one of the more balanced. 'Let their lives be saved, lest the wrath of the Lord be stirred up against us . . . But so let them live as to serve the whole multitude in hewing wood and drawing water.' (Joshua 9:20–1)

Aid is not a new phenomenon: ancient history contains accounts of settlements, cities and empires providing goods, food and coin to other communities in time of need or disaster. That Britain was expected to help when one of its colonies needed aid demonstrates that empires regarded themselves as having a responsibility (fulfilled or not) to provide for their peoples. Taking the 1899–1900 Indian famine as an example, it is interesting to note that the issues discussed and the response were not dissimilar to those of today. The monsoon rains had failed in 1899 leading to drought, which then continued for a second year, causing millions to die. Concern over India becoming dependent on handouts led to limited aid from Britain. The plight of the Indian people was highlighted by religious and philanthropic travellers from Europe and the USA, who spurred donations to charitable funds. These first tourists and aid workers were often accused of being odd and of gawking at others' misery. Later analysis showed that dissemination of images of the suffering encouraged British notions that Indians were incapable of self-government, while in India the perception that the British could have done more encouraged some to conclude that Britain and India's interests were not the same.

While aid is routinely criticized as an inefficient way of benefiting recipient nations, it should be remembered that altruism is only one of the motives for its distribution. At one end of the spectrum aid can be given with no strings attached, especially by private donors and NGOs. At the other, there are well-documented cases of so-called aid (including classifying interest-bearing loans as aid) which were of net benefit to the donor and almost certainly detrimental to the recipient. National aid programmes have significant political aspects. France, currently involving itself in Mali, tends to direct more of its aid to former colonies than elsewhere, at least partly in its own interests. Although governments rarely admit providing aid may be to their own benefit, *raison d'état* is a more efficient foreign aid policy than pure altruism.

For most of human history the surplus produced by any community, village or larger grouping over and above what was required for subsistence was small. Any interruption or shock to the food supply, natural or man made, could easily send communities into deficit, with attendant starvation, disease, social breakdown and death. While there are examples of secure, well-governed and affluent pre-industrial societies, significant improvement only came about with the modernization of agriculture and the Industrial Revolution. Subsistence is now only a fraction of richer nations' GDP, their surpluses now being employed in other ways – to raise standards of living (including social security and health services), to fund central government and to maintain standing armies being the most significant.

Industrialized societies do not need aid because external shocks have been minimized and they have solid institutions designed to produce surpluses and distribute them equitably to the entire populace – criticisms of widening gaps between the rich and poor notwithstanding. Nations which are currently recipients of aid do not possess these attributes. Inability to produce a surplus can be attributed to paucity of natural resources, an abundance of natural disasters, war (civil and cross-border), and political and social backwardness. There is also sometimes a legacy of foreign currency debt that cannot be repaid and/or a web of unfavourable tariffs and international agreements which negate if not reverse any natural advantages.

Taking each of these in turn, we can see that a lack of natural resources (or harsh climate) is no barrier to advancement. Nor are natural disasters (Japan) or war (Israel) so frequent or destructive in any nation that their adverse effects cannot be overcome by sound government. The remaining reasons must therefore be those primarily responsible for keeping nations from realizing their potential, yet it is precisely these which are least affected by foreign aid, sometimes deliberately (but not necessarily nefariously) so – the IMF refused for years to make loans conditional on political and economic reform, particularly land reform. In the few examples where interests have been so aligned to reorient and rebuild institutions effectively, we can discern a clear motive to decrease dependency. In a few other cases (Malaysia, South Korea, China), despite starting with apparently incredible handicaps, these were overcome to join the club of advanced nations. Strong central government pushing through exactly those modernizing reforms which aid packages and international institutions have been loath to do has been a common feature of such success stories.

The best-documented examples of successful aid recipients are probably West Germany and Japan following the Second World War.

Here, the donor (the United States) saw it to be in its interests (and those of the Western bloc which it headed) to create two strong independent states which would not fall to communism. Both Germany and Japan had their political, and to some degree cultural, institutions steamrollered for the dual purposes of de-Nazification (and its equivalent in Japan) and economic recovery, leading to autonomy without exploitative oligarchy. Unlike after the First World War, the USA did not insist on the repayment of past loans, and the result was a fresh start on the balance of payments ledger as well. (It's a pity the United States did not apply the same policy to the United Kingdom, which had to go to the edge of extinction to pays its debts in full.) West Germany and Japan were therefore primed for success in a way few current aid recipients experience: the diplomatic support of a superpower with geopolitical interests aligned largely with their own, an economic reset button on balance of payments in foreign currency, and rebuilt institutions designed to deliver economic prosperity to all. Hindsight may well be perfect, but until basket-case aid recipients realign their economic and political institutions and society in a similar fashion it is difficult to see aid being the difference between continued poverty-stricken dependence and autonomous prosperity.

What can we learn from history about successful aid policy? Post-war Germany and Japan are different from other aid recipients in that they had, in addition to the economic and geopolitical advantages mentioned, strong residual institutions: a judiciary, educational systems, cultural ties and an established commercial, religious, political and social order. Economists ranging from Jeffrey Sachs to Francis Fukuyama have identified institutions as the key foundation for successful and sustainable economic growth. Societies require social institutions in order to function well. The Germany of 1945 still possessed in essence the governmental institutions of 1914 imperial Germany. This ensured that 1946 was not Year Zero. Enforcing legal contracts, issuing legal tender, teaching children, providing healthcare and running public services require strong institutions to enforce basic rules and modes of behaviour. Money alone cannot build these but time and care can.

Tied aid is a controversial form of economic support regarded by many in the international aid community as a threat to effective anti-poverty programmes. It is when the provision of aid is tied to a specific response – typically aid is given by one country to another provided the latter purchases goods or services from the former. This may result in no net benefit for the recipient country but allows the donor to look good: the worst possible form of reciprocity. It has undoubted political attractions for those on the giving end, especially when tough domestic economic conditions make the moral case for aid difficult to sell. Fans of the BBC comedy series *Yes, Minister* may well remember the episode where Jim Hacker (the minister) provided an African country with aid in order to generate orders from British companies that equalled the amount of aid given. However, although the episode was clearly intended to lampoon tied aid, not many minutes will elapse in a discussion in a British pub about aid before it is championed as 'getting something for something' or 'making everybody a winner'. This takes us back to the argument about whether a successful aid programme is about the immediate alleviation of poverty and distress or fostering a long-term ability to avoid it being needed at all.

Steps like the Paris Declaration on Aid Effectiveness (2005) have been important in identifying what aid should be given, and why and where it should be spent. The aim of the declaration was to provide reliability and predictability for aid recipients. So far the jury is out, but it represents progress. One of the arguments likely to resurface is whether there should be more directly managed aid programmes or whether money should be given to recipient governments for them to determine their own priorities. I believe that while the latter would be acceptable in a perfect world, the levels of corruption, dysfunctional government and perverse priorities among many recipient countries mean that we should go carefully down this particular path. While the argument is put by some that project aid is condescending and demeaning, individual taxpayers, who ultimately provide the money, surely have a right to know that what is given in their name is spent in a way that is in line with their own ethical values.

Meanwhile, the whole rationale for aid has its critics. I do not normally tear out pages from airline magazines but a recent piece in British Airways' *HighLife* magazine by Ian Birrell struck me as particularly punchy and poignant. In pointing out that, contrary to widespread public perception, Ethiopia, Ghana, Rwanda and Uganda had average growth rates of 6.5 per cent between 2005 and 2010 he noted, 'The proportion of people in sub-Saharan Africa hit by famine averaged under one third of one per cent between 1990 and 2005. The harmful narrative was driven for decades by an unholy alliance of an ever growing aid industry, politicians claiming to be saving the world and lazy journalists happy to go along for the ride rather than challenging the conventional wisdom.'

The complex issues of external aid and global imbalances collide when we consider countries with large natural resources which exhibit extraordinary mismatches between the richness of the resource and the poverty of the population. When Britain struck oil in the North Sea, 'God's gift' to the economy created wealth for the nation that we continue to enjoy today. Helped by high oil prices, tax revenue from North Sea oil continues to run into billions of pounds. The British experience is not an inevitable one and natural resources are not a help for all countries. Some countries, however, fail to achieve meaningful development despite the value of their bounty: the resource may lead to external conflict, to civil war or to the corruption that has so widely hindered development.

Nigeria and Norway make for an interesting comparison. Nigeria has the world's 10th largest proven oil reserves with 37.2 billion barrels; Norway has the world's 23rd largest oil reserves with 5.7 billion barrels, less than a seventh of Nigeria's. Given these facts, you might expect Nigeria to be far richer than its Scandinavian counterpart. However, while Norway ranks 4th in the world by per capita GDP, Nigeria comes an astounding 137th. Norway has been shrewd at extracting revenues from its black gold for the benefit of its people and has set up a sovereign wealth fund to invest the money to benefit future generations when the oil runs out.

Of course Nigeria has a much greater population at 162 million than Norway's 5 million, but this does not entirely explain the discrepancies between them. Some are quick to point the finger at the international oil companies, which, they claim, have raided Nigeria's resources with scant regard for the local populace. It is certainly true that Royal Dutch Shell has made a lot of money, but in return Nigeria has enjoyed some $300 billion of revenue from oil in the past thirty years. Despite this the average Nigerian has become poorer.

While natural resources exist in many forms including gas, gold and diamonds, it is easiest to look at oil to explore the puzzling contrast between the possession of resources and development. There are several explanations for the 'paradox of plenty', which explains why a resource-rich country may not become rich de facto. Firstly, economic factors such as volatility in commodity prices may wreak havoc on the revenue streams of the resource-rich country. 'Dutch disease' may also affect the commodity exporting nation. This term was coined by *The Economist* magazine in 1977 to describe problems in the Netherlands after the discovery in 1959 of a large natural gas field. As foreign customers bought Dutch currency to purchase the gas they inadvertently inflated its value. This made Dutch manufactures less competitive on the international market, placing a brake on growth outside the commodity sector. The second explanation for the paradox is political. Resource-rich countries often have considerable scope for patronage, resulting in corruption and political elitism. Thirdly, conflict often develops over areas with valuable commodities. Finally, states rich in natural resources have become increasingly enmeshed in the environmental debate over the need to husband global resources for the long term and the search for renewable alternatives, especially in the energy sector.

How do we achieve a balance between the need of individual nations to generate enough wealth for their people and the global desire, particularly strong in the developed world, to exercise collective responsibility for the environment and the sustainability of resources? It was Theodore Roosevelt who said, 'The nation behaves well if it treats the natural resources as assets which it must turn over to the next generation increased, and not impaired, in value.' While Roosevelt's comment may seem idealistic, his sentiment holds true. I believe we have a moral obligation to the next generation, for whom we are the custodians of the environment. It follows that we should exploit our natural resources in a responsible manner such that they can continue to be enjoyed by generations to come. Whether or not we believe in global warming, I believe we should operate a precautionary principle and avoid any potential exacerbation of the phenomenon where we can. Irrespective of our views on climate change, I believe there is an overwhelming obligation to recognize that we have finite resources on our planet and to use them in the most sensible way. Given the potential for solar and tidal energy, to name but two, I can only imagine what future generations will think of us when they realize that we squandered precious, finite and complex hydrocarbons by simply burning them for energy.

In recent decades we have become more aware both of the impact we are having on our environment and the limited supply of certain commodities. Higher commodity prices, as resources run out, make investment in innovation more profitable and thus more likely. This reasoning suggests that we don't need to worry about depleting our reserves of commodities as long as we can bank on our reserves of innovative spirit to develop replacement technologies such as the hydrogen-powered car. I'm a great believer that, when push comes to shove, our natural ingenuity and creativity will generate the technological advances we need to satisfy our energy appetites. That is not, however, an excuse to ignore our personal responsibility for the good stewardship of our world.

The Holy Grail of a Free Trade World

One of the great drivers of the global economy is international trade, which enables creative or resource-rich nations to benefit from the consumer demands of others, ultimately creating a rebalance of wealth. Many of us have adopted the belief in free trade as a political article of faith, but why? For me, the traditional concept of free trade as a moral right has been augmented by the economic benefits it brings – improved living standards and better and cheaper goods and services – with the added benefit of minimizing the risk of conflict between states. Free trade is probably best described as a state of affairs in which national governments do not discriminate against imports, do not apply tariffs, subsidies or quotas, and allow trading partners mutual gains from the trade in goods and services. In a free trade system prices are ultimately dependent on the balance of supply and demand rather than any form of external influence.

Free trade is a relatively modern concept. As recently as the late eighteenth century, the dominant doctrine was not free trade but mercantilism. The mercantilist view was that wealth resided solely in money – at that time meaning gold and silver – so countries were wealthy if they built up gold and silver stocks, often plundering them from overseas and then preventing them from leaving. This was the economic motivation for the policies that followed the Spanish discovery of the New World. Mercantilism also promoted the view that control of foreign trade was essential for national security. It essentially demanded a positive balance of trade, and its application is almost always associated with high tariffs, especially on manufactured goods. Between the early sixteenth and late eighteenth centuries this was the dominant economic doctrine in western Europe and both reflected, and contributed to, the highly competitive colonial policies of the European powers of the day, resulting in both military conflicts and colonial expansion. Prohibiting colonies from trading with other nations, creating monopoly markets, subsidizing exports and banning goods being carried on foreign ships were only a few of the aspects of this policy. Ideas were, however, about to change.

Born in Fife in Scotland in 1723, Adam Smith was one of the moral philosophers at the centre of the Scottish Enlightenment. With the parliaments of England and Scotland having united just sixteen years earlier, Smith was one of the earliest examples of how the Scottish intellectual renaissance combined with the might of the developing English Industrial Revolution to power, intellectually and economically, the new United Kingdom and its emerging empire. Those who reflected Smith's views advocated the view that it was free trade that had enabled Mediterranean cultures such as Egypt, Greece and Rome to prosper, as well as the great trading empire of ancient China.

For those who find the 950 pages of Adam Smith's phenomenal work *The Wealth of Nations* impenetrable (which probably includes 99 per cent of those who quote or refer to it), Dr Eamonn Butler of the Adam Smith Institute has written *The Condensed Wealth of Nations*, a must-read for anyone who wants to understand the essence of the arguments put forward. Smith argued that far from being beneficial to a country's wealth, monopolies and tariffs were positively harmful. If foreign goods were cheaper, then it was wasteful to make at home what could be bought cheaper from elsewhere. In a vivid example he says,

> By means of glasses, hotbeds, and hot walls, very good grapes can be raised in Scotland, and very good wine too can be made of them at about 30 times the expense for which at least equally good can be brought from foreign countries. Would it be a reasonable law to prohibit the importation of all foreign wines, merely to encourage the making of claret and Burgundy in Scotland?

Most importantly, in my view, Smith challenged the assumption that lies at the heart of mercantilist thinking – that there has to be a winner and a loser in any trading exchange. The idea that a nation was more likely to become wealthy from trade if its neighbours were also rich, industrious and commercial – rather than poor – might seem like common sense to us today but was economically revolutionary in the mid-eighteenth century.

So, according to Adam Smith and those of a similar philosophical outlook, free trade was a moral right. I believe that to be true still. Free trade allows people to voluntarily exchange their hard work for goods or services, without artificial barriers erected by a government. Conversely, tariffs or subsidies restrict the right of an individual to buy what they want at the price they think is fair, and equally they restrict someone else's right to sell a product or service at the price they consider reasonable. Trade is based on voluntary exchange, and politicians should not arbitrarily decide which exchanges are good, which are bad, and which should be changed. If they do, they should expect this interference to have adverse consequences.

Another philosophical argument in favour of free trade is that it benefits the many at the expense of a few vested interests. Free trade allows specialization – leading to better-quality goods and services at cheaper prices – which is good for consumers. Protectionism, on the other hand, aims to help the minority who produce a certain item or service from having to compete, thereby placing the majority at a disadvantage. Therefore, protectionism favours sectional interests at the expense of the majority.

Free trade brings significant economic benefits and has already raised the living standards of hundreds of millions around the globe. There has never been a more potent force for the liberation of the world's poor than global capitalism. The genuine opportunities that come with open markets and free trade will always be more beneficial than any international aid programme. The percentage of the world's population living on less than one dollar a day has fallen from nearly 11 per cent in 1970 to around 2 per cent today, largely liberated by free trade in a capitalist global economy.

Creating an environment free from artificial distortions boosts overall trade and thereby increases economic growth and output. Countries develop specializations, and capital and resources are moved into those sectors where there is an existing competitive advantage and away from areas where there is a disadvantage. Countries can then build on their existing strengths to produce more goods and services at a higher quality. This process, described and advocated by Adam Smith and contemporaries such as David Ricardo, remains as true today as it ever has been: capital and labour are allocated where they are most efficiently used.

Nobel Prize winner Muhammad Yunus wrote in 2008, 'There are many things that free markets do extraordinarily well. When we look at countries with long histories under capitalist systems . . . we see evidence of great wealth . . . The emergence of modern capitalism three hundred years ago made possible material progress of a kind never before seen.' The intellectual triumph of capitalism reached its apogee in the twentieth century with the collapse of Soviet communism at the end of the Cold War. The myth that the command economies of the Soviet bloc could compete with Western capitalism dissolved under the costs of the arms race, with the economic might of the United States, in particular, proving to be the decisive factor. Today, another communist giant is being forced to embrace its own form of capitalism.

China is perhaps the most striking and visible example of how trade can dramatically improve living standards. In 1978, under Deng Xiaoping, China started to open up to the world. It was a far-sighted decision in a world where the Cold War was still in full swing. Prior to the Deng reforms, clothing and food were rationed and housing was of generally poor quality – except of course for the party hierarchy. China was not only closed to the world economically, but it had been subjected to the vindictive horrors visited upon its population first by Mao Zedong's Cultural Revolution and then by the infamous Gang of Four, who distorted its culture and stunted its intellectual development.

Conversely, in the period 1978 to 2008, 400 million Chinese emerged from poverty to become part of a burgeoning middle class, and this figure continues to rise today, bringing with it political as well as economic change. The liberalizing economic reforms of the Deng government are seen today as the key drivers behind this story of growth and prosperity. As state diktat was gradually replaced by individual initiative, the imbalances built up under the previous system started to diminish, with effort and reward being more closely linked than was ever possible under the rigid Maoist system. Today China is the world's second-largest economy, with hundreds of millions of people lifted out of poverty and into a new era of prosperity and expectation. With China 'the world's factory' – at least for the present – Western nations have benefited from the deflationary effects of cheaper goods prices. So our budgets stretch further and cover more products than before, and the Chinese have benefited from improved standards of living in a real life example of Adam Smith's argument that in a free trade system there need not be a winner and a loser, but everyone can benefit.

Free trade has other tangible benefits too, particularly for the populations of the relatively more prosperous nations. For example, free trade can help secure stable food and energy supplies. This means cheap good-quality food sourced from the best agricultural regions globally with what would otherwise be seasonal items available all year round. Instead of expensive and poorer quality foodstuffs, improved free trade links make up for domestic shortfalls by supplying what consumers want at a fair and reasonable price. Free trade therefore allows family budgets to stretch further and to cover more goods and services than might have previously been affordable. There are those who argue that the environmental cost of transporting goods across the world has its downside – perhaps to the point of being unacceptable. This, however, is hardly likely to cut any ice with producers, who have found a way to trade themselves out of poverty, and Western consumers, who are able to reap the benefit of fresh produce all year round.

Another advantage of free trade is the constant push towards innovation it produces through competition. Lower barriers force businesses to be more competitive, to focus on productivity improvements and to invest in order to maintain profitability and market share. Of course there is always the temptation for governments to protect vulnerable industries from competitive pressures by erecting tariff walls. In the short term this might allow companies to remain competitive with better-managed foreign rivals. Ultimately, however, the better companies will expand their market share, and the inefficient will be forced to change or go under. Since the public – consumers – benefit from free trade through being able to buy better and cheaper goods and services, protectionism – of whatever sort – is never in their long-term interests. Finally, because free trade builds commercial links between countries it is argued that it reduces the risk of conflict, since countries with strong trade links are unlikely to go to war with one another because of the mutual economic damage that will occur.

It all adds up to a very attractive picture – at least to a growing number of nations around the world – so, if it is so good, why do we still have so much trouble getting real global free trade? The main impediment continues to be the protectionist mindset, the false belief that if the competitive forces of the market are ignored, then their pressure to produce change will simply disappear. Since competition is usually seen as threatening when domestic producers are less productive and innovative than foreign competitors, the protectionist mindset can be powerful in national politics. In pluralistic nations pressure groups can have a marked effect on political outcomes. While producers tend to be organized into groups, those who will have to pay for their inefficiency – taxpayers and consumers – usually are not. It is special interests – for example, auto manufacturers or agricultural producers – who tend to gain in the short term when competition is impeded by government action.

An argument used in favour of protectionism is the risk of 'unfair competition', for example, foreign companies 'dumping' products at significantly below-market prices onto domestic markets. Again, in such cases consumers do not complain about the lower prices but domestic manufacturers do. Recently European solar panel manufacturers wrote to the European Commission protesting at dumping by Chinese competitors. China responded to the allegation (and others) by taking the dispute to the World Trade Organization (WTO). But domestic manufacturers only complain about unfair competition when they are on the losing side, and many EU states manipulate the market to support their domestic industries with hidden tariffs and barriers. The chutzpah is palpable. For those unfamiliar with Yiddish, probably the best example of chutzpah is the apocryphal child accused of murdering his parents who asks for clemency because he is an orphan.

The WTO sets the rules by which international trade is conducted. It is a forum for countries to negotiate, and is generally accepted as having been useful in promoting global commerce. Sadly, this does not yet mean that the WTO is always helpful or successful, but it is the best mechanism we have so far devised. It is important to understand what the World Trade Organization is and what it does. The WTO grew out of what is known as the Uruguay Round of multilateral trade negotiations, which started in 1986 under the auspices of what was known as GATT – the General Agreement on Tariffs and Trade – with a remit to act as a forum for trade negotiations, to liberalize trade and to settle trade disputes around the globe. This will not lead to end of all trade barriers any time soon, but the WTO has been able to secure a number of multilateral trade agreements on the road to a genuine system of international free trade for the benefit of peoples around the world. As a sign of its growing maturity and relevance, the WTO has now expanded to take on trade issues that go beyond simply goods and increasingly deals with services and intellectual property. It is to be hoped that the gradual progress of the WTO towards real global free trade will eventually silence the siren voices raised against it, but we must remain very vigilant indeed.

As we become more globalized and interdependent, the question of identity and ownership in the transnational business world inevitably arises. What does the term 'British company' mean today? What does a 'Buy American' campaign achieve? In an era dominated by global cross-border ownership, production, supply and distribution chains, what actually constitutes a national company? These questions are pertinent because during times of economic distress there is a natural tendency to close ranks and back 'our own'. While this view of business and commerce is likely to feel increasingly anachronistic as time passes, we need to reassure those who are threatened by the pace of global change.

'There will be no national product or technologies, no national corporations, no national industries.' Is this a quote from an ivory-tower academic? No, it is the start of Professor Robert Reich's 1991 book *The Work of Nations* (the author subsequently become secretary of labor in the first Clinton administration). The demise of the concept of national companies may seem new to many, but these and similar developments have been discussed for more than twenty years. What is a national company if the majority of shareholders are foreign and a majority of operations, supply chain and revenue are derived from overseas?

In the past the domestic economy was vitally important to deliver the goods required for production. This meant that, other than the sourcing of raw materials, the manufacture of the product was contained within either the national borders or the company itself. Today there have been profound changes to both this process and its accompanying mindset.

For example, when President George W. Bush agreed to the $17.4 billion bail-out of the American car industry at the end of 2008, this was primarily because of the impact its bankruptcy would have on the supply chain for automobile manufacture both in the US and across the globe – although of course US politicians focused more on the impact on domestic supply chain producers. The next time you board a passenger airline you are likely to see British Rolls-Royce engines or be dependent upon Japanese battery parts. Is a Boeing plane really American when the majority of its component parts were manufactured overseas? The concept of a national company may be getting close to its use-by date. If we want to see a demonstration of the inter-connectivity of modern international trade we need look no further than the supply chain disruption caused by the 2011 earthquake and tsunami in Japan, which led to severe shortages of any number of highly elaborate manufacturing goods worldwide. British investors and entrepreneurs own businesses, work and export all over the world, and the rest of the world reciprocates in Britain.

In 1998 30.7 per cent of shares in the London Stock Exchange were owned by overseas investors. By 2010 this increased to 41.2 per cent. Even more starkly, in 1963 individual British investors owned 54 per cent of the shares listed on the London Stock Exchange, but only about a fifth of that, or 11 per cent, in 2012. Can a company be seen as British when only the head office is in Britain, the majority of its shareholders are foreign and most of its operations and revenue are derived from overseas? This is a complex topic, and it gets more complex still. How does the concept of a national business stand up when a company can have its operations based in multiple countries, the notional head office in a tax haven, its owners are spread across the world and the legal documents are written under the law of yet another country? With the documents of a company drawn up under English law, an English judge could decide the fate of a company headquartered in Holland but primarily owned by east Asian investors with subsidiaries in France regulated by completely different legal requirements. This happens more often than most people probably realize.

Many people will look at the Byzantine example above and scratch their heads. It was all so simple in the past: a British company would be owned by Brits, with operations in Britain employing British workers. Some see this as a better world and changes in the global economy purely as a threat, but it is just as easy to see them as a great opportunity for British entrepreneurs. New technology, reduced trade barriers and the growing importance of intellectual capital make it easier for British businesses to benefit from the internationalization of the global economy by picking the best brains from across the world.

So do 'I'm backing Britain' or 'Buy American' campaigns really work as their organizers intend? The short answer is no. Global manufacturing and trade are just far too intertwined. Such campaigns actually often scare capital away from where it can be best used. The world has changed, almost certainly irreversibly.

The T-word: Tax

If global trade and commerce are inextricably enmeshed, as they are, then this has implications for the taxation of both corporations and individuals around the world. It is a general economic rule that people don't like taxes. It was Edmund Burke who said, 'To tax and please, no more than to love and be wise, is not given to men'. It is hard to go anywhere in the world where people don't complain about having to pay tax whatever the rate that is being levied.

The economic debate in most developed democracies tends to revolve around tax and spend policy. Citizens argue about how and where tax revenues are raised and spent, although in Western countries, including the United States, state spending has long outstripped income from taxes, resulting in ever higher government borrowing and public debt. In Europe, which, as Chancellor Merkel of Germany has pointed out, has 7 per cent of the global population but is responsible for 25 per cent of the world's GDP and 50 per cent of its social spending, there has tended to be a consensus about non-negotiable areas of state spending. What we might call the four universal pillars of education, law and order, defence and health consume a large proportion of our total tax revenues. Add to these welfare entitlements and the pension costs of an ageing population, and it does not take a genius to see why tax rates are high.

As well as the level of tax, one of the main complaints is the complexity of the tax system. Labyrinthine regulations have become a licence to print money for legal and accounting professionals. The archaic tapestry of market-altering rules which pass for tax codes already provide a barrier to domestic economic activity, and with globalization such problems are exacerbated as countries must now increasingly compete for ever more mobile tax revenues.

In the United Kingdom in 2012 this issue hit the headlines in a big way when the story broke that Starbucks was avoiding UK tax by using a fairly common and legal strategy known as transfer pricing, which would have been agreed in advance by the UK tax authorities. There was an almighty outcry among politicians and in the press against multinational companies which make money in the United Kingdom but use tax avoidance mechanisms to reduce their tax bill here. 'If you make money in Britain, you should pay tax in Britain' was the almost universal refrain, which sounds perfectly fair and reasonable to most people. There is however another side to the argument which needs to be made, especially as this is likely to become an increasingly prominent and frequent issue in the future. It is worth pointing out that the firm employs over 8,500 people in the United Kingdom and is making heavy capital investments here as well as paying employers' National Insurance contributions for all of its staff. There is no moral obligation on any company, any more than there is on an individual, to pay any more tax than the law requires – the idea that tax is some sort of voluntary contribution that we make to the state is laughable. Whether or not we believe that Starbucks is trying to avoid paying its legitimate dues, there is no doubt that the high street coffee market is a highly competitive environment in which it will be looking to boost value for all its stakeholders, which includes shareholders but is primarily the consumer. If we effectively ask these multinational companies to stop competing with each other, using all the tools they can within the law, then we are likely to be presented with lower-quality products or higher prices or both.

The main point of the story is that there is no such thing as a victimless tax. It may make us feel better to beat up faceless corporates in order to generate a small increase in short-term government funding, but in the long run there is a risk of lowering standards and raising prices for any commodity in an economy. With every government tax and revenue hike, another entrepreneur is disincentivized from taking risks, creating an extra job or starting up a new business. If we want to build a stable and prosperous society, the enterprise of the human spirit must be celebrated, not shunned for the sake of short-term political expediency. So the challenge is how to raise the revenues which make our countries the sorts of societies we want to live in.

Corporation and personal taxes have become unbelievably complex, with reams of laws and regulations to comply with. Complex regulation is a burden on an enterprise society, and without the wealth creation that such a society brings, a prosperous and stable future is hard to achive. Small businesses are at a disadvantage to large corporations when there is a lot of red tape. Red tape makes it harder to get new businesses off the ground, which means competitiveness falls as large corporations dominate the market. So where does this leave a government needing to raise revenue? Ultimately start-ups and existing companies will go elsewhere if taxes are too high and too complex, and the country will lose out on the investment necessary for production and employment, and tax receipts will drop. However much governments and the media scream about multinational companies trying to pay as little tax as possible, they will eventually have to come to terms with the fact that the market applies to policymakers and treasuries too.

The Debt Quicksand

The United Kingdom, along with a number of other Western debtor nations, if not drowning in debt is barely keeping its collective head above water. Overspending is a time bomb waiting to explode, with government debt standing at over £1 trillion in the UK and total public debt over $16 trillion in the United States. In Britain we owe over £17,000 for every man, woman and child, and that's before the bank bail-outs are considered or the off-balance-sheet debts hidden by previous administrations. The more we borrow, the more we burden our children with having to repay our debts. In other words, debt is simply deferred taxation. But does it matter? The UK received a bail-out of £2.3 billion from the IMF in 1976 as the economic policies of the Wilson/Callaghan Labour governments disintegrated. Will we find ourselves in this situation again?

'Credit' is derived from the Latin word *credere*, to believe or trust. Our nation's creditors have lent us money in the belief that they will receive this money back, plus interest, at some point in the future. That belief is already being challenged with Britain's credit rating – along with those of many other Western countries – being downgraded by the ratings agencies. Obviously, the less the markets believe that any country will repay its debts the more expensive it will be for that country to borrow. This is important because currently we can only afford to make interest repayments on our present debt by borrowing even more!

History is littered with examples of great empires humbled by debt. Spain defaulted on its debt fourteen times between 1557 and 1696 and suffered rapid inflation as a result of an influx of New World silver. Coupled with the outcome of the Nine Years' War and the death of Spain's Charles II, this saw the eclipse of Habsburg Spain. Another case is pre-revolutionary France. By 1788 France was spending 62 per cent of royal revenues on servicing its debt. It is no coincidence that some historians identify 1788 and not 1789 as the true start of the French Revolution. It was on 7 June of that year that one of the first disturbances occurred over an attempt by the government to implement new taxes to deal with France's public debt. More recently we have the example of Ottoman Turkey. The Ottoman empire was spending 50 per cent of its budget on debt interest payments by 1875, with the final payment being made by the Republic of Turkey in 1954, even though the empire had been abolished thirty-six years previously. Britain's own history is also instructive. The contraction of its influence in the twentieth century was driven as much by economic exhaustion as a result of two world wars as it was by decolonization. As a result of the First World War, in the 1920s and 30s Britain's national debt was regularly over 150 per cent of GDP. After the Second World War it peaked at around 250 per cent of GDP.

The United States, with its huge debt interest payments burden, not only over-borrows and overtaxes the American people, but is of necessity cutting its defence spending to help make ends meet. The irony seems to be lost on some that much of this debt interest will end up in Moscow and Beijing. In other words, America has been more enfeebled by welfarism and big government than it ever was by the ideology or practice of communism. There is no doubt a wry smile or two inside the Kremlin when Mr Putin reads his morning papers.

If we are not to default on our debt then we must be able to afford to service it. In 2012 the United Kingdom spent £44.8 billion on interest payments alone. This year (2013) debt interest is the fourth biggest call on taxpayers' money after welfare, health and education. Next year it will overtake education. Currently, each taxpayer is being asked to contribute over £1,200 just for debt interest payments, for which they will receive no services or benefits. By 2015 this will rise to around £1,700. In the US, which is spending around $400 billion on debt interest this year, this figure is more than the federal government is spending on education, transportation and veterans affairs combined. Debt isn't purely a governmental phenomenon: households are drowning in debt too, although there is some evidence that households, unlike government, are reducing their exposure. In the UK households owe a whopping £1.42 trillion. With one person declared bankrupt every 282 seconds, our addiction to debt is surely a cause for concern.

UK debt has ballooned in recent years because of the failure to pay it down in times of economic expansion, a problem which was then exacerbated by borrowing more in the global financial crisis. But has our addiction to debt always been this bad and how does the UK compare to other countries? The stock of debt outstanding relative to the value of goods and services produced in any country is known as the government debt-to-GDP ratio. Today this stands at 87.8 per cent in the UK. This statistic matters because it shows the affordability of our debt relative to the size of our economy.

Greece hit the headlines in 2009 after it began to struggle with its debt, with an eye-watering debt-to-GDP ratio of over 152 per cent. Greece has now received bail-outs worth over €160 billion, but fears still persist over its ability to repay its debts and remain in the Eurozone. Other countries enjoy apparently astronomical debt-to-GDP ratios without fear of default, such as Japan (225 per cent) because of its high domestic savings rates and the US (74.2 per cent) because of its position as the world's reserve currency.

While our debt as a percentage of GDP is alarmingly high relative to that of our counterparts, things have been much worse. Debt was, it can be argued, in many ways the foundation of the British empire. The successive wars to achieve global dominance were financed by borrowing. At the time of one of Britain's greatest triumphs, the Duke of Wellington's defeat of Napoleon at the battle of Waterloo, national debt as a percentage of GDP had hit 237 per cent. Much of the rest of the nineteenth century was spent paying this off, and at the same time. When the industrial age arrived, Britain became the richest country in the world, enabling us to export our way out of debt (alongside of course taxing the colonies, a state of affairs that led to such disagreements as the Boston Tea Party which triggered the American War of Independence). In the eighty years up to 1914, debt was reduced to a low of 25 per cent of GDP.

Debt is a strategic issue, and governments can face threats from their own debt-to-GDP ratios. When countries have to cut spending on internal and external national security because of the need to finance debt repayments, alarm bells sound. Furthermore, the economic growth required to generate the wealth that pays debt interest can be hampered by the size of the debt itself as the debt-to-GDP ratio spirals out of control. Given the economic malaise faced by most Western governments this is a cause for concern. There is a striking irony, for example, that the US is having to cut its defence budget, partly as a result of the huge levels of government debt interest payments. In other words, they are cutting their defences, potentially against Russia and China, so that they can pay their debt interest to Beijing and Moscow!

So when, if ever, will the tipping point be reached? In a sense, it doesn't matter whether the tipping point is 77 per cent or 90 per cent. The point is that when it is reached, not only is growth reduced, but it can be reduced for many years. On top of this, as governments become more deeply embroiled in domestic debt crises, they are less able to respond to global events.

Whom exactly do we owe all this money to? Given the UK owes the staggering sum of £1.3 trillion, who is lending to its government? The investor base matters because some investors can be forced to hold UK gilts (government bonds) while others cannot, and it is the demand for gilts that ultimately determines the interest rate we pay to borrow as a nation. The Bank of England, through the Asset Purchase Facility (APF), has lent the government 29 per cent of its debt. Of course, while the BOE is technically an independent entity, the chancellor always has the ear of its governor (whom he appoints), and the APF was authorized by the chancellor in 2009. In the third quarter of 2012 £386 billion was held by the Bank of England, £335 billion by insurance companies and pension funds and £106 billion by monetary financial institutions such as banks and building societies. Banks, pension funds, insurance companies and other such bodies own 38 per cent of UK debt. These institutions are required by law to hold certain levels of capital to protect them from going bankrupt, and, cleverly, the government allows these institutions to hold UK government debt as capital!

The group that the government cannot force to hold UK debts is overseas investors, who hold 30 per cent of outstanding UK gilts. In the third quarter of 2012 some £398 billion of UK government debt was held overseas. By contrast, in Japan overseas investors account for only 7.5 per cent of Japanese government debt holders; 92.5 per cent of government debt is held domestically. One of the most alarming global statistics is China's dominance of the debt markets. China holds $1.16 trillion of US debt and its status as the United States' number-one creditor enables it to wield considerable political power.

Our reliance in the UK on overseas investors to finance our debt has increased markedly in recent years. Until 2005 overseas investors held less than 10 per cent of outstanding gilts; since then this figure has increased by 200 per cent, so we are increasingly reliant on investors who can choose to hold or sell UK government debt. It is therefore ever more important to have a fiscal policy which these investors believe in. Only in this way will they continue to offer us credit at a rate low enough for us to afford the repayments on our debt. The IMF suggests that the greater the share of overseas investors holding any government's debt, the greater the volatility of yields on that debt.

Moving away from government debt, how does personal and corporate indebtedness fit into the globalization picture. There is certainly no shortage of advice in the personal sector from religious and literary sources. The issue of interest is dealt with in Exodus Chapter 22: 'If thou lend money to any of My people, even to the poor with thee, thou shalt not be to him as a creditor; neither shall ye lay upon him interest.' In literature, advice is offered in *Hamlet* by Polonius: 'Neither a borrower nor a lender be/ For loan oft loses both itself and friend/ And borrowing dulls the edge of husbandry.'

For much of history lending money for interest was illegal across medieval Christian Europe. Israelites were forbidden from levying interest on loans to other Israelites but allowed to charge interest to gentiles. Today the practice of charging interest on loans is still regarded as sinful in Islam. The first evidence of lending appears as grain loans in the ancient civilizations of Assyria and Babylonia in 2000 BC. Between 650 and 600 BC the first coins were minted in Lydia, modern-day Turkey. The first evidence of personal debt in the form of money comes from the Roman empire: moneylenders would carry out their business from benches or *bancae* – hence the word 'bank'. It seems that the idea of personal debt, whether monetary or non-monetary, is at least as old as civilization itself.

Today we live off tomorrow's expected income as we spend relentlessly on credit. In November 2012 there was a whopping £54.9

billion of debt outstanding on our credit cards in Britain. But we also borrow in the form of loans to finance major purchases, including mortgages to finance the purchase of houses. In the run-up to the global financial crisis UK debt-to-income ratios increased markedly, though since households enjoyed a buoyant equity market coupled with rising house prices creating a wealth effect, household debt-to-asset levels remained fairly constant. It is nonetheless worth looking at how household debt-to-income ratios have changed over the past decade. In the US they have risen by about 12 per cent, in the UK 45 per cent, in Denmark a whopping 82 per cent and in Ireland a massive 100 per cent. Does this matter?

Probably. The IMF found a positive correlation between the increase in the household debt-to-income ratio between 2002 and 2006 and the loss of consumption in 2010. Countries such as Ireland, which enjoyed around an 80 per cent increase in this period in the household debt-to-income ratio suffered a 20 percentage point fall in consumption in 2010. Debt has to be paid back sometime, and when it is, spending on other things drops.

The allocation of corporate debt in a globalized economy is more complex. How do we allocate this on a country-by-country basis given the multinational nature of ownership and the allocation of debt down into international subsidiaries? 'Globalization' was coined in the 1980s to describe the process of international integration. Synonymous with companies such as McDonald's, Nike and Apple, globalization has made owning shares in foreign companies easier and more likely, and at the same time it has distorted our idea of what foreign means. James Bond no longer drives a British Aston Martin, he now engages in high-speed chases in a car owned by a consortium of Middle Eastern, American and English investors. In fact more than 40 per cent of the UK's listed firms are owned by foreigners. Today many companies and brands thought of as quintessentially British are not. Weetabix is majority-owned by a Chinese company; Harrods is Qatari owned; Cadburys Chocolate has been bought by Americans, and Tetley Tea belongs to Indians. The quintessential American company, Apple, puts 'designed in California' on its computers, detracting from the small print which says 'made in China'.

The question of debt in the context of multinational corporations has two facets. Firstly, differing tax rates affect the locations in which companies raise money and post profits. Secondly, ownership affects how corporate debt is allocated by country. Debt offers the owners of corporations a tax advantage because interest payments are tax-deductible. For example, in the UK this means that for every pound of interest payments a UK-based company makes, it saves itself twenty-three pence in Corporation Tax (since April 2013). In this way companies can use debt to reduce their tax burden. It follows that there is an incentive to push debt into subsidiaries in high-tax locations to reap a larger tax benefit. In a similar way, companies may shift their profits into jurisdictions with low rates of corporate tax. This much-maligned technique saw companies such as Google, Amazon and Starbucks hit the headlines in 2012, as discussed earlier, but exactly how should debt be allocated in multinationals? Take Cadburys as an example. It operates in the UK, is headquartered in Switzerland and owned by the American company Kraft. To complicate the problem further, some companies raise money through special purpose vehicles. SPVs are often located in places outside where the company operates or is headquartered, such as the Cayman Islands, and provide it with a vehicle through which the company can avoid reporting the debt on its balance sheet, thereby improving its credit rating.

In theory the question of allocation of corporate debt isn't important in national debt accounting. The debt is the responsibility of the owners of the company to service and repay; unless the debt is assumed to be the obligation of the government to settle in the event of a bankruptcy, then the allocation is only of interest from a statistician's perspective. But while we can assume, for the most part, that governments will not bail out corporations, the global financial crisis showed us that governments *will* bail out banks. Thus the allocation of financial debt by country is important if we assume governments are implicitly 'on the hook' for it. Alarmingly Britain has a financial debt-to-GDP ratio of almost 200 per cent. This raises the important question of whether in a democratic society in which a failing entity may lay claim to taxpayers' money, anything should ever be allowed to become 'too big to fail'. The loss of moral hazard at that point surely becomes unacceptable. If the consequences of success and failure are substantially the same, an underlying principle of the capitalist system has been violated.

Perhaps the most controversial but potentially most important of the issues relating to the financial aspects of globalization is whether the whole system of global credit is trying to defy economic gravity. Our paper money system will end in failure, predicts the doomsayer and Austrian School economist Detlev Schlichter in his book *Paper Money Collapse*. In it he recounts how all paper money systems have either ended in failure or reverted to commodity money. The problem with paper money, in his opinion, is that its supply is not fixed, whereas commodity money such as gold has a relatively finite supply. Governments have the ability to print money, to borrow more and overextend themselves, a process which sooner or later results in a systemic collapse of the paper money system.

Economic policy has been written such that we meet economic contraction with the provision of cheap money resulting in greater indebtedness. Many argue that when Alan Greenspan cut interest rates after 9/11 to avert a recession, it contributed to the debt-fuelled bubble which burst in 2007. In recent years successive rounds of 'quantitative easing' have sought to paper over the problems of paper money. The central banks of Europe, the USA and England have printed money to boost confidence and growth in their beleaguered economies blighted by debt. Schlichter and those who hold similar views argue that in order to avoid impending collapse, governments have used regulation to force banks and pension funds to hold ever greater proportions of their debt. In effect, governments and central banks have created a Ponzi scheme to perpetuate the illusion that the global economy is functioning.

What if Schlichter is right? Should we wipe the slate clean and revert to commodity money now? His argument is strong, yet confronted with the possibility of a Eurozone break-up, confidence in paper money remains high, and in the face of risk it has been the US dollar, the currency of the world's most indebted nation, that investors have flocked to.

So the equilibrium of an ever more globalized international economy depends on maintaining the balance between savers and borrowers, between immigrants and long-term citizens and between aid recipients and donors. It also requires an open, balanced and fair system of trade. Yet it is not only how we sell that matters, but also the commodities that are traded – what we sell. Will competition for these commodities threaten this precious equilibrium and push countries away from peaceful independence to conflict? This is the next pressing question.

Chapter Six

COMMODITIES

Since I have been aware of current affairs and politics, there has been an ongoing debate about how we will feed a world in which there is a constantly growing population. From the black-and-white television images I can remember from the war in Biafra, through the celebrity glitz of Live Aid to today's debate about international aid, the refrain has always been 'Feed the world.' And it remains a real if changing problem as the global population demands an ever more protein-rich diet and threatens fragile ecosystems. Increased demand for meat means that although more food is being produced than ever before, a greater proportion is going into animal feed, resulting in less available for human consumption. According to the United Nations Food and Agriculture Organization, the world will have to produce 70 per cent more food by 2050 to feed a projected extra 2.3 billion people with rising incomes and increasingly sophisticated tastes.

Yet we hear a lot less about watering the world. Famine and drought go together as partners in misery and death, but the issue of water, so vital for the survival not only of mankind but all living creatures, seems only to merit second billing. We have all seen so many images from space of our beautiful blue and green planet that they perhaps do not have the awe-inspiring impact they did only a generation or so ago – but beauty can be deceptive. It is true that over two thirds of the world's surface is covered by water, but most of it is too salty for us to use. Only 2.5 per cent of the water on earth is the fresh water we need, and two thirds of that is locked up in ice caps and glaciers. When we subtract the water located in remote areas and the rain which falls at the wrong time and place, we reach the shocking conclusion that less than 0.1 per cent of all the earth's water is actually available for human use – only a tiny speck of the blue on our planet.

According to the United Nations, almost 800 million people – just over one in ten people worldwide – lack access to safe drinking water. With rapid population growth and increased industrial consumption, the demand for water has tripled over the last fifty years. Every day more than 30,000 children die before their fifth birthday either from hunger or through preventable diseases, with drought a major aggravating factor. Only half the world's population has safe sanitation. According to the OECD, by 2030 some 47 per cent of the world's population will be living in areas of high water stress – and that means high human stress too.

As resources become more scarce, it is likely that conflict for their control will become more common. The US director of national intelligence forecast in a report of March 2012 that the risk of conflict would increase because water demand is likely to outstrip sustainable current supplies by 40 per cent. The US secretary of state at the time, Hillary Clinton, agreed: 'these threats are real and they do raise serious national security concerns'. Part of the trouble is that the areas where water is scarce tend to coincide with places where political conflicts fester and tensions simmer. According to UN studies, thirty nations will be in water scarcity by 2025, up from twenty in 1990. Eighteen of them are in the Middle East and North Africa, including Egypt, Israel, Somalia, Libya and Yemen.

There is a real chance that water will replace, or at least join, oil as a primary source of conflict in the twenty-first century. Where nations fought for black gold in the twentieth century, will they fight for blue gold in the twenty-first?

The War for Blue Gold – the History of Water Conflict

In the 1980s the Pacific Institute, one of the world's foremost authorities on water issues, began to categorize events in which there was a relationship between water and conflict. The list has become longer over the years, with events from China through India to the Middle East adding to the total. The institute's typology of water conflicts comprises: for control of water resources (where water supplies or access to water contribute to tensions); the military tool (where water resources or systems are used as a weapon in military actions); the political tool (where water resources or systems are used for a political goal); terrorism (where water resources or systems are either targets themselves or tools of violence or coercion, usually by non-state actors); the military target (where water resources are themselves the targets of military action); and development disputes (where water sources or systems are a major source of contention in dispute in relation to social or economic development). These categories are not mutually exclusive, and there is a degree of overlap particularly when wider geopolitical factors come into play – for example, when multinational development results in environmental damage with contamination of water supplies.

In cases where water is either the military tool or its target, history suggests that there are three favourite ways of utilizing it: the denial of water, using flooding as a weapon and the poisoning of water. The first recorded occasion when flooding was used as a military weapon is probably the most famous of all. According to the book of Exodus,

> Then the Lord said to Moses, 'Stretch out your hand over the sea so that the waters may flow back over the Egyptians and their chariots and horsemen.' Moses stretched out his hand over the sea, and at daybreak the sea went back to its place. The Egyptians were fleeing toward it, and the Lord swept them into the sea. The water flowed back and covered the chariots and horsemen – the entire army of Pharaoh that had followed the Israelites into the sea. Not one of them survived.

Presumably, subsequent commanders have justified similar tactics on the basis that if it was all right for God it was all right for them. In 1672, at the beginning of the third of his Dutch wars, Louis XIV invaded the Netherlands. The response of the defenders was to flood their own country by opening the dykes, creating an almost impenetrable barrier to the French forces. In a similar vein, when threatened by the Japanese army in 1938, Chinese general Chiang Kai-shek destroyed the flood control dykes of the Huayuankou section of the Yellow River, flooding an area estimated at between 2,000 and 30,000 square miles. Although this was successful in destroying part of the invading army and slowing the rest down, it resulted in casualties among the civilian Chinese population estimated at between tens of thousands and one million. During the Second World War one of the most famous missions of the British Royal Air Force was its attempt to destroy the dams on the Möhne, Sorpe and Eder rivers. The 'Dam Busters' raid resulted in the breaching of the Möhne dam, the water released destroying all downstream dams for 30 miles with the loss of over 1,200 lives. The breach in the Eder dam discharged at its peak over 26,000 cubic feet of water per second, nine times higher than the highest flood recorded, submerging a huge number of houses and bridges. The raid had achieved its military objectives.

The denial of water to military opponents and civilian populations alike has been frequently used as a weapon, often by defenders destroying their water infrastructure to deny it to an invader. Again, one of the earliest examples is contained in the Bible, in 2 Chronicles 32:4: 'So there was gathered much people together, who stopped all the fountains, and the brook that ran through the midst of the land, saying, Why should the kings of Assyria come and find much water?' The actions of King Hezekiah would be mirrored in the same region many centuries later when Saddam Hussein ordered the destruction of Kuwait's desalination capacity during his retreat in the Gulf War of 1991. This action in turn has echoes of the Muslim leader Saladin, who denied the invading crusaders water by filling wells on their route with sand and destroying the villages of the Maronite Christians, who would have supplied the Christian army with water, given the chance. Using water as a siege weapon has been a frequent tactic from the earliest times. As the Roman empire continued its decline, the Goths besieged Rome in the sixth century and cut all the aqueducts, resulting in the taking of the city in AD 537. Only the Aqua Virgo, whose course is almost entirely underground, survived. The US bombed irrigation systems in North Vietnam during the 1960s, destroying or damaging over 650 sections of dykes.

Poisoning water supplies is also a tried and tested tactic. In the sixth century BC the Assyrians, denied water themselves during their invasion of Israel, poisoned the wells of their enemies with rye ergot. When a plague broke out in Athens during the second year of the Peloponnesian War, the Spartans were accused of poisoning the cisterns of the Piraeus, the primary source of Athens's drinking water.

In his memoirs of the American Civil War General William Sherman gives accounts of Confederate soldiers dumping the carcasses of animals into ponds in order to contaminate the water – although Confederate soldiers would make the same accusations against their Union counterparts. In the brutal conflict that raged in Kosovo from 1998 to 1999 Serb forces were accused of disposing of the bodies of Kosovar Albanians in wells and Yugoslav federal forces of poisoning wells with animal carcasses. In Angola in 1999 a hundred bodies were found in four wells during the civil war.

In 1944, on the Italian coast south-east of Rome, the Germans flooded the Pontine Marshes by opening dykes and disabling pumps. While this was partly intended to slow down the advancing Allied armies, its primary purpose was to bring mosquitoes and malaria back to the area to punish the population for its 'disloyalty' to the Nazi cause. It had a limited impact on the invading forces but succeeded in its aim of bringing devastating illness to the local people. In another act of biological warfare, in 1945 German forces polluted a large reservoir in north-western Bohemia in Czechoslovakia with human sewage with predictably horrible results. Water supplies may also be unintentionally disrupted during a war. During the 1991 Gulf War, for example, Baghdad's water supply and sewage systems were badly affected by Allied bombing, with four of seven major pumping stations damaged, leading to sewage pouring into the Tigris River. The *New England Journal of Medicine* reported that, as a result of the damage, childhood deaths in Iraq during the first eight months of 1991 increased by 47,000 and the country's infant mortality rate doubled to 92.7 per 1,000 live births.

Water has unsurprisingly found itself used in terrorist activity, a trend that seems to be accelerating today. In 1970 a group of left-wing extremists (whose slogans included, 'Freaks are revolutionaries and revolutionaries are freaks') who attacked both the Capitol building in Washington DC and the Pentagon allegedly attempted to obtain biological agents to contaminate the water supply system of major American cities. This was echoed two years later, when two members of a right-wing group, the Order of the Rising Sun, were arrested in Chicago with around forty kilos of typhoid cultures with which they apparently planned to poison the water supply of Chicago, St Louis and other American cities. According to a textbook of military medicine written for the office of the Surgeon General of the United States Army, however, the plan was unlikely to cause major damage due to the chlorination of supplies, but the psychological impact can be easily imagined. A decade later in Oregon a religious cult known as the Rajneeshee successfully contaminated the water supply of Wasco County with salmonella, resulting in over 750 cases of poisoning.

Today an increasing number of water conflicts fall within the Pacific Institute's 'development disputes' category. Unsurprisingly, international conflicts over water – rivers, sea or groundwater – are more common in areas of scarcity. The Middle East has only 1 per cent of the world's fresh water, which is shared among 5 per cent of the world's population. There are disputes over the Euphrates and Tigris between Turkey, Syria and Iraq, and over the Jordan between Israel, Lebanon, Jordan and the Palestinian territories. In Africa Mauritania and Senegal fought a war starting in 1989 over grazing rights on the River Senegal, and there are ongoing problems related to the Nile between Egypt, Ethiopia and Sudan. The Aral Sea is the cause of conflict between Kazakhstan, Uzbekistan, Turkmenistan, Tajikistan and Kyrgyzstan.

In 1975 a dispute flared between Syria and Iraq over the building of dams and the filling of upstream reservoirs on the Euphrates. The Iraqis complained that the quantity of water reaching their territory was intolerably low, while the Syrians countered that the river was below half its normal flow. As tensions rose, Syria closed its airspace to Iraqi flights and both nations went as far as transferring troops to their mutual border. Although the confrontation was mediated to a peaceful conclusion by Saudi Arabia, it is an example of how quickly water disputes can escalate. In 1990 the flow of the Euphrates was once again interrupted, this time for a month, as Turkey finished construction of the Atatürk Dam. Syria and Iraq both protested. Fears that Turkey might use water as weapon were to prove prescient when, later in the same year, the Turkish president, Turgut Özal, threatened to restrict water flow to Syria in order to force it to withdraw its support for Kurdish rebels operating in southern Turkey.

On the African continent in 2002 President Festus Mogae of Botswana sent troops to destroy the wells of the Bushmen of the Kalahari Desert. Supposedly, the plan was to force the Bushmen away from their ancestral homes and to assimilate them into the rest of Botswana, but critics believe that the underlying motive was to open up the desert for mining. Against all the odds, a group of Bushmen retreated into the desert and have survived for years with little outside interference, a small victory over both politics and nature.

Not all development disputes are caused by humans. In 2002 reports emerged from a drought-stricken village in north-eastern Kenya that ten villagers had been hurt by monkeys. According to the *Daily Nation*, a Kenyan newspaper, the trouble started shortly after villagers began drawing water from three tankers, when a troop of thirsty monkeys approached them and began throwing stones and biting and clawing at them. The startled villagers fled, leaving the monkeys to drink as much water as they wanted, but returned later with knives and axes to drive the monkeys away, killing eight of them in the process. Reports say that the whole incident took two hours with the monkeys initially standing their ground before eventually retreating. It is a reminder that we are not the only species whose very existence is dependent on our ability to drink.

Syria: Where Water and Politics Mix

Syria is where, some 12,000 years ago, many believe mankind first experimented with agriculture and cattle herding. Between 1900 and 2005 there were six significant droughts in Syria, but five of these lasted for only one season, allowing farming communities to use secondary water resources and to benefit from government support. The most recent drought, the seventh and by far the most devastating, lasted from 2006 to 2010, and it is estimated that more than 1.5 million people were displaced as a consequence. Whole communities of farmers left their homes and took themselves, their families and their few possessions from the north-east of the country, previously the most agriculturally productive region, to the urban centres of the south, already overcrowded and with creaking infrastructures. How much did this contribute to the political crisis that is now overwhelming the country?

The *Bulletin of the Atomic Scientists* has been published continuously since 1945, when it was founded by former Manhattan Project physicists after the atomic bomb attacks on Hiroshima and Nagasaki. Shahrzad Mohtadi is the bulletin's 2011 Leonard M. Rieser Fellow for Research. In August 2012 he produced a paper looking at the interaction between agricultural and water management and social unrest. Looking back on it now, it shows tremendous understanding and foresight. In his paper Mohtadi sets out how the current Syrian president's father guaranteed the Syrian people food security and economic stability, and underpinned his promises with subsidies to bring down the price of food, fuel and water (the wider implications of such policies will be dealt with later). At the same time, ill-thought-out projects like growing cotton – a water-intensive crop – meant that more water than ever was being consumed by agriculture at a time when water management was barely considered at all.

Many analysts, right up to a few days prior to the first protests, predicted that Syria under Bashar al-Assad would remain immune to the Arab Spring. However, with hindsight, we can see that the seeds of unrest were in fact present, and one of the causes was shortage of water. The regime had criminally combined mismanagement and neglect of Syria's natural resources resulting in desertification. One factor was the licensing system for new wells. The majority of irrigation in Syria uses groundwater as its source, since the amount of water available from rivers is insufficient. In 2005 the government began licensing the digging of agricultural wells, but its policy of keeping the Kurds in the north-east of the country economically underdeveloped resulted in licences being denied there. Unsurprisingly, the result was that more than half of the country's wells were illegally dug, and hence unregulated, leading to rapidly depleted groundwater reserves.

In 2009 it was reported that over 800,000 Syrians had lost their livelihoods as a result of the droughts, and in a UN report published a year later it was stated that 'up to 80 per cent of those severely affected live mostly on a diet of bread and sugared tea, which is not enough to cover daily calorific and protein needs for a healthy life'. The results were all too predictable, with hungry and thirsty people establishing temporary settlements on the edges of Damascus, Aleppo, Hama, Homs and Daraa. This worsened an already bad situation created by the arrival of nearly 2,000,000 refugees from outside the country, mainly Iraq and Palestine. In 2008 the American embassy in Damascus sent a message to the State Department quoting the Syria representative of the United Nations Food and Agriculture Organization, Abdulla bin Yehia. What he termed a 'perfect storm', the confluence of drought conditions with other economic and social pressures, bin Yehia believed, could undermine stability in Syria. I'm sure it is little comfort to him to realize how accurate his predictions were. To exactly what extent drought and migration were instrumental in tipping Syria into protest and then civil war is difficult to say, but the conflict is a warning to all governments, of whatever nature, of how humans can react when the taps are turned off.

Trouble at the Roof of the World

We are used to the concept of how few countries in the world control most of its oil and gas, but how many people are aware that only ten countries in the world control 60 per cent of our planet's fresh water? It might also come as a surprise that nowhere exercises more control over a higher proportion of the world's human water drinkers than Tibet, the highest plateau on earth, which stretches 1,500 miles from east to west and 900 miles from north to south. The Tibetan Plateau is a landscape of giant waterfalls, more than a thousand huge lakes and phenomenal glaciers. With more fresh water than anywhere else on the globe, apart from the Arctic and Antarctic, it is the water tower of Asia and the driver of the monsoon. Tibet includes the headwaters of many of Asia's largest rivers, including the Yellow, Yangtze, Mekong, Sutlej and Brahmaputra; it has 1,100 billion cubic feet of surface water resources and 1,000 billion cubic feet of glacial water resources.

Almost half the world's population lives in the basins of the rivers whose sources lie on the Tibetan Plateau, and almost all of the main plant species from the tropics to the frigid zones of the northern hemisphere are present in Tibet. Total forestry reserves exceed 6 billion cubic feet, and there are about 925,000 hectares of pine forest. There are more than 1,000 wild plants used for medicine, 142 species of mammals, 473 species of birds, 49 species of reptiles, 44 species of amphibians, 64 species of fish and more than 2,000 species of insect.

Black bears, leopards, little pandas, Rhesus monkeys, Mongolian gazelles, blue sheep and snow leopards are among the many wild animals who roam here. Tibet is also an enormous and, until recently, untapped source of minerals and energy. There are more than 90 known mineral types in Tibet including lithium, copper, chromite, boron and phosphorus. It produces around 200 million kilowatts of natural hydroelectric energy per year. It also has one of the largest geothermal fields in the world, the Yangbajain near Lhasa, China's largest high-temperature steam geothermal field.

Things at the top of the world, however, are far from the ideal of Shangri-La. According to the environmental group Circle of Blue, deforestation in Tibet has led to large-scale erosion and siltation. Mining, manufacturing and other forms of human activity have resulted in unprecedented levels of land and water pollution. To make matters worse, according to the Intergovernmental Panel on Climate Change, Tibet's glaciers are receding faster than anywhere else in the world. Increased rates of melting and evaporation are causing serious problems inside and outside China. Rajendra K. Pachauri, the 2007 Nobel Peace Prize winner and chair of the Intergovernmental Panel on Climate Change, has said that at least 500 million people in Asia and 250 million people in China itself are at risk from the decline in glacial flows from the Tibetan Plateau.

China is one of the world's most arid countries with more than a quarter of its land classed as desert, so it is little wonder that Tibet's water resources have become an increasingly crucial asset that the Chinese are intent on managing and controlling. While the rest of the world is concerned with the political aspects of the Tibet issue, China retains a clear focus on what it needs most – water. Estimates suggest that around 70 per cent of China's rivers are polluted due to agricultural chemicals and untreated industrial waste, leaving an estimated 300 million Chinese with limited access to clean water. Tibet has had a long and turbulent relationship with its Chinese neighbour. The current conflict began in 1950, when China invaded Tibet with around 40,000 troops. The Dalai Lama fled the country and settled in India, establishing the Tibetan government in exile, which has repeatedly raised the issue of China's management of Tibet's water and warned that China's plans will seriously decrease water supplies to India, Bangladesh, Vietnam, Cambodia, Thailand, Laos and Myanmar. They also claim that the plans would affect the Yangtze River basin as far as Shanghai. In the meantime, they maintain that Tibetans continue to suffer high rates of hepatitis and waterborne infections.

If fears about what China will do with the waters of the ten major river systems that originate in Tibet have been steadily rising, they were greatly exacerbated by the publication in 2005 of *Tibet's Water Will Save China*, by Li Ling, a former officer of the Chinese People's Liberation Army. This publication, which advocated among other things the diversion of the Brahmaputra to northern China, resulted in considerable anxiety in Delhi and other Asian capitals. The Chinese authorities have also talked about building dams to generate hydroelectric power and spending eye-watering sums of money on a series of canals to take water from Himalayan snow melt and glaciers hundreds of miles north-east to Chinese farms and industry. Increasingly, these issues, as well as the mining of minerals precariously close to riverbanks and the consequent potential pollution of water supplies to the rest of Asia, make Tibet a growing source of tension in east Asia. The rest of the world's indifference to the plight of its people since 1950 and the unwillingness of trade partners to raise the issue of Tibet with China will need to be re-examined given the possibility that China will turn off the Tibetan tap to the rest of Asia in order to relieve its own water problems. Brahma Chellaney, professor of strategic studies at the New Delhi-based Centre for Policy Research, says,

The Tibet issue has been presented more often than not in the international literature in political or cultural terms, with the Chinese government and ethnic Tibetans supposed to be the principal players. But the Tibet issue is much larger and more fundamental: it is about Asia's water and climate security and its ecological interests. It is also about vital resources. Fundamentally, it is about securing Asia's future.

Before we are too condemnatory of China, however, it is worth trying to understand the deeply unpleasant predicament that the Chinese people and their leaders face when it comes to water. In 2005 I attended a private meeting with President Hu Jintao and his advisers in London. Often these meetings are very formulaic, with standard answers given to predictable questions in a pretty dry encounter – not exactly a laugh a minute. At the end of this particular meeting I was asked if there were any other questions I would like to raise, so I asked the president what he was more afraid of – the nuclear ambitions of his neighbours (North Korea) or drought. There was an instant and animated response from both the president and his staff, who burst out laughing and said, 'Why, a drought of course.' It was a very revealing reaction and one which has always stuck in my mind. I very much admired President Hu's grasp of detail during the meeting and his down-to-earth descriptions of his country's problems. In essence he said that China was simply a very large developing nation, which had all the problems of other developing nations, only writ large, with the West being mesmerized and obsessed with the size of the numbers. It was very clear that he ranked the shortage of water as among his biggest political headaches.

China's water shortages and its problems of pollution are the result of a growing population with a rapidly developing economy and historically lax environmental oversight. While China has seven per cent of the world's freshwater reserves, it is also home to 20 per cent of the world's population – in other words, four times the population of United States but only a fifth of its water. China's current water management system evolved under Chairman Mao in the 1960s, when a series of disastrous floods resulted in the construction of a range of dams, reservoirs and spillways. Although this infrastructure was successful in its primary purpose – helping to prevent floods – it created enormous ecological imbalances by restricting the rivers that had flowed into the North China Plain. As lakes and rivers began to dry up, farmers depleted well supplies. This was exacerbated by the massive rise in the Chinese population, with the OECD estimating that China's use of water has increased more than fivefold since 1950. One of the drivers of this increase has been the Chinese Communist Party, which aimed to make China grain self-sufficient. The result has been that areas have continued to grow crops that are highly water-intensive rather than focusing on types of agriculture better suited to their particular environment. In 2004 the World Bank warned that scarcity of water would lead to conflict between rural interests, urban interests and industrial interests – at the moment 65 per cent of China's water is used in agriculture, 23 per cent by industry and 12 per cent by domestic households.

For most of the 1990s northern China's major river, the Yellow River, failed even to reach the sea, and water tables around Beijing and other cities of the north have fallen so low that some wells are over 600 feet deep. Chinese environmental activist Ma Jun claims that 400 out of 600 cities in China are now facing some sort of water shortage, including 30 out of the 32 largest conurbations. Even worse, there is a huge mismatch within the country between the population and water supplies, with about 80 per cent of all water resources in the south of the country, beyond the Yangtze. As a result of the over-extraction of groundwater and falling water tables, more than 37,000 square miles of land have sunk in the north of the country with more than fifty cities suffering from serious subsidence, problems on a scale difficult for most of us to imagine.

The mismatch between the north and the south threatened to cause a major embarrassment for China during the 2008 summer Olympic Games, and the authorities reacted by diverting water from Shanxi and Hebei provinces, areas already suffering from drought, to Beijing. In the area around Baoding city alone around 31,000 residents lost their land and homes due to the water transfer. In recent years the Chinese have thrown money at the problem. According to a 2007 World Bank report, there was major financial investment in Chinese water infrastructure between 1990 and 2005. One piece of good news is that the continued increase in the consumption of water by the growing population has been counterbalanced by a decrease in the water used by industry, stabilizsing water usage levels overall. However water is used extremely inefficiently by Chinese industry, which requires three to ten times more water than factories in developed nations to produce equivalent goods.

The problems have been made worse by constant and worsening pollution. In the spring of 2013 the Chinese authorities were acutely embarrassed and the public outraged when more than 12,000 dumped pig carcasses were washed ashore in Shanghai and Jiaxing in full view of thousands of international tourists and the world's business community. This was by no means an isolated incident, and deterioration in the quality of drinking water remains a significant problem in China and a major source of public discontent. While emissions from factories are the biggest threat to water quality, badly treated sewage, industrial accidents and the widespread use of agricultural fertilizers and pesticides have all contributed to the problem.

According to Elizabeth C. Economy, senior fellow and director for Asia studies at the US-based think tank Council on Foreign Relations,

20 per cent of China's rivers are so polluted that their water is rated too toxic for human contact. Part of the explanation, she says, may be the proliferation of up to 10,000 petrochemical plants along the Yangtze River and 4,000 along the Yellow River. The cost in terms of human life is around 60,000 premature deaths annually, with many Chinese not knowing whether their water is safe to drink. Economy quotes a report by *Century Weekly* which gives a number of reasons for unreliable assessment of the country's water quality. The first is that the frequency of testing at water treatment plants is simply too low, with only 40 per cent of the plants in China's thirty-five major cities having the capacity to test for all the necessary indicators. The second is that there are too few independent monitoring bureaus, with most water testing being done in-house. There is also little transparency by local authorities about the results of the tests, and in any case testing at plants cannot pick up contamination from the dilapidated and degraded pipes through which the water is transmitted to China's households.

The fall in the level of water tables also brings its own danger. As wells are drilled deeper and deeper they can tap into arsenic-rich aquifers. Arsenic poisoning, first seen in China in the 1950s, is on the increase, with more than 30,000 cases already reported and around 25 million people exposed to dangerously high levels of arsenic in their drinking water.

Two main policy tools have been utilized by the Chinese government in an attempt to deal with the massive water imbalance. The first is to attempt to transfer water, on an almost unimaginable scale, from the south of China to the north. Initially considered under Chairman Mao, the South to North Water Transfer Project was finally approved in 2002. It plans to move more than 12 trillion gallons every year from the Yangtze basin to the north of the country, where it is needed more. This may be less of a benefit to northerners than they imagine as around 40 per cent of China's waste water is dumped into the Yangtze, often untreated. In any case, the project, which is likely to cost up to $100 billion (and outside estimates are substantially higher), will not be completed until around 2050 – more than two decades after the forecast peak in the Chinese population, which is likely to coincide with maximum water demand. The issues around Tibetan water go further than plans, which may or may not exist, to divert rivers originating on the plateau to China. Diversion of the Mekong River, on which China is building at least three more dams (two already exist), is causing tension with Vietnam, Laos, Cambodia and Thailand. Diversion of the Brahmaputra would stoke the already fractious relationships with India and Bangladesh.

China's other main attempt at a solution has been to build dams. The country is currently the home of half of all the dams in the world, with the largest, the Three Gorges, unveiled in 2008, the biggest hydroelectric power structure in the world and able to generate over ten times the power of the Hoover Dam, around the same amount as fifty nuclear reactors. Ecologists argue that it has had disastrous environmental and social effects including a series of deadly landslides and the displacement of around 1.5 million people. These costs are likely to rise, as the announcement by the Chinese government, under international pressure, that it intends to cut its carbon emissions by 17 per cent by 2015 will require it to add 120 gigawatts of conventional hydroelectric power by that date – the equivalent of building one Three Gorges Dam each year for five years. So while one environmental target will be reached, a whole new range of issues are being created. Whether this represents progress is debatable.

So what does the future hold? According to the most recent US National Intelligence Council (NIC) report, climate change alongside China's move towards greater organization and more middle-class lifestyles will increase water demand and thereby create crop shortages by 2030. As the report says, 'Water may become a more significant source of contention than energy or minerals.' This will occur against a global backdrop in which demand for food is estimated to increase by more than 35 per cent by 2030, which in turn means that the world will need more water, since agricultural and livestock use accounts for 70 per cent of our water consumption. China may be particularly vulnerable in this regard as it is a major wheat producer and the second-largest grower and consumer of corn after the United States but with considerably less water than North America. By 2030, the NIC report goes on, China may no longer be self-sufficient in these crops and could be forced to increase its imports, triggering significant price rises on international markets, with all the consequences that these would have for developing nations. Three technologies need to be developed: genetically modified crops that are drought resistant and require smaller amounts of fertilizer; precision agriculture robotics to reduce the amount of water, fertilizer and seed required; and high-tech micro-irrigation systems to boost yields and stop waste, which currently accounts for around 60 per cent of the water used in agriculture.

Scott Moore, research fellow in sustainability science at the Harvard Belfer Center for Science and International Affairs, argues that Beijing cannot keep increasing its water supplies indefinitely, whatever technologies the Chinese employ. Already those regions of the south earmarked to lose water to the north are facing shortages themselves. 'Ultimately,' he argues, 'China needs significant political reform to meet the challenge of water scarcity. In order to make difficult decisions about who gets how much water, the country needs robust, transparent and participatory decision-making mechanisms. Moreover, in order to make policy ideas like water-rights reform work, the legal system and the rule of law must be strengthened.'

The Glorious Nile

Of all the world's rivers, probably none has been so influential in human development than the Nile. The cradle of Egyptian civilization, it played a pivotal role in the development of agriculture and architecture, and its history and culture continue to fascinate. Having played a prominent role in the struggle between the Israelites and the Egyptians, it is unsurprising to find a number of references to the Nile in the Bible. Typical of these is Isaiah 19:5–8.

> and the waters of the sea will be dried up, and the river will be dry and parched, and its canals will become vile, and the branches of Egypt's Nile will diminish and dry up, reeds and rushes will rot away. There will be bare places by the Nile, on the brink of the Nile, and all that is sown by the Nile will be parched, will be driven away and will be no more. The fishermen will mourn and lament, all who cast a hook on the Nile; and they will languish who spread nets on the water.

The Nile is the world's longest river, flowing over 4,100 miles and through eleven countries in north-east Africa – Tanzania, Uganda, Rwanda, Burundi, the Democratic Republic of the Congo, Kenya, Ethiopia, Eritrea, South Sudan, Sudan and Egypt. The river has two main tributaries, the longer White Nile and the Blue Nile. The White Nile rises in the Great Lakes region of central Africa while the Blue Nile begins at Lake Tana in Ethiopia. They meet near the city of Khartoum, and the combined river eventually empties into the Mediterranean, forming a large delta. Some 90 per cent of the water and 96 per cent of the sediment carried by the Nile originates in Ethiopia, with 59 per cent of the water coming from the Blue Nile. While the flow of the White Nile is more stable and predictable, the Blue Nile varies considerably over its annual cycle with almost fifty times the flow during the wet season as during the dry period.

The drainage basin of the Nile covers around 10 per cent of Africa and contains around 160 million people; almost 300 million live in the eleven countries sharing the waters of the Nile. With the population of the basin expected to double within the next quarter-century, the demand for water from agriculture, industry and domestic households will rise enormously. This comes in a region which already has problems with water scarcity. A recent world water development report ranked 180 countries for water availability per person per year. Uganda came 115th, Egypt 129th, Ethiopia 137th, Kenya 154th and Sudan 156th.

As North Africa became desertified between 6000 and 4000 BC, those fleeing the expanding deserts joined those who had already built settlements along the Nile and together they created a critical mass of population which enabled the development of a new culture with sufficient labour for agriculture and building. By 3100 BC the Nile Valley and Delta had coalesced into a single entity which we now recognize as the world's first large nation state.

This budding civilization lived on a strip of land along the Nile, never wider than sixteen miles and often much narrower. The population owed their existence and prosperity not only to the life-giving waters of the Nile itself but, the silt it carried from the high Ethiopian Plateau, which was deposited along the slower-flowing lower course of the river in annual inundations. This fertilized the earth, turning it black and enabling it to retain moisture. Over time the area of cultivable land increased, development continued and the population continue to grow as the annually predictable replenishment of the soil created political stability and the conditions for cultural advancement. During the pharaonic period the fauna and flora along the river were much more varied than they are today but, in common with the rest of the world, the growing human population saw the natural habitats of hippos and crocodiles, lions and ostriches gradually destroyed.

The river itself became a major economic lifeline with goods being traded along its length. Nature provided a helping hand since the winter winds blow south, upriver, so boats could sail against the flow of the river and then return with the current. The ease of boat travel on the Nile was a socially unifying force and contributed to political stability, although the Nile's flow is disturbed at several points by cataracts, small islands and rocks separated by shallow or rapidly flowing water, which form an obstacle to navigation. These points often became areas of settlement where goods were stored or traded and where slipways were created to enable boats to be dragged overland. The Greek historian Herodotus described Egypt as 'the gift of the Nile'. It is equally true that plentiful grain was the gift of Egypt. In a region historically plagued by famine, Egypt's ability to export wheat was central to the trading system, the alleviation of hunger and Egypt's economic and diplomatic strength.

For thousands of years, the level of the Nile began to rise in southern Egypt in early July, reaching flood stage around Aswan by mid-August. From there the flood steadily moved northwards, reaching Cairo around six weeks later. The waters started to recede in the south in early October and within two months most of the valley was dry, enabling farmers to plant their seeds in naturally fertilized, well-watered fields. By the time they harvested their crops, in mid-April to early May, the river's flow was sustained only by the more constant White Nile, and subsequently much diminished. The inundation was relatively reliable, although high floods at times caused great destruction and occasionally brought famine and disease. The main crops grown were cereals, including emmer wheat for beer, and flax, which was used to produce fine linen cloth and rope. Much of the success of Egyptian agriculture was due to basin irrigation, a system of earthen banks enclosing basins, into which flood waters were directed by a network of sluices. This enabled water to be retained until the soil was saturated, when it was drained off into another basin or a canal. The swamp plant papyrus, whose roots are edible, was used to make anything from boats to the classic Egyptian writing material. The river in addition produced the main protein source for the population in the form of fish.

The Egyptians understood well the link between the flood level of the Nile and the season's agricultural potential and they developed a system for measuring the height of the Nile in different parts of the country. In conjunction with meticulously kept records, this enabled them to compare daily river level readings with those of the past and to predict with great accuracy the levels that would be reached in the coming year. In *Antony and Cleopatra*, Antony tells Octavius Caesar,

> Thus do they, sir: they take
> the flow o' the Nile
> By certain scales i' the pyramid; they know,
> By the height, the lowness, or the mean, if dearth
> Or foison follow: the higher Nilus swells,
> The more it promises: as it ebbs, the seedsman
> Upon the slime and ooze scatters his grain,
> And shortly comes to harvest.

Given the dependence of Egypt on the Nile, it is perhaps surprising that Egyptian texts say little about irrigation and the provision of water, and while in tombs there are many representations of agriculture and animal husbandry, the Nile itself is largely absent, being represented only with depictions of large ships used in trading expeditions.

While the pharaohs controlled the nation's agricultural resources through ownership of the land, taxation and compulsory labour, they were also responsible for the administrative measures through which it was cultivated and the storage of surpluses against any annual failure. Egypt was known as the 'breadbasket of Rome' both prior to and during its domination by the Latin empire, but many historians regard this as hyperbole. However, the grain needed by the city was certainly not supplied by the surrounding countryside, which tended to produce only fruits and vegetables for the urban aristocracy, and it became dependent on supplies from other parts of Italy and from further afield, notably Sicily, North Africa and Egypt. A number of scholars have tried to assess the total amount of grain that Rome imported from North Africa, and there is some consensus that around 300,000 tons were probably imported annually, with two thirds coming from other parts of North Africa and one third from Egypt. Nonetheless, this is a very significant proportion and meant that whoever controlled Egypt had, at the very least, considerable influence in Rome.

The great civilization of the Nile Valley has existed for over 5,000 years largely due to the sustainability of Egyptian agriculture. Only in recent years with the phenomenal increase in Egypt's population – from three million in the early 1800s to almost eighty-three million today – has the country dispensed with the Nile's time-tested natural annual flow rhythms in favour of new methods of flood management and irrigation. The annual inundation, the life-giving relationship between the Nile and the people of Egypt, ended in 1970 with the building of the Aswan Dam.

Much of the tension around the issue of the Nile relates to two agreements signed during the mid-twentieth century – the 1929 Nile Water Agreement and the 1959 Agreement for the Full Utilization of the Nile – which gave Egypt and Sudan the lion's share of the water. In 1929 Britain was seeking to create a secure, stable and prosperous

Egypt as part of its empire, and Nile water was seen as a fundamental part of that process. By the terms of the agreement, Egypt was given 157 billion cubic feet annually and Sudan 13 billion cubic feet. The 1959 agreement between Egypt and Sudan allocated 182 billion cubic feet to Egypt (three quarters) and 60 billion cubic feet to Sudan (one quarter). Unsurprisingly, especially in recent years, the upstream countries, especially Tanzania, Uganda and Kenya, have argued that the treaties have worked against their interests and given them too little control over the waters of the Nile.

In 1998 discussions began to create a better regional framework for managing the river, and in November 2002 the Secretariat for the Nile Basin Initiative was established in Entebbe, Uganda, with funding from the World Bank. Most of the countries in the region share similar problems – poverty, high population growth, environmental degradation and political instability – and the NBI is intended to help deal with these by devising schemes to harness the basin's water for irrigation and provide power for all countries involved. It may not yet work perfectly, but at least there is now a framework with the potential to defuse potential conflicts at an early stage. This might face a major challenge soon. Recent political changes in Egypt have exacerbated tensions in the region, especially between Egypt and Ethiopia. A suggestion of obstinacy in the new Egyptian regime has raised suspicions among many Ethiopians, who remember decades of intransigence under Mubarak and wonder whether Egypt is still committed to a fair deal on water. In November 2012 relations were further strained by the publication by WikiLeaks of documents claiming that Egypt and Sudan had considered plans to attack the massive Grand Ethiopian Renaissance Dam project in order to protect their water supply.

The challenge for the future is ensuring a fair share of the Nile's waters for everyone. While it is perfectly reasonable to use its powers for electricity generation, we must ensure that Cairo gets its water too. Eighty-three million people can get very thirsty.

India and Watering the Neighbourhood

Over 1.3 billion people live on the Indian (south Asian) subcontinent, over a billion in India alone. The sheer scale and rate of growth of this population has unavoidably brought it into conflict with nature, and has resulted in increased desertification, a dramatic decrease in wildlife, soil erosion and widespread pollution by developing industries and densely populated urban centres. Environmental issues have become critical.

The mighty rivers of the Indus, the Ganges and the Brahmaputra originate high in the Himalayas before flowing down onto the Indian plains and then either east to the Bay of Bengal or west to the Arabian Sea. These rivers have been the focus of international security and environmental issues. Up to now the dispute in the east, between India and Bangladesh, has been the more tense and aggressive, although India's military dominance over Bangladesh means the risk of contagion is limited. In the west, even if the disputes between India and Pakistan have been better managed by treaty, the fact that both are nuclear powers raises the stakes, were tensions over water ever to escalate into military action.

The dispute over the Ganges River as it flows east through India and into Bangladesh and then the Bay of Bengal has had a higher environmental impact than the Indus River dispute with Pakistan. The decrease in the flow of the Ganges through Bangladesh has disrupted fishing and navigation and resulted in the contamination of rich farmland with salt deposits, severely damaging agricultural production, changing the characteristics of the river and bringing about catastrophic changes in the ecology of the Ganges Delta.

If the Nile can claim to be the river that has had the greatest influence on history and culture, then the Ganges has a strong claim to today's title of the river that plays the greatest social and cultural role in the lives of the largest number of people. The Ganges emerges spectacularly from an ice cave under the Gangotri Glacier – which is receding rapidly like many of the other glaciers in the Himalayas – and along its course provides water and drainage for over 350 million people. By the time it leaves Kanpur, a sprawling industrial city 300 miles south-east of Delhi, the level of human, animal and industrial waste in the Ganges is so great that it threatens the survival of the increasingly rare species of fish, dolphins and turtles that live in the river. Although an ambitious plan was devised by the Indian government back in 1986 to clean up the river, little has been achieved other than the containment of pollution, with no real reduction taking place. According to campaigners, over $600 million has been spent on useless technology including sewage plants which require constant power supplies when none are available. The river, according to Shiv Kant of the BBC's Hindi service, is 'a meeting point for both the rich and poor, who believe it is a divine route to heaven'. This belief may be sabotaging the river at its very origins. Although scientists calculate that global warming is at least partly responsible for the recession of the Gangotri Glacier, the huge increase in the number of huts and tents occupied by the ever rising tide of pilgrims, who increase the temperature on the glacier by burning fossil fuels, may be contributing to its own demise.

The Ganges forms the boundary between India and Bangladesh for 80 miles and flows for a further 70 miles within Bangladesh. Before leaving India, the Ganges splits off a distributary called the Hooghly, which flows south to Calcutta, continues into Bangladesh, where it is known as the Padma, and spreads out to flow through the

350-kilometre-wide Ganges Delta and empty into the Bay of Bengal. Four fifths of Bangladesh is straddled by this delta, and as half of the country's GDP is based on agriculture its economy is highly sensitive to changes in its ecosystems. The topography of Bangladesh makes it very vulnerable to typhoons and monsoons, which produce mass casualties on a seemingly annual basis, and during the dry season river levels may fall disastrously, affecting both agriculture and fisheries.

One of the main disputes between India and Bangladesh arose as a result of the construction of the Farakka Barrage in India. This was built to divert Ganges water into the Hooghly during the dry season, from January to June, in order to increase its flow and so flush out the accumulations of silt which had become a problem for the port of Calcutta, which lies on the river. The conception of the Farakka Barrage dates back to when Bangladesh was still part of Pakistan, and the project was caught up in the convulsions that surrounded its independence. After alternating periods of freeze and thaw between India and Bangladesh, a treaty was eventually signed in 1996, which has survived even nationalist Bangladeshi governments. Tension continues, however, between those sections of Indian society who maintain that Bangladesh does not deserve to receive any water at all and those in Bangladesh who do not believe that India should draw any water off at Farakka. In time the dispute may be resolved by the intervention of nature, as the Ganges is gradually shifting eastwards, and before long the Hooghly will no longer be able to support a deep-water harbour in Calcutta.

Even with the diminution of tension with India, Bangladesh's problems remain considerable. As a result of the reduced water flow the salt front has travelled upstream by almost 200 miles and salinity in surface water has increased almost sixty- fold. The reduced flow has also produced a shortened growing season and resulted in the depletion of groundwater tables. With the river's reduced ability to flush out weeds, insecticides and other pollutants, fish and prawn stocks, the staple diet of Bangladeshis, have been dramatically reduced.

All of this has had a huge impact on the GDP of Bangladesh, and the result has been large-scale emigration, with over two million Bangladeshis moving to neighbouring regions of India since the 1970s. Not only has this led to ethnic conflict in Indian states such as Assam and West Bengal (with over 4,000 people killed in clashes in the 1980s), but there is a growing pattern of movement to centres like Delhi and Bombay, where conditions for migrants are extremely poor and clashes with native residents likely to increase. This is another graphic reminder of how imbalances in both the global economy and the environment are likely to lead to mass migration and potentially serious social consequences.

The dispute on the other side of the subcontinent, between India and Pakistan, has been less tense than that over the Ganges but nonetheless has many common roots. The Indus has a flow volume twice that of the Nile and travels some 1,800 miles from its origins high on the Tibetan Plateau to the Arabian Sea, while its basin has a long history as a vibrant and agriculturally productive area dating back 4,000 years. During the Raj Britain actively encouraged agriculture in the Punjab (meaning 'land of five rivers') as a way of keeping busy the many Sikhs who had resisted British authority. In a remarkable feat of engineering, the British military created an extensive irrigation system, diverting the main tributaries of the Indus into a series of interlocking canals to make the Punjab the breadbasket of the region.

When Partition came in 1947, India and Pakistan signed an agreement to maintain water supplies at pre-independence levels, but the disputes which quickly arose saw India cut off water from canals flowing to Pakistan in 1948. After years of tension between the neighbours, the Indus Waters Treaty was signed in 1960, by which the quantity of water available from the Indus would be increased by engineering works paid for by the World Bank, and the six primary rivers of the Indus basin would be split evenly between India and Pakistan. Interestingly, and many would say amazingly, the treaty is still in effect today, notwithstanding the many conflicts that have occurred in the interim between the two countries. Of course the treaty was signed and initially implemented before the massive rises in population which have been a feature of recent decades; however, it remains a victory for pragmatism over religious and ethnic extremism. It is a small beacon of hope, indicating that calm and constructive leadership can defuse even the most delicate and tricky of problems.

The most recent source of friction has been India's plan to build dams for hydroelectric power on the rivers of the Indus system. This has been used in Pakistan as a means of diverting attention away from the fact that its water management policy is haphazard, its agricultural practices unproductive and its water distribution and storage facilities outdated, dilapidated and collapsing. Although such dams would give India strategic leverage over Pakistan, we should note that it has never abused its water in this way. Nonetheless, extremist groups in Pakistan have been quick to jump on the bandwagon, with leaders of groups such as Jamaat-ud-Dawa (which many see as a front organization for Lashkar-e-Taiba, the perpetrators of the Mumbai terror attacks) threatening, 'if water doesn't flow into these rivers, then blood will'. Even at an official level, Pakistan's foreign minister, Shah Mehmood Qureshi, has said, 'Water I see emerging as a very serious source of tension between Pakistan and India.'

Although dismissed as Pakistani paranoia by Delhi, such remarks are worrying when the situation facing Pakistan's policymakers is more fully considered. Somewhere between forty and fifty-five million Pakistanis do not have access to safe water, which has resulted in high rates of infant mortality because of contamination and low agricultural output. Estimates suggest that more than three million Pakistanis become infected with waterborne diseases each year. Industrial pollution is a major threat in Pakistan. Water flowing through the city of Karachi, for example, contains high levels of lead, chromium and cyanide, and more metals have been found in Karachi's harbour than in any other major world port. In a 2007–8 survey of drinking water in Karachi 86 per cent of samples had levels of lead higher than the WHO recommended maximum.

What is particularly galling for many Pakistanis is that large quantities of water have been diverted upstream in Punjab to satisfy a growing middle-class desire for agricultural goods and, even worse, Pakistan has allowed agribusiness companies to develop large areas in order to produce food for Gulf states by tapping ever deeper into Pakistan's already diminishing aquifers. While this provides valuable export income, it also worsens the plight of many of Pakistan's own poor.

Is there anything that can be done through politics, diplomacy or technology to alleviate the plight of poor people worldwide who simply want access to clean water and sanitation? Efficiency is a useful starting point. If irrigation waste could be cut by a factor of 10 per cent, another two million hectares of crop land could be irrigated. This could be done by such simple measures as ensuring that fields are flat so that some parts are not saturated while others are dry. International aid agencies could also put more pressure on recipient governments to ensure that water is a priority and that spending goes into essential infrastructure rather than on more politically prestigious projects.

Across the globe, and in some unexpected places, water continues to rise up political, economic and environmental agendas. More than half Europe's major cities are exploiting groundwater at unsustainable rates. Ever since the 1960s I have spent part of the summer with family and friends in north-east Spain, in Catalonia. In the picturesque fishing villages surrounded by hillsides covered in pine trees it is hard to imagine that the authorities are currently pressing for a pipeline to be created to divert water from the Rhône in France to Barcelona because of worsening water shortages. On the other side of the world the Australian experiment to divert the Snowy River for inland irrigation is not only threatening to deprive Adelaide of fresh water, but the water table under the land it feeds is now rising, pushing salt towards the surface and destroying some of the country's best and most productive farmland in the Murray–Darling basin.

In west Africa half of Nigerians have no access to clean water despite the enormous oil wealth that the country has produced. Neighbouring countries such as Ghana and Mali are totally dependent on hydroelectric power, and when water levels fall will find their economies seriously affected. In southern Africa the countries of the Zambezi River basin experienced the worst floods in living memory in early 2010 when heavy rains were exacerbated by Zimbabwe opening the Kariba Dam gates. In a region where neighbouring countries compete to harness the power of water to generate electricity, lack of coordinated water management has shown itself to be a major cause of human misery.

International law to deal with such disputes continues to develop although its enforcement is weak. The equitable utilization of river resources, the prevention of significant harm to other states, the obligation to notify and inform on future actions relating to rivers, the sharing of data, the cooperative management of international rivers and an obligation to resolve disputes peacefully are principles which all need to be fortified. Politically, governments need to see the benefits that greater cooperation will bring, including the alleviation of economically expensive and socially divisive migration and improved energy production. Data sharing is an area of particular promise. Remote sensing satellites able to better determine groundwater prospects can improve supply in many of the worst affected areas. In an age when science and technology are able to bring so many answers to the problems that we face, our desire – indeed our duty – to improve the quality of the most basic element in human life should be at the forefront of our endeavours.

Water – or its lack – is not the only commodity likely to produce conflict in the future. Competition for finite resources with an ever expanding global population is likely to fuel tensions in many different ways and in many different places. The outcomes can be dramatic and swift.

The Arab Spring: Prelude to the Global Spring?

On 17 December 2010 a twenty-six-year-old man named Muhammad Bouazizi set fire to himself in the small rural town of Sidi Bouzid in Tunisia. His death was to spark profound and widespread political changes across the Middle East and North Africa, overthrowing dictators and bringing new uncertainties to an already febrile part of the world.

How did one man's protest spark a regional revolution; what were the predisposing factors, and what are the likely consequences?

Bouazizi – known locally as Basboosa – worked as a street trader to support his mother, younger siblings and uncle. It is estimated that he earned around $140 per month selling fruit and vegetables to his fellow villagers. Life was tough: he had to buy goods on credit one day to sell them the next. Accordingly, he did not have money to bribe the local police and officials, who regularly harassed him. On 17 December he started working at around 8 a.m. and around two and a half hours later the police confiscated his electronic weighing scales and overturned his cart, ostensibly because he did not have a permit to sell his fruit and vegetables. This incident was too much for him to bear, and he angrily attempted to see the governor to complain. When the official refused to see him, he acquired a container of gasoline from a nearby outlet, stood in the middle of the traffic outside the governor's office and shouted, 'How do you expect me to make a living?' Seconds later, he was on fire. It was less than an hour after his clash with the police, and the pent-up anger that ignited in the region, no less than the gasoline with which he doused himself, caused shock waves across the world.

In Tunisia itself President Zine El Abidine Ben Ali was ousted after twenty-three years in office; the ruling party was dissolved and its assets liquidated. Political prisoners were released and elections to a new constituent assembly took place on 23 October 2011. In Yemen President Ali Abdullah Saleh was overthrown, although granted immunity from prosecution. Within a year a new president had been elected and inaugurated. In Libya the government was overthrown in August 2011 following a widespread civil revolt backed by UN-mandated military intervention. Colonel Gaddafi, who had gone into hiding, was eventually shot and killed by rebel forces. The greatest upheaval occurred in Egypt, where protests centred on Cairo's Tahrir Square. After almost three weeks of disturbances President Hosni Mubarak dismissed his government and appointed a new cabinet. However, Mubarak was forced from office and subsequently sentenced to life in prison for ordering the killing of protesters. In other parts of the region there were major protests in Algeria, Jordan, Kuwait, Morocco and Sudan with continuing civil clashes in Bahrain. The unrest in Syria developed into civil war. Smaller protests also occurred in Oman, Mauritania and Western Sahara.

What is clear is that the region will not be the same again; what is not clear is what the picture will look like when the pieces of the jigsaw eventually settle.

These events, which have come to be known as the Arab Spring, were welcomed by leaders in the West as a new dawn and an expression of pent-up desire for pluralistic liberal democracy. This interpretation is only to be expected from those who already enjoy such systems, but it may be much closer to hope than real expectation. I believe we have been too quick to describe the motivations for these changes to values that we take for granted in Western political discourse. It is much more likely that we have witnessed a commodity revolution than a value-inspired political one, although that is not to say that one cannot metamorphose into the other over time. We should, however, beware that we do not set our expectations too high or expect events to move too rapidly, or we may make political and economic miscalculations which might tip the scales in the wrong direction.

A number of theories have been set forward to account for the Arab Spring. Many experts in the field see the trigger as being a backfiring of the food subsidies which had been used as a political tool by repressive regimes for many years. When food prices rocketed in 2008, and then again in 2010, the cost of subsidies became unsustainable – by 2010 the Egyptian government's bread subsidy bill alone was more than $3 billion a year. Not only was this highly inefficient and wasteful but it was a recipe for corruption, with bakers reselling subsidized bread and flour onto the black market, where prices could be five times or more the subsidized rate. The flaw in the democratic revolution theory is that the populations of these countries were willing to tolerate the regimes under which they lived as long as their basic commodity prices were controlled. Nothing is more likely to push a man onto the streets than the inability to put food and water on his family's table. There are many, including myself, who believe that widespread unrest does not arise from long-term failings in a political system but from its perceived failure to provide essential security to the population. In other words, in the case of the Arab Spring a certain threshold was crossed when the deal to sacrifice political liberty for affordable commodities fell apart and the whole system rapidly disintegrated.

An additional consideration is how much past Western policy towards the region may have contributed to the building tension in the Middle East. Stephens argues that the United States supported the 'democracies of bread' by supplying cheap wheat to its allies during the Cold War, including Mubarak of Egypt and Saddam Hussein in Iraq. When food prices spiked, governments in the region responded in the only way they knew how – by raising wages and raising subsidies, both of which rapidly became unsustainable. Egypt, Yemen and Jordan all raised food subsidies, while Algeria, Morocco and Tunisia lifted customs duties and import tariffs on food.

So, what is driving up commodity prices in the first place and what can be done to stop this inexorable rise before the Arab Spring turns into the Asian Spring, the African Spring or, indeed, the Global Spring? One of the factors appears to be the appetite of the world's growing middle classes for a higher-animal-protein Westernized diet. This has a very direct link with the price of animal feed and thereby the price of grain on world markets. It takes around 4.5 pounds of feed to produce a pound of edible chicken meat, 7.3 pounds of feed to produce one pound of edible pork and a staggering 20 pounds of feed to produce a single pound of beef. Burger culture looks hugely expensive in global environmental terms. Another driver of global food price rises may well be the growing of crops for conversion to ethanol, which at a time when global cereal production is at an all-time high results in less food being available for the world's population and consequently higher prices. A third factor may be increased financial speculation on commodity prices in recent years, with journalists like Frederick Kaufman pointing the finger at banks such as Goldman Sachs for setting up an index fund pegged to commodity futures, including corn and several varieties of wheat. Kaufman suggests that the model proved so successful and appealing to investors that commodity index holdings soared from $13 billion in 2003 to a massive $317 billion in 2008. Just how much this accounted for the food price spike in 2008 is hotly debated, but it is an issue that policymakers need to examine urgently and in great detail.

The final suspect in the line-up to find the cause of the sharp rise in commodity prices is the response of Western governments, primarily the United States, to the economic slowdown following the bank crisis of 2008. Quantitative easing, the purchase by central banks of their own governments' debts, has been blamed for driving money into the global economy which has manifested itself as commodity price inflation. Andrew Lilico, director and principal of London-based consultancy Europe Economics and one of the most interesting commentators in the United Kingdom today, believes that there is a correlation between the price of food and the US QE programme, particularly its second phase. He says, 'We see how the food price index broadly stabilized through late 2009 and early 2010, then rose again from mid-2010 as quantitative easing was restarted with prices rising about 40 per cent over an eight-month period.' Naturally this connection is hotly rejected by US policymakers, but Lilico argues that the effect is exactly as theory would predict. He maintains that excessive easing by the Federal Reserve solidified expectations in economies pegged to the dollar that monetary policies would have to remain exceptionally loose, driving inflationary booms in those countries reflected in rising commodity prices.

My own instincts tend to lie with those who believe that it is not possible to push ever increasing amounts of money into the global financial system without it being manifested somewhere. Initial QE measures may have been a suitable offset for the deleveraging that individual households in Britain and America have undertaken in recent years as they have paid down their personal debts (something that governments could learn from), but to continuously pump money into an economy is to beg for inflation, which, let's be frank, has been the immoral way in which financially incontinent governments in the West have reduced the value of their debts in recent years, irrespective of the impact on their own domestic savers or the struggling global economy.

So what are the risks ahead? As the global population heads beyond seven billion, as competition for natural resources hots up – not least for water supplies – as scarce crops are turned into biofuel and prices of basic commodities rise, governments are becoming increasingly concerned about their own commodity security and their ability to prevent the sort of social and political upheavals manifested in the Arab Spring.

One factor driving this concern is what is known as entity concentration risk – the dependence on only a few companies or countries for sourcing. Not all countries have responded at the same rate to this phenomenon. While China has been acquiring mines and farmland abroad in order to ensure its access to commodities, India does not seem to have followed any structured approach to this issue. When the surge in commodity prices for items such as rice, wheat and soya beans occurred in 2008, the state-owned China Investment Corporation (CIC) made an $856 million investment in Noble Group – a Hong-Kong-based international commodities trading company – sending out a clear signal about Beijing's intention to secure agricultural commodity supplies. The policy of ensuring commodity supplies by the purchase of assets has increasingly been underpinned by what is known colloquially as land grab. This practice, by which wealthy states acquire land in poorer countries and grow commodities for their own use rather than that of the native population, might reasonably be described as food colonialism. An academic study published in 2013 showed that somewhere between 0.7 and 1.75 per cent of the world's agricultural land is being transferred from local landholders to foreign investors – an area bigger than the combination of France and Germany.

Who is buying the land? The United States, China, the United Kingdom, the UAE, India, South Korea and Israel are all among the club of purchasers, and have mostly been spending in Africa – in Sudan, Tanzania, Congo, Ethiopia and Mozambique – but even as far away as Indonesia and Australia. China alone is now thought to have acquired around 5,000 square miles of farmland around the world as it tries to feed its 1.3 billion citizens. Chinese officials have regularly boasted that Beijing has been able to feed 23 per cent of the world population with less than 11 per cent of the world's arable land. Recently, however, the shrinking supply and increased pollution of its own arable land has seen the Chinese government encourage individual companies to buy foreign assets with subsidies and cheap loans. Particularly sought after is land with abundant fresh water supplies from rainfall or aquifers. A study by the World Bank in 2010 found that about 37 per cent of this land is used to grow food crops, 21 per cent to grow cash crops and 21 per cent to grow biofuels. There is no reason to jump to the conclusion that this is necessarily bad for the host country, especially if it results in more food reaching the indigenous population, but recent experience in places such as Ethiopia should give us pause for thought, as I describe later.

Desert, Water and Oil

Saudi Arabia is one of the driest countries in the world, with no permanent rivers or lakes and very little rainfall. One of the world's biggest oil producers and with a growing middle class, the desert kingdom epitomizes the issues of energy supply and use, food production and water usage, and their impact on the global economy and the world's populations, from the power-hungry consumers of the United States to subsistence farmers in the poorest parts of Africa. In many ways the story of Saudi Arabia is the story of globalization, the interface between economics and environment and the constant battle – even by one of the world's richest countries – to feed and water its people.

Several decades ago, in a bid to become self-sufficient in wheat, Saudi Arabia began to tap into its aquifers in a bid to create agriculture in the desert. By 2008 the plan had been abandoned because of its environmental and economic costs, and the Saudi government now says wheat growing must cease by 2016. The project may have been misguided but no one can blame the Saudi government for wanting to feed its people. As one senior official has commented, 'We cannot eat oil.' The fundamental mistake, however – trying to grow a crop in a place for which it is unsuited – is something we have already discussed in the context of the Syrian attempt to grow cotton for export.

Fred Pearce, reporting for *National Geographic*, gave a vivid insight into another attempt at food production in the desert when he visited the al-Safi dairy farm, one of the world's largest, a hundred miles south-east of Riyadh in the Arabian desert: 'Some 40,000 Friesian cows survive in one of the driest places on the planet, with temperatures regularly reaching 110°F. The cows live in six giant air-conditioned sheds, shrouded in a mist that keeps them cool. They churn out 53 million gallons (200 million litres) of milk a year.' It is anyone's guess if Saudi Arabia's dairies go the way of its wheat farms, but what is certain is that the financial and environmental costs of producing food in the wrong place and climate are enormous.

In September 2011 an article carried by Reuters quoted the Saudi deputy minister of agriculture as stating that per capita water use in the kingdom was already double the global average and increasing with its rising population and industrial development, but most especially because of the needs of agriculture, which consumed 85–90 per cent of supplies. About 70 per cent of drinking water comes from desalination, 25 per cent from the extraction of non-renewable groundwater and the rest from surface water, particularly in the mountainous south-west. Riyadh, the capital, is supplied with desalinated water pumped almost 300 miles from the Gulf. Although the quality has improved, reliability is low (in Riyadh water was available only once every 2.5 days in 2011) and pressure is often poor.

The Saudis have hugely increased water reuse. On the personal level, ablution water from mosques is reused to flush toilets, and at city level treated waste water is used for landscaping, irrigation and industrial purposes. In the mountains the government has built dams to capture surface water from the frequent flash floods. This is used primarily for agriculture, distributed through thousands of miles of irrigation canals and ditches. In Riyadh a leakage control programme has been implemented and a higher water tariff introduced. The Saudi authorities have also been at the forefront of promoting more water-efficient domestic appliances, which are provided free of charge, and residential water use has fallen by around 25 per cent.

The desalination of seawater on a massive scale has been the Saudis' main response to its permanent water shortage, and it now accounts for 25 per cent of the world's desalination capacity. In 2011 the volume of water supplied by the country's twenty-seven government-operated desalination plants was around 10 million cubic feet per day, delivered from seventeen separate locations. Most desalination plants use distillation technologies which remove all the minerals from water, and it requires further treatment to add appropriate minerals again before it is distributed. The real problem with desalination, however is cost. Desalination requires a great deal of electricity, and for the Saudis this means burning oil, their only real export. The more oil they burn to desalinate water to satisfy the needs of their own population, the less they have to export, and the revenues on which they depend will fall. Estimates by HSBC and the International Energy Agency suggest that between 2008 and 2010 direct oil burning for energy generation more than doubled. If significantly more oil is used for desalination and less becomes available for export (assuming constant production rates), then the consequences for oil prices could be profound, with knock-on effects on the global economy, especially in developing countries only just keeping their heads above water with the current oil price. Hence, the Saudi interest in nuclear power generation.

A nuclear power programme may seem illogical given Saudi Arabia's oil reserves, and it is limited anyway by a number of realities, including the time needed to build power stations due to supply constraints, something the United Kingdom is currently experiencing. Even if it were possible to achieve before oil exports had to drop, the geopolitical implications would be considerable. Saudi Arabia is perfectly entitled under the Non-Proliferation Treaty to implement a civil nuclear programme for energy generation – and we should support them if they operate under IAEA auspices – but it does not take a genius to work out what the reaction might be in the region, especially from Iran.

Perhaps the water issue of most concern in Saudi Arabia – both for the authorities there and for outside observers – has been the use of aquifers deep below the desert. According to the Saudi government, in the 1970s they undertook a major programme to locate and map these aquifers and estimate their capacity. This water was once part of one of the world's largest underground water reserves. Lying more than a mile under the desert, the water was laid down tens of thousands of years ago during the last ice age when the Arabian peninsula was still a wet part of the world. Forty years ago there was an estimated

120 cubic miles of water beneath the Saudi sands, enough to fill Lake Erie in North America. So much has been pumped out for use on farms that experts estimate that four fifths of this fossil water has now gone, and one of the greatest and oldest freshwater resources in the world has been all but emptied in a generation. The al-Ahsa aquifer in the country's Eastern Province has dropped a staggering 500 feet over the past twenty-five years, and it is not clear how long groundwater mining can be sustained.

With other options running out, the government of Saudi Arabia has turned to another, complex and controversial, means of trying to address its problems. In doing so, it has run into a whole range of interlinked global commodity issues. Saudi Arabia is one of the top rice importers in the world and has depended in the past for much of that rice from India. Faced with out-of-control domestic food inflation, however, India banned certain rice exports in 2008. (There is another irony here – the fact that the production of this water-intensive crop, in a country with its own depleted groundwater, consumes about one sixth of the nation's electricity to power its irrigation pumps. The result of excess demand is regular power shortages in many parts of the country, particularly rural areas, aggravating the already serious plight of the people there). So the Saudis, along with some other nations, have leased land from countries which have the natural resources to increase their food production but are unable to do so for themselves because of lack of finance.

In 2010 the government of Ethiopia leased some 300 million hectares of land to investors from China, India and Saudi Arabia and in doing so secured funds to invest in schools, energy and transport. However, this resulted in clashes with the indigenous population, who resent their ancestral lands being sold for foreign commercial exploitation. Fred Pearce described meeting a member of the Anuak tribe in the Gambela region of Ethiopia close to the source of the Nile.

The man complained that the forests and marshlands in which his ancestors had hunted for generations were being taken away, but he was not willing to give up without a fight: 'We have decided, each of us, that in the rainy season we will go back and cultivate our ancestral land. If they try and stop us, conflict will start.' This was tragically prophetic. Following the death of five workers in the camp of a Saudi agribusiness, Ethiopian government soldiers retaliated with more killings and destruction. Ethiopia's former prime minister, Meles Zenawi, who died on 12 August 2012, answered his critics thus: 'We want to develop our land to feed ourselves, rather than admire the beauty of fallow fields while we starve.' The question is, even if such lease arrangements are acceptable to locals and environmentally sound, where does the money go? Zenawi died with an estimated net worth of $3 billion. Discuss.

Chapter Seven

A DIFFERENT WORLD

An unavoidable conclusion from all the changes we have looked at is that the world that we have known in the past is slipping away and a new one is emerging. The following is, I promise, the last historical tangent that I will take, but I think it offers a final bit of context for some of the problems we are currently facing, which our leaders will have to resolve in the very near future.

At the end of the First World War the great powers assembled in Paris for a peace conference to determine the appropriate punishment for Germany, to decide on reparations and to reshape Europe and the Middle East following the near-simultaneous collapse of the German, Austro-Hungarian, Russian and Ottoman empires. Woodrow Wilson became the first American president in office to visit Europe, and his 'fourteen points', championing among other things the self-determination of peoples, formed the centrepiece of the American negotiating position at the conference. Not everyone had unquestioning admiration for the US president. Constantly reminded of Wilson's fourteen points, the French president, Georges Clemenceau, quipped to British Prime Minister Lloyd George, 'Even God himself had only ten.'

There was a certain ambiguity in Wilson's ideas, which was to plant the seeds of instability in an international system built on the concept of nation states. When Wilson talked about self-determination he envisaged it in civic terms (closer to what we would describe today as human rights), but the term was to raise nationalist hopes both across the collapsed empires and in the imperial possessions of the Allied powers in Asia and Africa. Robert Lansing, Wilson's secretary of state, pointed out in 1918 that national self-determination was 'a phrase simply loaded with dynamite'. Seldom in recent history can we have seen such accuracy expressed in such an understated way. The Treaty of Versailles was signed on 28 June 1919. A number of other treaties complemented it in the shaping of this new world. The consequences continue to affect our geopolitics today.

As the twentieth century came to a close, issues of self-determination re-emerged with a vengeance, especially following the collapse of the Soviet Union. A number of nationalist and religious tensions which had been contained by the communist regime were unleashed with bloody and terrifying ferocity. Having seen at first hand the consequences of these forces in the Balkans, I can completely agree with the distinguished historian Eric Hobsbawm, who said, 'The national conflicts tearing the continent apart in the 1990s were the old chickens of Versailles coming home to roost.' One of the reasons why the Balkans was, and continues to be, such a flashpoint is that the region, fought over for so long by Austria-Hungary, tsarist Russia and the Ottoman Turks, is where three competing cultures and religions meet – the Christian but increasingly secular West, eastern European Orthodox Christianity and the Islamic Middle East. Just like the geological faults which produce such damaging earthquakes in the area, these three cultural tectonic plates continue to cause tensions which occasionally explode on the surface.

In the First World War Turkey chose to ally itself with Germany and the Austro-Hungarian empire. Already weak before the war, 1918 began the process of its dismemberment at the hands of the victorious Allies, and all those parts of the Middle East formerly controlled by the Ottoman empire came up for grabs. Many of the current conflicts in the region can be traced back to the settlement which followed. Around the table of the Paris Peace Conference, politicians displayed a trait that is still on display today – that we are hard-wired for the cartographers' world. There is a belief that, if we draw a boundary on a map, it defines a nation. Try comparing an ethnic map of the region that includes Afghanistan with the national boundaries. Any similarities are largely accidental. In 1919 European politicians drew many of the Balkan and Middle East national boundaries we have today, with scant regard to local geography, tribal affiliations, religious beliefs or national identity. It was almost inevitable that these arbitrary lines would foster resentments and bitterness among the diverse groups in the artificial states they created, and that the tensions, mounting over time, would explode when the restraints of imposed authority were removed.

In eastern Europe a number of new small states were created. These tended to have substantial ethnic minorities who not unnaturally wanted to unite with the neighbouring states where their ethnicity dominated and where their family, cultural and historic links had a strong resonance. Millions of Germans, already resentful about their defeat in the war and what they regarded as humiliating treatment at the hands of the Allies, found themselves in the new countries. One third of ethnic Hungarians ended up living outside Hungary. The national minorities often found themselves isolated or even persecuted in countries whose new rulers sought to define their national character through the dominant ethnic group, whatever the cost in discrimination or alienation of often substantial minorities. As a result, the era after the First World War saw the European continent awash with refugees.

In an attempt to deal with the problem, the newly formed League of Nations sponsored various so-called Minority Treaties, but with its own decline in the 1930s, as memories of the horror of war diminished and Germany increasingly ignored the terms of Versailles, these treaties became more and more unenforceable. In one part of the Balkans a federation of various southern Slav groups was put together. Bosnia and Herzegovina, Croatia-Slavonia, Dalmatia, Slovenia and Vojvodina were joined with Serbia to form the Kingdom of the Serbs, Croats and Slovenes, later Yugoslavia. From 1945 to 1980 Yugoslavia was ruled by Josip Broz Tito, communist leader of the Yugoslav partisans during the Second World War. Yugoslavia lasted until 1991, when it all fell apart amid increasing ethnic tensions and the collapse of the Soviet Union. It was a disaster waiting to happen.

Just as in the Balkans, almost every Middle Eastern country that we are familiar with today was created by European and American leaders drawing arbitrary lines on a map. What we know today as Iraq and Jordan, for example, were the creations of British politicians. A British civil servant named Mark Sykes was responsible for the borders of present-day Saudi Arabia, Kuwait and Iraq. Their creation in 1922 was seen by many Arab leaders as a betrayal of the promises made by Lawrence of Arabia during the war and fostered simmering resentment. The French carved the new Christian-dominated country of Lebanon out of the predominantly Muslim region of Syria. The Russians drew the boundaries, and set the scene for future conflict, between Armenia and Azerbaijan.

How did all this fit with Wilson's goal of self-determination, which sought to diminish, not stoke, tensions? As a step towards this goal the mandate system was devised by the League of Nations as a provision for nurturing and helping a nation until it was ready to run its own affairs. Essentially, a League of Nations mandate transferred a certain territory from the control of one country to another. It was a legal instrument containing the internationally agreed terms for administering a territory on behalf of the League. The process of establishing a mandate consisted of two phases: the formal removal of sovereignty of the state previously controlling the territory and the transfer of mandatory powers to one of the Allied powers. Critics maintain that while Wilson might have meant mandates as philanthropic instruments, Britain and France effectively used them as imperialistic tools to create spheres of influence and take over German colonies from Africa to the Pacific Ocean, and in particular that Britain used the system to acquire substantial parts of the territory formerly controlled by the defeated Ottoman empire.

At the end of the war the Allies had occupied parts of Turkey including Istanbul. This prompted the formation of the Turkish national movement led by Mustafa Kemal Atatürk. The plan devised by the Allies to dismember the Ottoman empire, the Treaty of Sèvres, was signed on 10 August 1920, although it was never accepted by the Turks. Things were to change in Turkey's favour, however, when Atatürk responded to a Greek invasion in May 1919 by raising an army of revolutionaries and, with its backing, publicly rejecting the treaty's terms. When Atatürk won the conflict against the Greeks in the west and also defeated the Armenian forces in the east, Turkey had effectively recovered its lost territory.

Turkey then became the only belligerent in the First World War to overturn the terms of its defeat and negotiate with the Allies on an equal footing. The 1923 Treaty of Lausanne replaced Sèvres and led to international recognition of the new Republic of Turkey. Nonetheless, Lausanne formally acknowledged the new League of Nations mandates in the Middle East, the loss of the old Ottoman territories on the Arabian peninsula and British sovereignty over Cyprus. The League of Nations granted mandates to the French in Syria and Lebanon and British mandates over Mesopotamia (today's Iraq) and Palestine.

Some areas of the Ottoman empire on the Arabian peninsula became part of what are today Saudi Arabia and Yemen. Thus was created the Middle East we know today with all its conflicts and hostilities.

So how have the rulers of these artificial constructs attempted to hold on to power? Sadly, the all-too-frequent answer has been by trying to unite populations of diverse tribes, religious sects, customs, languages and traditions through hatred or fear of a common enemy. If there is none available, the solution has been to create one, as the enmity of the Serbs towards the Muslim population of the former Yugoslavia and the demonizing of the Zionists in what is now Israel can attest.

The resolution of the Balkan conflicts in recent years and the events of the Arab Spring may signal that we are near the end of the post-Versailles world. It is easy to be critical in hindsight, yet contemporary politicians, facing urgent and apparently intractable conflicts, will sympathize with Clemenceau's verdict on the treaty, negotiated on his own soil: 'In the end, it is what it is: above all else it is the work of human beings and, as a result, it is not perfect. We all did what we could to work fast and well.' Few would disagree that the conflicts in Iraq and Syria probably represent the final disintegration of the 1919 agreements, but what about the impact of globalization and a world that has become much more multipolar (at least economically) than before?

Even as the post-Versailles world fades into history, new powers are rising to shape the new global economic and security architecture. The most important of these without doubt is China. China's economic transformation has been astonishing. It has averaged growth rates of 10 per cent over the past thirty years and is now the world's second-largest economy after the United States in both nominal GDP and by purchasing power. It is the largest exporter and the second-largest importer of goods in the world.

Whether this stellar economic performance is sustainable is open to debate. We have already looked at issues relating to water, one of China's biggest natural-resource limitations, and there are other hurdles on the road ahead too. The World Bank has recently cut its forecasts for Chinese growth as Beijing policymakers seek to rebalance its economic model. Much of China's spectacular economic progress has depended upon strong export performance and government-led investment, but the recent sluggishness of Western economies has resulted in reduced demand for Chinese goods. In raising concerns over China's investment-led growth model the World Bank warned, 'The main risk related to China remains the possibility that high investment rates prove unsustainable, provoking a disorderly unwinding and sharp economic slowdown.'

The internal political situation in China is also a cause of concern. On a recent visit to Hong Kong a leading business representative, well-versed in the ways of Beijing told me:

[The government of] China is no longer ideological, as it was before, but about how to divide up the spoils between the three or four hundred elite families? Corruption is worse than in the 1940s, when the communists came to power. Internal strife is widespread. There is no social entitlement for those moving from the countryside into the towns. They are second-class citizens. Income disparity is increasing, with a wider and wider social gap. At least in the early days of communism, everyone was equally poor.

At a dinner with a range of political, media and business figures, we discussed whether too many in the West are turning a blind eye to internal difficulties because we need to do business with Beijing. 'China is becoming an enormous pressure cooker with very few outlets,' I was told. 'More money is now spent on internal security than on national defence. There is greater repression of the press and increasingly severe treatment of dissidents. The West is so seduced by what it sees in terms of economic growth that it can't see what lies beneath.'

There are also increasing numbers of voices being raised internationally about the political and economic impact of China's global market penetration. Those alarmed at China's increasing commercial acquisitions point to its current attempts to buy two major and iconic Western companies – the French resort company Club Med and the American pork producer Smithfield Foods. The authors of *China's Silent Army*, Heriberto Araújo and Juan Pablo Cardenal, point out that Chinese companies overseas act as agents of the state. In a recent comment piece in the *New York Times* they wrote, 'When Chinese state-owned companies go abroad and seek to play by rules that emanate from an authoritarian regime, there is grave danger that Western countries will, out of economic need, end up playing by Beijing's rules.' We should not assume that the Chinese have accepted capitalist values.

It is not only China's rising economic power but also its military strength and its growing regional dominance that generate concerns. Linking the economic and military spheres is the issue of China's cyber capability and in particular fears of cyber attacks on Western business. When the whistle-blower Edward Snowden ('whistle-blower' being an interesting euphemism for his actual offence) spoke out about the US National Security Agency's spying activities in China and Hong Kong, he provided the Chinese authorities with a golden opportunity to label American complaints about its own cyber activities hypocritical. Yet it was nothing of the sort. China's cyber incursions have been well and widely documented. In May 2013 *ABC News* ran a story about the hacking of plans for the headquarters of the Australian Security Intelligence Organization. Officials in Canada have accused Chinese hackers of compromising several departments within its federal government. Fears in India of Chinese cyber attack have resulted in the blocking of deals with telecoms companies such as Huawei because of their ties to the Chinese military.

Cyber attacks on the United Kingdom are at 'disturbing' levels, according to the director of GCHQ, Iain Lobban, who wrote in *The Times* in 2011, 'I can attest to attempts to steal British ideas and designs – in the IT, technology, defence, engineering and energy sectors, as well as other industries – to gain commercial advantage or to profit from secret knowledge of contractual arrangements. Such intellectual property theft doesn't just cost the companies concerned; it represents an attack on the UK's continued economic wellbeing.' In the United States a congressional advisory group called China 'the single greatest risk to the security of American technologies' and reported, 'There has been a marked increase in cyber intrusions originating in China and targeting US government and defense-related computer systems.'

Perhaps the most high-profile case was in January 2010, when Google reported theft of intellectual property from the company resulting from attacks on its corporate infrastructure originating in China. The attacks, which compromised the accounts of two human rights activists in China, were quickly connected by American security experts to other political and industrial espionage efforts, and officials in the Obama administration characterized the attacks as 'an increasingly serious cyber threat to US critical industries'. Other major companies such as Yahoo, Adobe Systems, Northrop Grumman and Symantec have also been targeted, with cyber attacks being aimed at areas in which China tends to lag behind the developed world militarily and commercially.

The Chinese have of course denied all accusations and counter-claimed that they themselves have been the victims of US cyber attacks, legations which were given a media boost by Edward Snowden, who claimed that the NSA had 61,000 hacking operations globally with hundreds of Chinese targets, giving it access to hundreds of thousands of computers. Is this an example of double standards? Absolutely not. Is anyone surprised that Western security agencies actually carry out spying overseas? Of course not. What is really significant is that Chinese cyber activities, often carried out by their military and its associated offshoots, are regularly involved in the theft of intellectual property from Western companies and aimed at gaining access to sensitive market and company data. It was a gift to Beijing to have its activities overshadowed by a debate about civil liberties in America, but this should not distract us from the threat to the very essence of Western prosperity, the ability to utilize the creativity of free people to generate innovation and wealth.

It is essential that as China becomes an even bigger economic player and competitor, we recognize the degree of control the state exercises over Chinese business and the threat that poses, understand what underpins our own success and redouble our commitment to our own political liberty, fair competition and the rule of law. The same vigilance must be maintained when it comes to the military sphere. China has recently announced a 10.7 per cent increase in its military budget as it continues to make itself the dominant western Pacific power. This is in stark contrast to the USA and its Western allies, where rising debts are forcing defence cuts, conclusive evidence that debt is a strategic issue. As Washington implements cutbacks so that it can repay its debt interest to Beijing (among others), China is able to finance its own military growth courtesy of American taxpayers and the US government's profligacy.

In late 2011 President Obama announced what has become known as America's Pacific pivot. He said, 'With most of the world's nuclear power and some half of humanity, Asia will largely define whether the century ahead will be marked by conflict or cooperation . . . The United States will play a larger and long-term role in shaping this region and its future . . . I have directed to my national security team to make our presence and mission in the Asia-Pacific top priority.' Whether such a reorientation is possible with continuing instability in the Middle East, the ongoing threat of nuclear proliferation in North Korea and Iran and an as-yet-unfinished operation in Afghanistan remains to be seen, but it also does not appear to take fully into account that China is becoming a global military player. With the focus of nuclear disarmament centred on Moscow and Washington, few have noticed that China may be close to reaching nuclear parity with Russia and the USA. China has over 3,000 miles of reinforced underground tunnels for its fixed and mobile strategic nuclear weapons, and is believed to possess around 850 warheads ready to launch and an inventory of nuclear weapons numbering somewhere between 1,600 and 1,800 warheads. It seems highly likely that any future strategic arms reduction talks will have to take into account China's stock of weapons.

However, some military strategists in the United States are contemplating ways in which China's global military capabilities can be effectively countered. The former commander-in-chief of the US Pacific Fleet, Admiral James A. Lyons, has suggested putting anti-ship ballistic missiles on US ships, submarines and aircraft and extending this capability to American allies. Whether this is an overreaction or not, and leaving aside how such a development would be viewed by Beijing, it is clear evidence of the increasing nervousness that China's military expansion is producing.

On the Chinese side disquiet has been expressed following the Obama administration's announcement that the US will expand its ballistic missile defence shield in the Asia-Pacific region. The prime driver of this change is of course the nuclear threat to America's allies posed by the regime in North Korea, but some in the Chinese leadership perceive it to be a longer-term move towards containment of China. The official English language newspaper in China *Global Times* has warned that 'if Japan, South Korea and Australia join the system, a vicious arms race in Asia may follow. It is not what China wants to see, but it will have to deal with it if the arms race happens. The US is creating waves in Asia. The region may see more conflicts intensify in the future. China should make utmost efforts to prevent it, but prepare for the worst.'

The People's Liberation Army, with 2.3 million active troops, is the largest standing military force in the world. It is now complemented by an increasingly modern and capable range of military hardware. China maintains a substantial fleet of submarines including several nuclear-powered attack and ballistic missile submarines. Its first aircraft carrier entered service in 2012. The Chinese air force has been substantially modernized over the past decade with Russian fighter jets being purchased to augment domestically manufactured modern aircraft, notably the Chengdu J-10 and the Shenyang J-11, J-15 and J-16. China is also developing its own stealth aircraft, the Chengdu J-20, to rival the American F-35, the subject of numerous accusations of cyber attempts to penetrate American defence technology.

American officials have long been sceptical about the officially declared level of Chinese defence spending, with a 2007 report by the US secretary of defense noting, 'China's actions in certain areas increasingly appear inconsistent with its declaratory policies.' This is very likely to be fair comment, but it is worth keeping a sense of proportion about the current military balance. China's official spending on defence is now around $166 billion, about 20 per cent of US expenditure. Even allowing for the fact that real Chinese spending is likely to substantially exceed the published figure, there remains a huge gap. In 2013 US defence spending accounted for 39 per cent of the global defence total. The current military advantage undoubtedly lies to a substantial extent with the United States, but there is no room for complacency in the medium or longer terms.

Leaving aside China's growing regional and global rivalry with the United States, there are plenty of local disputes to keep the Chinese authorities occupied. China and Japan are both pressing their claims to the Senkaku Islands, an uninhabited archipelago in the East China Sea currently controlled by Tokyo. The dispute over the islands, known as the Diaoyu in China, has severely damaged diplomatic relations between the two nations. This already poor situation was worsened recently when the Chinese Communist Party newspaper, the *People's Daily*, ran an article in which Chinese academics challenged Japan's sovereignty over the nearby Ryukyu Islands on the basis that they had been a vassal state of China. This claim is particularly sensitive since this chain includes Okinawa, home to thousands of American troops. A two-star general in the People's Liberation Army, Luo Yuan, almost certainly with the full approval of the Chinese government, claimed that the Ryukyus had started paying tribute to China in 1372, half a millennium before they were seized by Japan.

China is also in dispute about maritime boundaries off the coast of Vietnam, Malaysia, Brunei and the Philippines as well as the waters near Indonesia's Natuna Islands. The ongoing disputes over the status of the island chains of the South China Sea basin are really about three valuable interests – fishing rights, oil and gas rights and control of internationally vital shipping lanes. It is generally agreed that the South China Sea is an area rich in oil and natural gas deposits. There is some dispute about the scale of the oil reserves, with the Ministry of Geological Resources and Mining of the People's Republic of China estimating that the seabed may overlie 17.7 billion tons of crude oil (bigger than some small Gulf states), while the US Energy Information Administration geological survey puts the figure at only a fraction of this. The same dispute exists over the scale of natural gas resources, but there can be no doubt that in a region of fuel-hungry economies these fossil fuel reserves represent a real source of potential future conflict.

The need to access basic commodities such as oil and gas, as well as the shortages of water previously discussed, are ongoing headaches for the Chinese leadership, and recently a new worry has been added to the list – China's growing problem with adverse demographics. On 18 January 2013 the Chinese National Bureau of Statistics released information showing that China's working-age population (15–59 years) had declined in 2012 by 3.45 million, or 0.6 per cent, the first drop in the working population in many years. It was widely expected that this decline would start around the middle of the current decade, but these latest figures suggest that it will be faster than previously expected. Figures produced by the United Nations predict that China's total population will start to fall after 2030, a number that senior Communist Party officials suggest should be revised to 2020. The China Development Research Foundation estimates that the working-age population will then decrease by another twenty-nine million, raising fears among the authorities that the inward investment on which China's growth policy has been so dependent may move to other countries of the region where population patterns are more favourable. China is certainly ageing quickly. In 1982 the proportion of the population over the age of sixty was 8 per cent, a figure that has already grown to 14.3 per cent, and it is estimated that the number of elderly people will rise from 200 million today to around 360 million by 2030.

These problems are largely the result of China's one-child policy, introduced in 1979 and responsible for up to 400 million fewer births. The situation has been exacerbated by a huge gender discrepancy brought about by the country's selective abortion policy. Compared to the global average of around 105 boys for every 100 girls, China has 118 boys for every 100 girls.

Demographic change is just one of the social problems that China will have to deal with in the years ahead. I think it is too early to make a clear judgement as to the risk that China may pose to the security of the region and beyond – this will be entirely dependent upon how it responds to its own growing social tensions. A totalitarian state has three broad responses to internal tensions: repress them through the use of the internal security apparatus; liberalize to try to diminish and dissipate them; or externalize them, using the notions of a common enemy and heightened nationalism to provide a suitable distraction. Which route will China take? It is impossible to do anything other than speculate, but those who remember the events surrounding Tiananmen Square will not be encouraged about the Chinese Communist Party's willingness to loosen its grip.

Some commentators take comfort from what they see as the inevitable triumph of liberty and the rule of law. 'China portrays ideas of democracy and the rule of law as being Western or foreign. They do not see that there are universal values . . . No external force will make China change – it will have to come from inside. The people are not strong enough now, but one day they will be.' They also scold those who are afraid of challenging Chinese ways: 'The West is wrong to believe that speaking up will get you trampled on by China. It is quite the reverse – they pay attention to what countries outside think of them. They care about their reputation.' Perhaps the only thing we can say for certain is that in this new global giant titanic forces are at play and they are likely to play out in a uniquely Chinese way, but are equally likely to have a profound effect on east Asia and the rest of the world.

Another arena where there is massive turbulence is in the world of Islam (I prefer this term to the 'Islamic world', which suggests a geographical rather than ideological sphere). How will the interaction of current geopolitical struggles and tensions between the different strains of Islam play out? Condoleezza Rice believes that the religious element should not be understated. 'The Sunni–Shia split is very important in all of this. Unfortunately, because of the way many of the states [in the Middle East] were constructed, unresolved confessional conflicts were perpetuated by monarchy and dictators.' There is no doubt that the battle between secular and theocratic states is currently at its most intense in the Middle East, though some see some glimmers of hope. Tony Blair, for example, argues,

> We need to put religion in its proper place. The sooner this argument comes the better. In Europe it took a long time to realize that you can have religion, but you have to be willing to allow other people to believe differently or not at all. At last there is a real debate about these issues occurring in the region – if you watch Al Jazeera you will see genuinely different views being represented. This didn't happen in the past.

Is he optimistic about the future? 'Can the region transition; can you get freedom to worship? I believe they can but transition will take a long time.'

There are those who believe that religion is often used as a pretext for nationalist and geopolitical aims. The crown prince of Bahrain told me,

> Much of the current situation facing the wider region is rooted in power politics and is set against the backdrop of, and driven by, nationalist agendas. There is a broader battle for influence playing out, but this is not simply consigned to countries like the Kingdom of Saudi Arabia and Iran, but also, regionally, to the likes of Egypt and Turkey and, in turn, the interests of Western allies and global powers.

I believe that both political and religious forces are important in the region and must confess that when I began writing this book I tended towards the view that the intra-Islamic divide is often used as a cover for wider political aims. While I still believe this to be true, over time I have drifted more to Condoleezza Rice's view. I think we cannot avoid the conclusion that the Shia–Sunni split has become more bitter in recent years, and its conflation with wider nationalist issues has made it all the more toxic. However, the crown prince believes that steps being taken in Bahrain could be important in diffusing what increasingly appears to be a regional time bomb.

> Bahrain is not insulated from the rest of the region, and in many ways it is a microcosm of it, impacted by a geopolitical agenda which has evolved domestically into a sectarian agenda, but this does not mean that Bahrain cannot effectively demonstrate a way forward. An equitable political solution will be forged, which can subsequently help inform other parts of the region undergoing varying stages of development.

Naturally with the advent of the Arab Spring, some of my discussions with Condoleezza Rice revolved around the withering of the concept of Arab nationalism. As she put it, 'I don't think Arab nationalism ever dealt with the problem of the Sunni–Shia split – it simply suppressed the Shia. Arab nationalism was Sunni nationalism.' I asked if she thought Bahrain was becoming the new Berlin, at the centre of a new Iranian–Saudi cold war and/or a protracted Sunni–Shia conflict, as some regional commentators have suggested. She very much reflected my own view when she said, 'The tensions in the region are both geopolitical and religious, but trouble is being stirred up [by Iran] in both Saudi Arabia and Bahrain . . . The crown prince's reforms have begun to give the Shia a voice and economic reforms have helped.'

In a number of speeches and lectures in the Middle East I have continued to make the point that if reform is not a process then it can all too easily become an event, as we have seen in the fall of the dominoes from Tunisia to Egypt. Encouraging reformist elements in the Arab world is a much more constructive role to play than the knee-jerk condemnation that we see too often in the media and politics. It is important that we keep emphasizing that it is not a coincidence that those nations who have embraced liberty most fully have been the dominant global economic and political powers. Free, democratic nations who allow their citizens to express themselves openly and without fear also unleash the powers of creativity and entrepreneurship which are the basis for success in a free market.

In the current struggle to turn the events of the Arab Spring into something more sustainable a number of forces are battling with one another. As Tony Blair puts it,

> There are three elements jostling for power: people who have been in power for a long time in what we thought were sustainable positions – but those institutions haven't held; modern-minded and open-minded people – new more tolerant leaders who are more secular, and the good news is that they are numerous but they are not well funded or organized; and a third group who are hard-line Islamists, and the bad news is that they are organized and well funded.

Clearly, in the Gulf and the wider region, the ramifications of the war in Iraq continue, and the debate about its strategic consequences is as robust as ever. The hopes of those involved remain clear. Condi Rice maintains, 'Saddam was the greatest human rights criminal in the Middle East . . . We hoped we would be replacing a dictatorship with institutions in which different communities could remain in a single entity. [Today] in Iraq we have a Kurdish president, a Shia prime minister and a Sunni speaker.' Whether or not Iraq stabilizes into a balanced religious, if not a secular, state largely depends on whether Iraqi nationalism, which became particularly strong at the time of the Iran–Iraq War, reasserts itself. Tony Blair is optimistic: 'I tend to the view that Iraqi nationalism will prevail in the end. It depends on outside interference – they have Iran on one side – and extremist Sunni elements inside trying to destabilize the country. I would be 100 per cent more optimistic about the outcome in the region if there was a different regime in Teheran.'

Malcolm Rifkind believes that the conflict in Iraq has left Teheran in an improved position. 'The single most important outcome of the Iraq War is the strength and position of Iran in the Gulf. Iraq is not a decisive player in the region and will not be in the foreseeable future.' I substantially agree. Surely one of the most important strategic consequences of the war, at least in the short term, has been the growing and largely unchecked influence of Iran in the region.

One of the things that interests me most about the debate on the tensions and rivalries within Islam is the relative lack of discussion of the role of women. This issue is, I believe, of crucial importance if the world of Islam is to be fully reconciled with the globalized planet of the twenty-first century. Theoretically, many of the problems that relate to women in Islamic societies should not exist. Not only does the Koran state that men and women are equal, but the advent of Islam brought revolutionary changes for its time, raising the status of women to a hitherto unknown level in Arabia. For example, it brought an end to female infanticide, which was then quite widespread (and still exists in China today, although in the guise of selective abortion), as well as asserting the equality of the sexes in worship and society. Indeed, the Prophet Muhammad had just one daughter, Fatimah –to whom he was very close – and no son, and for this reason was viewed with suspicion by the more conservative of his contemporaries. This was, of course, the state of affairs that led to the great Sunni–Shia split.

This improved status for women was reflected in the role they played in the founding of many Islamic educational institutes, dating back to the University of al-Karaouine in AD 859. This trend seems to have reached its peak in the twelfth to fifteenth centuries, but then dropped away. Today a comparison of adult literacy rates shows that of the seven countries in the world with the biggest gaps between men and women, five are Islamic – Yemen, Pakistan, Niger, Mozambique and Guinea-Bissau. A similarly poor pattern can be seen in the relative percentages of girls and boys enrolled in primary school. By this measure the seven countries with the biggest gaps are all Islamic – Chad, Yemen, Pakistan, Mali, Iraq, Guinea-Bissau and Iraq. The World Economic Forum uses a range of measures to measure the gender gap. Its report puts seventeen Islamic countries in the bottom twenty. They include Algeria, Nigeria, Egypt, Morocco, Saudi Arabia, Pakistan and Yemen, yet some of the differences within Islamic countries are striking. If we look at women in employment, we find that, while only 16 per cent of Pakistani women are economically active, the figure is 52 per cent in Indonesia. This would appear to be a cultural rather than a religious problem, with those societies embracing a harder-line Sunni version of Islam less supportive towards female emancipation. Even so, the willingness of the Saudi Arabian government to see a large expansion in the number of women in higher education is a positive sign.

One area where there should be greater international concern relates to the treatment of women who are victims of crime. For example, according to the eleventh-century specialist in Islamic jurisprudence al-Mawardi, it should be possible for a woman who kills a man raping her to be exempted from a charge of murder. Yet we have seen the abhorrent spectacle of such women convicted of adultery or fornication and subjected to barbaric punishments such as stoning to death. This flies in the face of all international concepts of justice and deserves to have a higher profile in Western political debate. It amazes me that we have not seen more concern from the political left for the plight of women under the rule of the Taliban, for example.

Recently, the United Nations Commission on the Status of Women produced a declaration condemning violence against women. The Muslim Brotherhood in Egypt responded by asserting that implementing such a declaration would lead to the 'complete disintegration of society' and that it was a decadent and destructive document which undermined the ethics of Islam by saying that a woman had the right to work, travel and use contraception without first getting the permission of her husband. They went further, claiming that the measures called for would be the 'final step in the intellectual and cultural invasion of Muslim countries, eliminating the moral specificity that helps preserve cohesion of Islamic societies'.

Yet the outcry against such sentiments has been muted. Why? According to Condoleezza Rice, 'If you educate women, then they won't have twelve children and have the first at thirteen,' but she added, 'The left's first hobby horse is anti-Americanism, rather than women's rights.'

There are however hopeful signs that this issue might be addressed. Gita Sahgal, a great-niece of Jawaharlal Nehru and a lifelong human rights activist, particularly on issues relating to women's rights and religious extremism, used to head the gender unit at Amnesty International. She was sacked three years ago after making known her concern that the organization was embracing some deeply unpleasant elements within the Islamist movement and, in particular, had become close to Moazzam Begg, Britain's most high-profile Guantánamo Bay detainee. In 2011 she controversially and courageously set up the

Centre for Secular Space in order to counterbalance this harmful and distasteful tendency.

The *Spectator* magazine, which has helped promote her cause, believes that it is unfashionable it because exposes collusion between the Anglo-American left and the Islamist right. I fully agree, and it is time we put an end to this disgraceful and twisted form of political correctness and replace it with a debate founded on sound intellectual principles. The *Spectator*'s Nick Cohen has said that the failure of the liberal establishment and the left in Britain to combat reactionary religion, or even call it by its real name, is stunning.

> I can say from experience that if I talk about the 'American Christian right' or the 'Israeli right' no one will blink . . . When I use equally precise language to talk about the 'Muslim right', one of the great forces of reaction in the world today, my comrades either go blank, because I am using language they cannot understand, or accuse me of 'racism', lack of 'empathy', inappropriate 'language' or some other gross offence against modern etiquette.

I find it very encouraging to hear journalists talk in such a frank way. I believe there is a fundamental difference between tolerance and political and cultural surrender. If we do not learn the difference and redouble our efforts to promote our values wherever and whenever they are challenged, then we will not only fail the oppressed, who expect and require our help, but we will betray our own values and traditions. Such a betrayal will put us on a path leading away from those concepts of rights, liberty and the rule of law which have made us champions of freedom at home and abroad. If we fail in the endeavours that I have discussed then we are likely to fan the flames of both regional and global terrorism. We have seen how, with improvements in global communication, especially the Internet, extremists and fanatics have been able to distort events and distribute propaganda as never before.

One of the main lessons we should have learned from the history of terrorism is that it mutates and feeds off a wide range of sources of resentment and warped ideologies. In our own time it has mutated from national groups (Baader–Meinhof, the IRA and Red Brigades) through increased cooperation in the world of organized crime and drug trafficking to the global network of transnational terrorism we see today with groups such as al-Qaeda or Jamaat-e-Islami. The rise of transnational terrorism, or at least the speed and scale of it, has taken many by surprise. As Condi Rice told me, '9/11 exposed the problem of transnationalism that we had underestimated. The rise of non-state actors and the weakness of states shocked us in 2001, and we have never really recovered from it.'

Governments move slowly. As Bob Gates put it to me, 'Government is like a big dinosaur – a very large footprint, a very small brain and very poor motor control.' And we all know what history did to the dinosaurs. Belatedly, we have begun to react in the necessary ways. In the United States the barriers between law enforcement and the intelligence services have been broken down. In the UK heavy investment in both domestic and foreign intelligence gathering has prevented numerous terrorist atrocities, and improved information sharing between democratic nations has created a safer world for all our citizens.

There remains, however, a potent and divisive argument about surveillance and the quality and quantity of information that it is appropriate for government to gather. Those who take the libertarian view argue that our privacy must be protected from the intrusion of the state, even at the cost of an increased risk to our collective security. While I have some instinctive sympathy for this position (and I think all Conservatives are a mixture of libertarian and authoritarian in some proportions), our right to privacy has already been enormously compromised by the Internet. At the same time, traditional legal remedies when we feel our privacy has been invaded, such as the laws on defamation and libel, have been made much less effective by the Web. The libertarian argument is fine, indeed correct in the abstract, but does not take full account of the asymmetry of information created by today's communications revolution with all its consequences. This is not to argue that the state should have unlimited powers – far from it – but it makes no sense to tie the hands of our intelligence services to such a degree that they cannot fulfil their duty to protect us.

Imposing restrictions on government to the extent that they tip the balance in favour of the forces of terror will not help to defend our liberty in the long run. We must not become what we are trying to defeat, that is true, but we perhaps have more protection than we perceive. It is often said that terrorists do not need to answer to an electorate in the way that democratic governments do, and this is often cited as a weakness of democracy. It is also a strength. We are able to eject governments that we believe to be unnecessarily authoritarian, and we have the rule of law, and in some cases written constitutions, on our side. Sometimes, however, we need to take a longer-term more balanced view of risk and benefit. Purism has its intellectual comforts and philosophical clarity, but it can be dangerous. For example, habeas corpus is a preciously guarded legal tradition and a guarantee against over-mighty state authority, yet, if the principle of preserving it at all costs had been applied by Abraham Lincoln, he might not have won the American Civil War and defeated the evil of slavery. Would that have been a price worth paying? It is a dilemma that we have to come to terms with in every generation and decide what is best for our own time. Equilibrium is what nature prefers – a balance of forces over time. That is what we too must seek. I asked Bob Gates whether the changes to the American security apparatus that followed 9/11 had been successful. He was emphatic in his reply.

> Dramatically so. The bin Laden raid was a great example of joining the dots. The Patriot Act made a huge difference. Before then, if the FBI arrested a terrorist in the US and [they] testified in front of a grand jury, the FBI could not share information with the CIA. The legal and cultural divisions that prohibited cooperation between law enforcement and the intelligence community – stretching all the way back to Harry Truman – had been overcome. We need to make sure that barnacles do not grow over the system.

Bob and I have frequently shared our worries about the advantages that asymmetry (some of which we have already discussed) hands to terrorists and the state of complacency which it is all too easy for governments to fall into. As he put it,

> Terrorists are not a bunch of backward thugs – they are pretty sophisticated in their ability to find gaps in security . . . National state governments are filled with organizations that need to tell themselves they are doing a very good job – and they need to tell their political masters the same. We need red teams whose job it is to find gaps in our defences. We need to institutionalize how terrorists think. The longer we go without a terrorist incident, the more complacent we become. We need to keep our edge over time.

There is no doubt that we need to equip our security services with the tools they need to deal with the terrorist threat, but I also wanted to know if there were lessons we could learn from previous experiences with terrorism that might help us to deal with contemporary threats, especially from Islamists, so I asked John Major, who instigated the process which under his successor led to peace in Northern Ireland, what he had learned from that experience. 'The key development was working in concert with the Irish government. Their input was important in itself, but it also cut the terrorists off from the Catholic population and gave them no place to hide. We were also then working with political opinion in the USA – we isolated the IRA.' What I found even more interesting was his description of the need of those who had always operated through the medium of violence to find an escape route into the world of consensual democratic politics.

> When you box in groups like the IRA, you need to talk to them. There will be those who want to humiliate them – that is wrong. You need to think, 'What will they be thinking?' That enables you to construct a ladder down which they can climb with dignity. If we [politicians] don't keep our supporters happy we can find ourselves out of office. If they don't keep their supporters happy they can find themselves dead.'

It was obvious that John Major found some of this process extremely painful, especially after the Warrington bombings in 1993. The deaths of three-year-old Jonathan Ball and twelve-year-old Tim Parry caused widespread anger and revulsion in the UK and Ireland and something of a backlash against the incipient peace process. 'After Warrington the pressure to stop the peace process was huge, but if we didn't proceed then other children would be killed. We had to continue, even if it was distasteful.' I wondered whether this might happen in areas from which Islamist terrorism draws much of its strength and whether a willingness to talk was a prerequisite to being able to deal with non-state actors. 'There are not exact parallels today, but there are some lessons we can learn. We need to get the active support of Islamic governments, especially places like Pakistan. The West can't deal with this alone.'

This of course is much easier said than done as some of the governments involved tend to face both ways on security issues, telling the international community one thing and their own domestic pressure groups another. Yet increasing the presence of both our traditional diplomatic forces and increasingly our NGOs in such countries seems like a no-brainer if the prize, however remote, is a safer and more peaceful world. 'We should increase our diplomatic presence in the countries that matter. What do we have to lose? We need to talk to the people who can make a difference even if we find some of them distasteful. It is a prerequisite to solving some of the problems. There will be no quick fix, only a series of small steps. We will need small bits of carrot and stick along the way.' I have seldom seen John more animated, more serious or more convincing.

This reminded me of a conversation I had with Donald Rumsfeld about differences in American diplomatic tactics between the Cold War and the present. I asked him why Ronald Reagan had increased the US presence in Moscow at the height of the Cold War, yet the policy is now to hold Iran at arm's length. His answer was interesting from both the historical and contemporary perspectives. 'Ronald Reagan had a great thinker in George Shultz. He knew we would need to know more about those who would come after the fall [of the Soviet Union]. There's been a shortage of thinkers like Shultz. John Kerry [the current US secretary of state] is measured and thoughtful. He is a good choice'.

How we apply these lessons, wherever they are appropriate or possible, is extremely important as we enter the interdependent global age and see two worlds unravelling that were so familiar to us – the world of the Versailles Treaty at the end of the Great War, and the institutions and structures that shaped the environment following the

Second World War. And where does this leave the institutions that we have come to depend on – the United Nations, NATO, the IMF, the World Bank, the WTO and the EU?

Most of those I spoke to while writing this book had similar views. Donald Rumsfeld was frank: 'I don't think our institutions are working as well at the beginning of the information age as they did in the industrial age.' His views were echoed by Tony Blair:

> There is no doubt that many of our institutions are not functioning well, but how can we reform them? It's not an easy question, and I don't think I've got any easy answers. It is easy to say that they are not fit for purpose. The United Nations is a bureaucratic quagmire. Part of the answer is to make some of the structures more effective, and the World Bank could certainly be improved. When it gets to issues such as the Security Council it is much more difficult. Some of these institutions become a block on effective action. UN development programmes could be made to work far more effectively. The World Bank too.

Condoleezza Rice was equally blunt. 'We don't have a very good international institutional structure. NATO and the EU – at least until the Eurozone crisis – were doing all right on reforming themselves. I'd give them a B-plus. The biggest mistake for the EU was not to integrate Turkey. I'd give the UN a D. The WTO is kind of coming apart, which is unfortunate, and the IMF doesn't know what to do with itself.'

The United Nations was founded in 1945 to replace the League of Nations. From an initial 51 members it has now grown to encompass 193 nations. As well as its central bodies such as the General Assembly, Security Council and the International Court of Justice, it also operates agencies such as the WHO (World Health Organization),

UNICEF (now the United Nations Children's Fund) and the World Food Programme. From its early days reform has always been on the agenda, especially in the areas of peacekeeping and humanitarian operations, but possible changes to the Security Council have attracted most attention. The size of its membership and the veto rights of the five permanent members are the most contested issues. Those who advocate reform point out that global political realities have changed fundamentally since the formation of the Security Council in 1945, and its membership should change to reflect this. Among the main proponents of change are the members of what has become known as the G4, a group consisting of Japan and Germany (second- and third-largest financial contributors to the UN), Brazil (fifth largest in terms of territory) and India (second-largest population). As well as being of increasing economic importance, all are key players in their own regions and believe that their positions should be represented appropriately in the UN. Crown Prince Salman of Bahrain's view is typical and widespread. He says, 'Rapidly changing global dynamics are clearly testing the ability of multilateral institutions that were created in a different era. In many instances global problems are now being addressed with the increasing involvement of emergent powers, whose share of voice in these institutions does not necessarily match the scale of their importance in the new global order.'

Certainly the arguments seem compelling, but are they as strong as they might at first appear? Geographical territory or economic size do not equate with security commitment. It is, after all, the Security Council, not the GDP Council. Malcolm Rifkind put a different emphasis on the debate: 'The whole point about the Security Council is the contribution to security. It's not just a club. Those who want a permanent role will need to make a permanent contribution of the sort that Britain and France make. If they can't contribute to security in a meaningful way then their claim to a greater role will be much weaker.' There is surely an important point here. How, for example, can countries who have constitutional restrictions on their military capabilities and use (like Japan and Germany) be equal partners with those who are willing to fund, equip and use military forces in whatever circumstances are necessary?

The debate is also something of a red herring, given that the UN's ability to act is frequently blocked by Russian and/or Chinese veto. This results in coalitions of the willing coming together outside the UN framework when they feel intervention is required to quell conflict or prevent humanitarian disasters.

The World Trade Organization came into being on 1 January 1995, replacing the General Agreement on Tariffs and Trade (GATT), which was having problems adapting to the speedily globalizing world economy. Its main functions are the regulation of international trade and the resolution of disputes between members. In recent years progress has been slow and difficult, with the Doha Round of negotiations, started in 2001 and originally designed to address poverty in developing nations, still to be completed. This process, intended to make globalization more inclusive and to help the world's poor, has largely been hampered by the unwillingness of some developed countries to remove tariff barriers and subsidies to agriculture. The result has been the negotiation of a number of bilateral trade agreements outside the organization between countries frustrated by the inability of the WTO to deliver.

The World Bank and the International Monetary Fund (IMF) were established at the 1944 Bretton Woods conference. The World Bank provides loans to developing countries for capital programmes and aims to promote foreign investment and international trade with the goal of eliminating poverty. The IMF describes itself as 'an organization of 188 countries, working to foster global monetary cooperation, secure financial stability, facilitate international trade, promote high employment and sustainable economic growth, and reduce poverty around the world'. Member nations, through a quota system, contribute money into a pool from which countries can borrow temporarily to deal with financial imbalances.

In the 1990s the World Bank and the IMF forged what is known as the Washington Consensus. This set of policies, which includes the deregulation and liberalization of markets, privatization and the downsizing of governments, has become the default approach to economic management across the globe. It has, however, been widely criticized (usually by the political left) for placing too much emphasis on GDP growth and not enough on whether such growth is reflected in rising living standards. Crown Prince Salman described the current difficulties of the IMF neatly when he told me,

> The global economic crisis laid bare fault lines in the institutional ability of the IMF to successfully intervene. Not only did conflicting mandates with national and regional regulators hamper efforts, the IMF fundamentally lacked the financial capacity to immediately respond. A number of founder members either could not or would not help provide the resources needed, and emerging players became critical financial contributors. The IMF's future capacity to act has to be re-examined, as does the structural role of countries beyond its traditional core.

I have discussed a number of issues relating to the European Union in earlier chapters, especially in relation to the euro. There are however more fundamental matters which need to be addressed in relation to its future. Across the EU as a whole public sentiment has soured in an environment where the political class in Brussels and its unaccountable bureaucracy have been spared the economic pain that widespread austerity programmes have brought to ordinary people.

Regular opinion surveys undertaken by the EU itself have shown falling support for membership. A recent Gallup poll conducted in six EU countries showed that 55 per cent of Britons would vote to leave the EU altogether in a referendum, with 34 per cent of French and 31 per cent of German respondents wishing to do the same.

My own earliest political memory is of the referendum in Britain in 1975 to determine whether we should join what was then the European Economic Community. My parents campaigned and voted on opposite sides. My father believed in doing whatever was required to prevent another conflict in Europe, while my mother thought the construct would not work for the UK because it was too 'foreign'. There is no doubt that many of those who voted for what was usually known as the Common Market have felt dismayed, if not betrayed, by the political integration that has since occurred without their consent. The problem now, however, is not that Europe is foreign but that it is not foreign enough. In other words, it spends far too much time looking inwards and backwards rather than outwards and forwards. An introspective political class, in denial about Europe's declining position in the world, carries on without adjustment and with complete contempt for the views of ordinary citizens.

Recently, the European Union has started to create its own agenda in defence and foreign policy. Leaving aside the fact that five EU members are neutral, making a mutual security guarantee similar to NATO's Article 5 an impossibility, most member states are cutting their defence budgets and are unable to meet their current financial commitments to NATO, the continent's primary defence organization. A joint EU defence and foreign policy is a dangerous diversion, even a delusion, and one of the reasons why, if Britain is unable to renegotiate a looser relationship with Brussels, I and many others will campaign and vote to leave an organization in which the logical end point of the concept of ever closer union is union itself.

The collective defence provided by NATO since the signing of the North Atlantic Treaty in Washington DC on 4 April 1949 has been one of the great success stories of the era since the Second World War. Originally the membership consisted of the signatories to the 1948 Treaty of Brussels (the UK, Belgium, the Netherlands, Luxembourg and France) plus the United States, Canada, Norway, Denmark, Iceland, Portugal and Italy. The agreement of its members to regard an armed attack against any one of them, in Europe or North America, as an attack against all, has been instrumental in maintaining peace and stability in Europe for over half a century. Reflecting the feelings of his time, the first NATO secretary general, Lord Ismay, famously said the goal of the organization was to 'keep the Russians out, the Americans in and the Germans down'.

The Korean War, which broke out in June 1950, was the first armed confrontation of the Cold War, and led NATO to develop concrete military plans and establish Supreme Headquarters Allied Powers Europe (SHAPE) as a consolidated command structure in 1951. The gradual strengthening of the alliance and the incorporation of Greece, Turkey and especially Germany saw the creation of the Warsaw Pact in 1955. Despite some ups and downs, including the petulance of President de Gaulle of France, who in protest at what he saw as the closeness of the UK and US and wanting to maintain the option of coming to a separate peace rather than being drawn into a NATO–Warsaw Pact conflict, removed all French armed forces from NATO's integrated military command, the alliance successfully faced down the Soviet threat for over forty years. After the fall of the Berlin Wall in 1989 and the collapse of the Soviet Union, the Warsaw Pact was dissolved in 1991 and many of its former members are part of today's 28-nation alliance. Since the Cold War ended NATO forces have seen action in the Balkans and, following the 9/11 attack on the United States, formed the core of the International Security Assistance Force in Afghanistan.

All is not, however, as rosy in the garden as it might be. Despite the fact that the countries of the alliance account for 70 per cent of the world's defence spending, the European contribution has been steadily falling. In 1991 European countries made up 34 per cent of NATO spending, a figure that has since dropped to around 20 per cent. It is obviously unreasonable to expect American taxpayers to continue to fund European defence to this extent. The situation has been exacerbated by the fact that some of the more recent entrants to NATO have slashed their defence expenditure, reasoning that they are now protected by Article 5. On the other hand, some smaller nations such as Estonia, with relatively recent memories of oppression, have stepped up to the plate and given a lesson in commitment which some larger nations would do well to follow. There are wider debates too, about NATO's future role and its territorial reach, with a range of views being expressed from inside and outside the organization.

Crown Prince Salman is generally welcoming to the idea of a more outward-looking alliance:

NATO has progressively adapted to changing shifts, reacting to the genuine security needs of its members, recognized that their most immediate threats fall far outside its members' geographic borders. While NATO's role has yet to fully evolve and, internally, it is having to wrestle with the varying foreign policy demands of the EU bloc, it has the opportunity to broaden its horizon to meet both present and future security challenges and comprehensively meet its objectives.

Bob Gates was circumspect about whether or not NATO was the appropriate tool for wider international action and raised the prospect of more informal partnerships:

I felt that Bosnia was a legitimate NATO activity but I can't see how Afghanistan, Iran or North Korea could be seen clearly to be within the NATO remit. It may even be a drawback as it would make it harder to bring in Russia. What is NATO's real writ beyond Europe? The expansion of the alliance in the 1990s started to change NATO from a military alliance to a political one. We need flexible arrangements like the coalition of the willing – that is a better approach.

I asked him what the implications of expanding the core NATO membership would be. He replied, 'Would the people of the United States be willing to see their young people die in a conflict over Georgia or the Ukraine? I don't think so.'

The attitude of the United States is, and will remain, central to how NATO sees and performs its role. The experiences of Iraq, Afghanistan and Libya have undoubtedly had an impact on US political thinking, and the apparent semi-permanent blocking stance of Russia is likely to make the UN route to military action more difficult. I believe there is a 'cascade of legitimacy' for military intervention that most Western leaders would like to follow. Full United Nations authority via the Security Council is at the top of the list. Failing this, the next most-preferred position is legitimization via NATO agreement and cooperation. Next is a coalition of the willing, bringing like-minded nations together. Towards the bottom is bilateral action, and finally going it alone when exclusive national interests are threatened.

Donald Rumsfeld reflected on the new reality when we had breakfast in Washington: 'We [the US] will want to have all the help we can get and we will want it in a way that makes any partners feel comfortable.' Perhaps more importantly, he reflected concerns many of us have had post-Libya about the likelihood of getting unanimous NATO support for a particular campaign and the need to avoid having our hands tied.

'When it comes to military campaigns in future, the mission will have to determine the coalition. We can't allow the coalition to determine the mission.' Malcolm Rifkind added another nuance in the light of recent experiences: 'Much more important than the coalition of the willing is the coalition of the relevant. In the Iraq War, for example, the willing were often smaller client states of the US because we were unable to persuade larger regional players to join.' There is no doubt that a more flexible approach is necessary to cover a wider range of future options, especially with the emergence of increasingly assertive new powers and a NATO alliance with a larger, more disparate membership with different priorities and funding streams. If any reinforcement is required to this viewpoint, it has been provided by Putin's aggressive stance towards Ukraine and the illegal annexation of the Crimea. The West has been guilty of allowing wishful thinking to replace critical analysis, with the result that it has been outmanoeuvred in a strategic theatre, a situation in which implications are far from clear.

NATO needs to take a long hard look at how it assesses risk if it is to remain relevant in the years ahead. Ideally I think it should establish its own centres of analysis in some of the areas we have discussed if it is to avoid becoming simply a vehicle for tactical responses to short-term crises. In the Cold War we knew what we were for, politically and militarily. We war-gamed, planned scenarios and thought the unthinkable. We need to adapt our thinking and planning to the emerging world. To be an effective and relevant global security institution, NATO needs to understand and act upon the interactive range of risks posed to global stability: global imbalances and other dangers to economic security; threats to energy security; the growing capabilities of trans-national terrorism; the risk of contagion from failing states; the unresolved crisis within Islam; and the competition for resources, including food, fuel and water, inevitable in a world of rapidly increasing demand from a burgeoning human population.

EPILOGUE

Probably every generation reflects on how different the world has become. For the young the present is the dawn of a new world, a blank canvas on which to paint the picture of their age. For the elderly the present is the culmination of the past, often what has succeeded the 'good old days' and 'not how things used to be'. So, it is with some trepidation and a respectful nod to history that I begin this final section of *Rising Tides* with the assertion that not only are we entering a very different world, but that the rate of change is accelerating.

Nowhere is this demonstrated more clearly than in the mind-boggling advances of information technology. As someone who was barely computer literate only a few years ago, I cannot imagine how much more difficult it would have been to research a book of this nature without access to the Web or using the voice-recognition software with which the vast majority of it has been written. The Internet is now the primary source of information for countless millions of people, whether at home, at work or in education. Its use and evolution have been influenced enormously by the development of the social networking websites and the mushrooming of mobile technology. The increasing sophistication of mobile technology and its easy-to-use applications have made access to the Internet much simpler and has increased the number of users worldwide enormously.

Bill Clinton put it concisely when he said, 'When I took office, only high-energy physicists had ever heard of what is called the World Wide Web . . . Now even my cat [Socks] has its own page.' At the end of 1995, during President Clinton's first term, around 16 million people (0.5 per cent of the world's population) were using the Internet. By the end of 2012 this figure had ballooned to 2.75 billion, around 39 per cent of the world's population. It is astonishing to think that in the middle of 1993 there was a total of 130 websites. By the end of 2012 this had become an estimated 634 million. The Internet has also allowed us to change the way we communicate with the invention of email. It is already incomprehensible to many of us how we managed to live and work at anything other than a snail's pace without it. At the end of 2012 around 2.2 billion people were using email and some 144 billion emails are sent worldwide every day, although around two thirds of these are spam, the scourge of the net. Almost every month there seems to be a new addition to the social media landscape – first Facebook, then Twitter and now Pinterest and Instagram. (I must confess to never having heard of either of the last two before researching this subject on, of course, the Internet.)

The Facebook phenomenon has now reached a level of 665 million daily active users, and monthly active users have passed 1.1 billion for the first time. Twitter is the fastest-growing social network, with 645 million active registered users, and 15 million active users every month. In other words, around 21 per cent of the world's Internet population is using Twitter every month. Interestingly, Twitter's fastest-growing age demographic is the 55–64-year-olds, in contrast with other forms of social media. Lastly, the YouTube phenomenon attracts over 1 billion unique visitors every month with 6 billion hours of videos being watched in that time period. Around 20 per cent of personal computer time and around 30 per cent of mobile time are spent on social networks, with women dominating usage.

Many on the conservative side of the political spectrum say that they favour the notion of a small state with big citizens – where individuals have maximum control over their own lives with minimum interference from government. Have we reached this situation, or at least something like it, by default with these changes in communications? Certainly, the power of financial markets has increased significantly as compared to that of national governments, and if we accept that the markets are the accumulated wisdom and behaviour of millions of individuals, then we may have reached a milestone on that path. Likewise, the emancipation of information that has resulted from the Internet and social media has given individuals a much greater role in social and data exchange. The difference between this organic outcome and the traditional model is that today's position has been arrived at without the assent of government at all. It has happened irrespective of, and sometimes despite, the approval of our political masters. It is a genuine revolution of truly historic magnitude. As John Major put it, 'Politicians are less powerful and the public is more powerful. It is a source of pressure for politicians that just didn't exist before. For me, it was a good time to have been a politician. It is a difficult time to be one today.' Yet the sheer joy of the access to knowledge that the Internet brings is a dream come true for information seekers.

There are few changes, however, that only bring benefits, and there is a dark side to this advance too. The nosy neighbours, the busybodies, the haters and the downright sick have acquired the sort of access to information about others and their own editorial freedom that was impossible and unthinkable. We can all bring to mind truly repulsive examples of the hate that has been poured out under cover of the anonymity of the Internet, and the fewer occasions when the perpetrator has been identified. The concept of privacy has all but disappeared as individuals post tweets and photographs of neighbours, strangers and the famous alike on the net. How long before we see pictures of the rich and famous in their hospital beds or coffins (followed in time by our families, friends and neighbours), irrespective of the hurt or intrusion, simply because the freedom to post such images exists? It is likely that people will seek legal redress to ever more intrusive behaviour, but it is unlikely that the law will provide the remedies they seek.

Every action has an equal and opposite reaction – it is an elementary law of physics – so people will adapt to deal with the elements of the Internet age they dislike. The wealthy will find more exclusive and secluded ways to live their lives, increasing the gap between themselves and the rest of society. People will keep their personal data on memory cards or sticks or whatever the next technological equivalent may be, rather than storing or sending it via the Web. More secure methods of data storage will constantly emerge to keep ahead of those trying to steal it.

I asked Donald Rumsfeld what effect he thought the WikiLeaks episode would have on how governments collected and stored information and the relationship between governments.

The government doesn't know as well as it did what is going on out there. WikiLeaks has made it hard for people to talk to us – they feel that we have no capability of keeping a secret. Why would those in other countries talk to us about any sensitive controversial views, if they think it will all come out? Intimidation works. Not only will people not tell us what they think if they fear it will come out and affect them – it is worse than that. They may actually tell us things that, if they are leaked, will positively advantage them. It is a multi-dimensional problem.

Did he agree that it has undermined the ethical way in which diplomacy has traditionally been conducted? Has it not also been an own goal for those who believe they have the right to know everything, because it will generate more secrecy and more secure ways to store data? 'Absolutely right. I totally agree.'

Eventually, I think, the information revolution may provoke a counter-revolution, which will create its own exclusive groups, and the social wheel will turn again, at least temporarily. In the meantime, it provides wonderful new opportunities for learning, integrating and understanding. In this golden era of access to knowledge, whatever its drawbacks, we must use the opportunity to not only know but understand, and to recognize the difference between the two.

What have I learned from writing *Rising Tides*? It has been, as Tony Blair would say, 'a journey'. I have never written anything longer than a speech or a newspaper article before, and only the reader can decide whether I have the skills needed to produce a full-length book. Either way, I have seldom enjoyed any project as much as this. The amount of reading has been greater than anything I have done since I finished studying medicine, and the sheer quantity of open-source information available on almost every subject, made so much simpler to access by the net, is almost overwhelming.

I have been amazed, and a little horrified if I am honest, at some of the things I didn't know. Ones that stand out are that the name Pakistan is an acronym and that almost half the population of the world is dependent for its drinking water on rivers that rise on the Tibetan Plateau, so he who controls Tibet has an awesome strategic weapon. I have belatedly rediscovered the joy of learning. Politicians are so used to output that they simply don't have enough time, or put enough emphasis, on input.

In the course of writing this book I have become even more worried about the credit and debt imbalances in the world economy. The huge debts of the United States in particular, with its continuing need to fund a structural deficit, pose a threat to future global stability. In the short term the US may very well be able to cope, and the dollar may even be seen as a safe haven when other currencies such as the yen, the euro and the pound are being debauched by central banks printing more and more money – even if it is euphemistically called quantitative easing. In the medium and long term, however, such high levels of government and personal debt create enormous vulnerability. When interest rates rise from their present historically low levels, the burden of debt will become crippling. I wonder how many warnings we need about the potential effects of continuing global financial imbalances. Just as in the arenas of security and national resources, equilibrium will be established over time in the global economy; whether we manage our way towards it, or are propelled by events, is up to us. Western countries need to start living within their means and recognize that the world owes us neither a living nor a guaranteed standard of living. Failure to control our appetite for debt could ultimately affect not only the developed world, but also have a disastrous impact on some of the world's poorest if our irresponsibility results in a widespread global downturn.

If we are looking at the possibility of history repeating itself in an undesirable way, then perhaps we should be keeping an eye on events that are unfolding in Thailand. As that country heads towards what could potentially become a civil war, we might well want to remember that this is where the 1997 currency crisis had its origins. Despite this, it seems to be barely on the radar of either the economic or foreign departments of most Western governments.

However, I have been surprised and reassured by the large measure of consensus among those I have spoken to on the range of subjects considered here. John Major summed up the challenges and hopes that the era of global communication has brought when he told me, 'The Internet has changed everything – it is integrating the world. Young people wear the same clothes and listen to the same music wherever you go. China is no longer cut off – not because of government action but because their citizens can see what is happening in the outside world. The same will be true in Iran.' I believe he is right and that freedom and the rights of the individual will ultimately triumph over tyranny and theocracy.

If there is one subject in this project that has fascinated me more than any other, it is the competition for natural resources and global commodities. In particular, the potential for conflict and strife over water supplies should be high on the agenda of all those in positions of authority. One aspect of the commodity debate which is worth a book in itself (and which I have not really dealt with) is energy security, an area where domestic and international policy overlap. For years politicians, especially in the West, have sought the holy grail of energy independence – freedom from the forces that produced the oil price shocks of recent decades and the resulting economic difficulties. I wonder, however, whether this aim, achieved or not, has always been a mirage.

I recently spoke to a United States senator about how the huge amounts of gas made available by fracking has taken the United States to the edge of energy independence. I asked what the implications were for America, domestically and internationally. He told me the most important effect was that 'We don't have to worry any more about places like the Strait of Hormuz. It will be someone else's problem.' It struck me that this fundamentally failed to grasp the nature of the world's increasingly interdependent economy, and I asked him how long it would take the American economy to be affected if Japan or

China were unable to get their oil supplies. The point is that today there is perhaps no such thing as independence, energy or otherwise, such is the degree of mutual reliance and international commonality of interests. Certainly in extreme circumstances, for example in a time of global war, energy (or indeed food) independence may be a lifeline for a country, but in the normal scheme of things, in times of relative peace and stability, it has a limited value. Still, I would much rather have it than not, and the goal of breaking our dependence on imported fossil fuels remains as relevant as ever.

Energy security was certainly one of the issues that occupied the mind of Crown Prince Salman, and we spoke about it at length in Bahrain. He told me,

> The possibility of the US becoming a net exporter of energy within the next two decades, coupled with the growth in Asian economies, suggests that the global demand for oil may well shift eastward in relative terms. This will almost certainly affect strategic interests and partnerships in the Middle East and contribute to closer ties between the Middle East and Asia, but also has the potential to strengthen security ties between east and west. The importance of regional stability to oil price stability will mean that the strategic interest in Middle East security will remain a core imperative for all major economies for the foreseeable future.

Given the chronic instability of the Gulf region, I asked him what the best route to ensuring continuity of supply was, until such time as nations develop their own sources of energy. He replied,

> We can only achieve energy security by enhancing a shared interest in regional stability and, in doing so, we may be able to

encourage greater global cooperation across many more areas of shared interest. Ultimately, strong and lasting friendships and partnerships in the region, built on active engagement where lasting bonds have been established over time, will always be the best guarantee of supply and the best protector against risk.

Despite the consensus about the direction of travel and the nature of interdependence, there is some scepticism about how it will all work in the future. Condoleezza Rice does not dispute the advance of globalization but wonders whether, in terms of global security, the world is as multipolar as is often claimed.

> The world doesn't feel very multipolar to me at all. Only the US, the Brits, the Australians and occasionally the French have any notion of global responsibility. The Chinese have none – it is a totally mercantilist foreign policy. India could have a major impact, but they are too focused on their regional issues. Russia is now mainly a blocking power. Show me another power that is willing to shoulder the responsibility that comes with real global leadership.

Bob Gates is also sceptical about a multipolar solution to global governance: 'People are looking for a grand strategy to govern global issues, but the world is too complex for that. It's a fool's errand.'

How is the world likely to evolve? I have thought for some time that if the twentieth century was the era of the block – the economic block, the military block and the trade block – then the twenty-first century is likely to be the era of the organic solution. We will need to find new partnerships, new alliances and new mechanisms to deal with a whole new range of challenges. We will need to develop new levers to pull in a wide variety of situations – the age of the one-size-fits-all solution is, I think, behind us. Should this fill us with dread? Not at all. In fact, I believe there are reasons to be optimistic about our ability to create novel solutions to our common problems.

Having set out so many present and potential problems, it would be irresponsible not to show that we can learn from recent experience how to adapt in order to deal with some of the dangers we face. Let us just for a moment consider how the international community has developed an organic solution to the issue of piracy on the high seas. In order to counter the threat to international shipping lanes off the Horn of Africa, a problem estimated to be costing billions of dollars annually, Combined Task Force 150 has emerged as a coalition of twenty-five nations. The US, UK, Canada, Denmark, France, Germany and Japan have been joined by Australia, New Zealand, Singapore, Italy, Spain, Thailand, Turkey, Pakistan, the Netherlands and others. Perhaps more surprisingly, CTF-150 has engaged in anti-piracy operations off the coast of Somalia alongside independent operations by China, India and Russia. If we had tried to create such an international coalition in advance of deployment I fear we would still be negotiating. In the event, when there was a real and tangible threat to our common well-being we were able to act in an organized, coherent and credible way. What is more, we have been successful.

Much the same sort of phenomenon has occurred at the political and economic level as hard reality has intruded on the cosy relationships of those who saw themselves as the great powers of the world. As Malcolm Rifkind put it, 'Why has the G8 become the G20? Because we needed them. A global response needed to include the Chinese, the Brazilians, the Indonesians – within weeks the G8 became the G20. Circumstances will force the kind of change needed.' I agree. We are learning to adapt, which is encouraging, since the lesson of natural selection is clear – adapt or perish.

Having examined the complex linkages between failing states, transnational terrorism and the state of the world of Islam today, two conclusions seem inescapable to me. The first is that religiously tolerant societies have greater stability, creativity and prosperity. By the same token, states which allow or propagate religious intolerance are likely to wither socially and economically, creating a perfect environment for the growth of extremism. This should not surprise us, as societies that are religiously intolerant are also likely to stifle intellectual freedom and consequently to restrict individualism, creativity and political diversity. That such countries have failed (and will fail) to flourish in an ever more open global society should not come as a shock. Encouraging religious tolerance should be a key element of our foreign policy and even more our overseas aid programme.

The second conclusion is that societies that empower and liberate women, treating them as full equals with men, also do better economically and socially. It is obvious that any culture unable to tap into the talent pool of half its population will be at a global disadvantage, but the loss is more than just in economic potential. The role that women have played in peace processes, from Northern Ireland, where their input was pivotal, to their position at the forefront of Iran's democratic movement today, shows just how much women can contribute and how important it is they are full participants in society. This too should be a driver for foreign and aid policy, our contribution to a globally stabilizing influence.

Most if not all of the problems we face today result from the forces that have shaped both our planet and its civilizations over thousands of years. I have tried to put some of those forces into context to help explain the problems that we face and the complex difficulties that have to be overcome if we are to solve them. We can't do anything about the past. We can however write the history of our own time and pick up the gauntlet thrown down in front of us. Whether in our individual affairs or in affairs of state, we will either shape the world around us or we will be shaped by it. We need to constantly remind ourselves that we are not passive figures but can shape our destiny in line with our own beliefs and values. We simply need to have the courage to do so.

Almost every iteration of our world has been a triumph of man's ingenuity – a victory over adversity. If we can learn to use our knowledge to achieve a balance with the natural world, then we may gain the space and time required to mould our civilization in a way that allows the vast and gloriously varied species that we call mankind to have a more sustainable and secure future. Will we sink or swim in these global rising tides? Will we, in Shakespeare's words, take them at the flood and go on to fortune?

I am, and always have been, an optimist. I am grateful for that. I still believe the future will be worth getting out of bed for.

ACKNOWLEDGEMENTS

All books begin somewhere and this one would probably never have been written without the encouragement of my great friend and champion Clark Judge in Washington and the redoubtable Ali Gunn in London whose enthusiasm was a turning point. Susan Watt, my editor, has had the patience to guide me through writing this, my first book, and I am grateful to them all. Ali's tragic death in Switzerland has deprived so many of us of a great friend and source of inspiration. With her abundant kindness, wit and lust for life, she was always larger than life and will be so terribly missed.

The generosity and ideas of many people have been reflected in much of what I have written. I have already acknowledged the help from Sir John Major, Tony Blair, Malcolm Rifkind, Condoleezza Rice, Robert Gates, Donald Rumsfeld and Crown Prince Salman, but I must also thank those who have provided specific expertise in the relevant chapters: Michael Burleigh for his inspiration and knowledge on the issues surrounding global terrorism; Professor Ali Ansari for his insight on Iran and matters Islamic; Ali Azeem, James Symes, Sean Garman, Daniel Yates, Dr Raveem Ismail for their hard work on the range of complex issues involved in global finance; and my friend Pippa Malmgren whose understanding about the links between economics and security is both impressive and groundbreaking. I would also like to thank Anson Chan for her frank analysis on regional issues and the access she arranged for me to those with a wealth of experience and knowledge of Chinese matters.

Many have had their patience tested while I obsessed with the writing of *Rising Tides*. My long suffering staff Ione Douglas and Helene Vaughan have shown their usual forbearance. Eleanor and Iain, the Costa Brava two, have given their usual sound, hugely valued and thoughtful advice and along with Craig and Sue have endured my endless "did you know" pub conversations. They have all given unstinting support and enthusiasm for which I am enormously grateful, as have Pippa and Dylan in their own inimitable ways.

Amy Tinley and Oli Waghorn are both indispensable parts of all my projects and always bring a sanity and balance to everything we do together. They have suffered the whole writing process with their usual amazing equanimity and their value cannot be measured. The same goes for our much missed friend, Luke Coffey, who is always available with his sound and informed views from Washington whatever the hour. They are an exceptional team. I am grateful for the constant support and inspiration of Robert and Scott and all those who have strengthened our transatlantic bonds.

My thanks to Adam, whose contributions for this book are as valued as his loyalty and friendship, along with the terrific support of the lovely Lucy.

My parents, my brother Paul and my sisters Tricia and Louise have provided constant support and encouragement as they have always done, now supplemented by our wonderful wider family. We are so fortunate. It is a lucky man who gets to count such blessings.

Finally, my wife, Jesme, has borne her time as "the book widow" with her usual patience and calm. Without her unstinting support, enthusiasm and input, this book would have been so much poorer. She is a gem that I do not deserve.

To all of the above and to those I have omitted in the interests of space, much love and thanks.